Introduction to
Theory and Design
of Sonar Transducers

Introduction to Theory and Design of Sonar Transducers

Oscar Bryan Wilson

Professor of Physics
Naval Postgraduate School
Monterey, California

 PENINSULA
PUBLISHING
LOS ALTOS, CALIFORNIA USA

Introduction to Theory and Design of Sonar Transducers

First Published in 1985
Expanded and corrected in 1988 edition.

Copyright © Oscar Bryan Wilson, 1988.

1988 edition published by
Peninsula Publishing
P.O. Box 867
Los Altos, CA 94023 USA
Corrected in second reprinting in 1991.

Library of Congress Catalog Number 87-063306
ISBN 0-932146-22-8

ACKNOWLEDGMENTS

The financial support, without which this book could not have been written, was provided by Vice Admiral E.B. Fowler, Commander, Naval Sea Systems Command, and Captain Ray Witter, Naval Electronic Systems Command, PDE-124-40, and is gratefully acknowledged.

I am very appreciative for the hospitality of Dr. Joe Blue, Superintendent of the Underwater Sound Reference Division of the Naval Research Laboratory, Orlando, Florida, where I resided for a number of months during the writing and where I was provided significant help in the form of technical advice and clerical support. Especially appreciated are the careful review, comments, and suggestions for improvement from Ms. Mary Lou Miller and Mr. Theodore A. Henriquez during this time. I am also very grateful to Ms. Parma Yarkin whose very active blue pencil wielded in the painstaking editing of the manuscript helped make it more readable and understandable and to Ms. Joan Murray who had to deal with the manuscript typing during its final preparation. I also appreciate the careful draftsmanship of Mr. Alvin Lau in the preparation of figures. The numerous comments and suggestions from students who were exposed to an intermediate draft of the manuscript as a textbook for the course, and the comments and encouragement from colleagues at both NPS and NRL were most helpful.

PREFACE

For a number of years, I have been teaching a course on transducer theory and design for naval officer students in the Underwater Acoustics Curriculum at the Naval Postgraduate School (NPS). In recent years there has not been a really suitable textbook containing material on the topics and at the level I consider to be appropriate for this course. Most texts that my colleagues and I used were both out of date and out of print. Reading material for the students in the course was drawn from a number of sources so that a lack of uniformity in style, conventions, notation, etc., contributed to the student's problems in learning this complicated subject. This book, then, is an effort to combine within one cover a treatment of acoustic transducer topics related to problems of naval interest which can be employed as a textbook at NPS. Although this book has been designed for the student at the Postgraduate School, it is hoped that it will also be useful for engineers who have some background in acoustics and electrical engineering and are beginning to work in the area of transducers for underwater sound.

The typical student in the Underwater Acoustics Curriculum has a technical baccalaureate degree received five to eight years prior to beginning study at NPS. This course on transducers follows courses in underwater acoustics and in electrical engineering at the senior and first year graduate level. Therefore, this book is constructed on the assumption that the student already has acquired a good basic knowledge of acoustic waves in fluids and electric circuit theory, has some familiarity with impedance concepts and electromechanical analogies in vibrating mechanical systems, and has had some experience with acoustical and electrical measurements. Since the student at NPS normally has not been exposed to elastic waves in solids prior to taking this course, some introductory material in this area has been included.

The scope of this book is limited both by the author's background and by the amount of time available to the student in a one–quarter course. Thus, there has been a problem in choosing what materials must be omitted. In making these choices, I have tried to emphasize the fundamental principles and to illustrate their applications to one–dimensional models and by providing examples of simple designs. In spite of these limitations, the book contains more material than can be covered adequately in the one quarter course. There was not room for some new and important approaches to design and analysis, such as impulse response methods, bond–graph techniques, nonlinear goal programming, or finite–element methods for analyzing the behavior of more realistic three–dimensional vibrators. I justify this also on my conviction that the student learns the principles best from elementary examples and will want and need to use the more sophisticated and more correct models in actual design problems. In many cases, the simple models will give correct order of magnitude results. The electrical circuit analysis methods used in this book are limited to steady state, simple harmonic methods applied to lumped parameter elements because of the belief that electrical circuit methods will continue to be useful in acoustic transducer analysis and design for many years to come. Some references to newer methods have been provided.

In the writing of a book such as this, the work is naturally influenced by the advice of colleagues and the writings of others. Probably most important to me in preparation for both the teaching of the course and the writing of this were the writings of W.P. Mason[1], Berlincourt, Curran and Jaffe[2], Hunt's *Electroacoustics*[3], and the summary technical reports of the National Defense Research Committee[4]. Others include the works by Cady[5], Camp[6], and Kinsler and Frey[7]. The author also acknowledges the usefulness of examples of the design of composite vibrators developed by McTaggert and others for the notes of a short course on sonar transducers given by Catholic University[8].

O. B. Wilson
Monterey, California
June 1985.

[1] Warren P. Mason. *Electromechanical Transducers and Wave Filters*. 2nd Ed. D. Van Nostrand Co. Princeton, NJ (1948).
Warren P. Mason. *Piezoelectric Crystals and Their Application to Ultrasonics*. D. Van Nostrand Co. Princeton, NJ (1950).
Warren P. Mason. *Physical Acoustics and the Properties of Solids*. D. Van Nostrand Co. Princeton, NJ (1958).
[2] Don A. Berlincourt, Daniel R. Curran, and Hans Jaffe. Piezoelectric and Piezomagnetic Materials and their Function in Transducers. Ch. 3 in *Physical Acoustics*. Vol 1A. Warren P. Mason, Ed. Academic Press Inc. New York (1964).
[3] Frederick V. Hunt. *Electroacoustics*. Harvard University Press. Cambridge, MA (1954). Reprinted by the Acoustical Society of America (1982).
[4] Summary Technical Reports of Division 6, Vol. 12. *Design and Construction of Crystal Transducers*. National Defense Research Committee. Washington, DC (1946).
Summary Technical Reports of Division 6, Vol. 13. *The Design and Construction of Magnostrictive Transducers*. National Defense Research Committee. Washington, DC (1946).
[5] Walter Guyton Cady. *Piezoelectricity*. 2 Vols. Dover. New York (1964).
[6] Leon Camp. *Underwater Acoustics*. Wiley. New York (1970).
[7] Lawrence E. Kinsler and Austin R. Frey. *Fundamentals of Acoustics*. 2nd Ed. Wiley. New York (1962).
[8] Principles and Design of Sonar Transducers. Notes for a short course given in San Diego in 1981 by Catholic University of America.

PREFACE TO THE REPRINT EDITION

INTRODUCTION TO THEORY AND DESIGN OF SONAR TRANSDUC-
ERS, having gone out of print since it was first published in 1985, is
now republished by Peninsula Publishing. In this reprint edition, corrections to typographical errors have been incorporated and an
appendix providing answers to selected problems has been added.
Although it would have been desirable to have included additional
material in the currently active area of low frequency projectors, particularly flextensional transducers, it was not practicable to do so at this
time. However, the still valid basic material in the book and its references should make it possible for the interested reader to locate
desired information on the subject.

O. B. Wilson
Monterey, California
July 1988

CONTENTS

CONTENTS

CONTENTS

FIGURES

TABLES

SYMBOLS

A	Amplitude of a wave; area; constant in solution to an equation; amplification ratio
a	Radius of disk or ring
B	Magnetic induction vector; constant in solution to an equation
b	As a subscript, indicates a characteristic of wave propagation in a long bar
C	Electrical capacitance; heat capacity; constant in solution to an equation
C_M	Motional capacitance
C_m	Mechanical compliance
c	Wave speed for elastic waves
c_{ij}	Elastic stiffness constant. Superscripts E and D (or H and B) denote the values at constant electric (magnetic) field and constant electric displacement (flux density), respectively.
D	Electric displacement vector; constant in solution to an equation
d_{mi}	Piezoelectric (piezomagnetic) strain constant
E	Electric field strength vector
e	Rms voltage per unit bandwidth
e_{mi}	Piezoelectric (piezomagnetic) stress constant
F	Force vector
f	Frequency in cycles per second (Hertz)
f_s	Frequency of series resonance; subscripts p, m, n, r, and a denote, respectively, frequencies of parallel resonance, maximum and minimum impedances, resonance and anti-resonance.
G	Gibbs function
g	Piezoelectric (piezomagnetic) strain constant
H	Magnetic field strength
h	Piezoelectric (piezomagnetic) stress constant
I	Electrical current
i	Running subscript, usually for the elastic field variables; pyromagnetic constant
J	Acoustic reciprocity constant
j	Running subscript, usually for the elastic variables; imaginary coefficient in the complex exponential function ($j = \sqrt{-1}$)
K	Bulk modulus; spring stiffness
k	Propagation constant for elastic waves ($k = \omega/c$); electromechanical (magnetomechanical) coupling factor
$\bar{k}$	Spatial operator for magnetic transduction
L	Electrical inductance
L_M	Motional inductance
ℓ	Length; as a subscript, denotes load
M	Mass; transducer receiving sensitivity
m	Running subscript, usually for the electrical or magnetic field variables; Magnetodielectric constant
N	Transformer turns ratio
n	Running subscript, usually for the electrical or magnetic field variables.
P	Dielectric polarization vector
p	Pyroelectric constant; as subscript, indicates plate mode of wave motion
Q	Heat function; transducer transmitting response; quality factor; volume velocity
q	Charge
R	Electrical resistance
R_M	Motional resistance
R_m	Mechanical resistance
r	Radius
S	Mechanical strain
s_{ij}	Elastic compliance constant
T	Mechanical stress; electromechanical coupling parameter
t	Time; thickness of plate or disk

SYMBOLS

U	Amplitude of velocity; internal energy function
u	Velocity; in Ch. 3, displacement component
V	Electrical potential difference
v	Normal velocity
W	Power
w	Width
X	Electrical or mechanical reactance
X_M	Motional reactance
x	Displacement; Cartesian coordinate
Y	Electrical admittance; mechanical admittance; Young's modulus
y	Cartesian coordinate
Z	Electrical impedance; mechanical impedance
z	Specific acoustic impedance; Cartesian coordinate
α	Thermal expansion coefficient; fraction of pressure acting on interior surface of cylinder
β	Dielectric impermeability; fraction of pressure acting on exterior surface of cylinder
γ	Fraction of pressure acting on ends of cylinder
δ	Loss tangent
ϵ	Dielectric permittivity
η	Efficiency
θ	Phase angle; temperature
κ	Radius of gyration
λ	Wavelength; Lamé constant
μ	Magnetic permeability; Lamé constant; shear modulus
ν	Magnetic reluctivity; Poisson's ratio
ξ	Component of displacement
ρ	Mass density; ratio of inside radius to outside radius
σ	Entropy; surface charge density
ϕ	Phase angle
χ	Dielectric susceptibility
ψ	Phase shift
ω	Angular frequency

CHAPTER 1

INTRODUCTION

1.1 History

In its broadest definition, the word *transducer* refers to any device or agency that converts energy from one form to another. An electroacoustic transducer converts electrical energy to acoustical energy or vice versa. Probably the oldest known electroacoustic transducer, admittedly somewhat beyond human control, is the naturally occurring electrical discharge, lightning, and the sounds produced by it, thunder. Certain modern transducers use a controlled electrical discharge as a source of sound, e.g., the sparker used as a source in off-shore seismic studies.

Several physical laws govern basic mechanisms for the conversion between electrical and acoustic energy. These include Coulomb's law (1785), Faraday's law of induction (1831), Ampere's law and the Biot–Savart law (1820), the direct and inverse magnetostrictive effects discovered by Marion and Page (1837) and Villari and Joule (1842), the direct piezoelectric[1] effect discovered by the Curie brothers (1880), and the inverse effect discovered by Lippman (1881). Joseph Henry's investigations of magnetic effects and their practical aspects led to the invention of many tools. As the dates associated with their discovery or disclosure indicate, these phenomena were first explored and became well understood many years ago.

There is a long history of the application of these effects to electroacoustics. A very early electroacoustic device was Benjamin Franklin's invention, the electrostatic motor, which was used to actuate a bell. Romagnosi is credited by Hunt (*1*) with the experimental discovery of electromagnetic induction in 1802 and Oersted with its rediscovery in 1820.

The early history of transducers for underwater sound is closely associated with the development of electroacoustic transducers used for telephony. Bell's invention of the telephone (1876) and Edison's work on the carbon microphone, the phonograph, and the bipolar moving armature telephone receiver (1870–1880) were, of course, landmarks in the history of transducers. More recent applications have been the development of echo ranging equipment by Richardson (1912), the development of the Fessenden oscillator (1912), and its use for the detection of icebergs by Fessenden (1914). During World War I, 1915 to 1918, Langevin and others applied echo ranging methods to the

---

[1] Because there are so many mispronunciations of "piezo," it is worthwhile to give the recommendations of Webster's International Dictionary (1976 Ed.): pe̅ :a̅ zo; pe̅ :a̅ tso; pī :e̅ zo, with the stress on the second syllable varying between primary and secondary.

1

detection of submarines and developed an early form of composite projector transducer (the steel–quartz–steel resonator plate). Between 1920 and 1940, piezoelectric crystals were used for the frequency control of oscillators by Nicholson and Cady (1920), and equivalent circuits for piezoelectric resonators were developed by Van Dyke and Mason. Other efforts and inventions improved transducers for communications and home and theater uses.

The discovery of the large piezoelectric effects in ceramics (e.g., barium titanate (1946)) led to the development of the technology of modern piezoelectric ceramics and to significant improvement in the performance of electroacoustic transducers for underwater sound. For a more detailed history of electroacoustics and transducers, the student is referred to the first chapter of the book *Electroacoustics* by F.V. Hunt (*1*) and the collection of reprints *Acoustic Transducers*, edited by I.V. Groves (*2*). Further historical information on piezoelectricity and its applications may be found in refs. (*3*) through (*7*).

1.2 Conversion Criteria

For most applications of electroacoustic transducers there are general performance criteria. Among these are:
  a. Linearity. This implies that the output of the transducer is substantially a linear function of the input.
  b. Passivity. This implies that all of the output energy delivered by the device, electrical or acoustical, is obtained from the input energy, acoustical or electrical.
  c. Reversibility. This indicates the ability of the device to convert energy in either direction.

With few exceptions, this book will limit treatment to transducers that fulfill these criteria.

1.3 Conversion Mechanisms

Five basic motor–generator mechanisms have been useful in electroacoustic transducers and satisfy, at least approximately, the above requirements. These are:
  a. Electrodynamic. The motor and generator action is produced by current in or motion of an electrical conductor in a magnetic field.
  b. Electrostatic. The motor action occurs when a change in the potential difference between charged electrodes results in a change in electrical forces which may cause one or more of the electrodes to move. Generator action can arise from motion that changes the capacitance of the charged electrodes, resulting in charge flow and/or changes in potential difference between the electrodes.
  c. Magnetic. The motor action arises from changing the magnetic force in a magnetic circuit which tends to move the pole faces at an air gap in the

circuit. The generated electromotive force (emf) is induced in a conductor surrounding the magnetic circuit when the magnetic flux varies due to changes in the magnetic reluctance in the circuit.

d. Magnetostriction. A change in the magnetic polarization in the material causes an elastic strain. The generator action occurs when an elastic strain changes the flux density and induces an emf in a conductor which surrounds the material.

e. Electrostriction and piezoelectricity. An externally applied electric field causes a change in the dielectric polarization in the material which in turn causes an elastic strain. The generating action takes place when an elastic strain causes a change in the polarization that induces a charge on the electrodes.

1.4 Transducer Operating Environment

As Hunt (1) points out, whenever a source or a receiver of sound is required, the designer must take account of the particular environment in which it is to be used. The circumstances attending the use of acoustic transducers in the ocean or in liquids differ substantially from those in which transducers are used to produce or detect sound in air. The acoustic properties of the water medium are the most important design considerations for transducers to be used under-water, and impose problems that are significantly different from those of air. In addition, transducers operated in the ocean must withstand the often severe effects of the conducting and corrosive sea water, biological activity, and hydrostatic pressure.

1.5 Symbols and Conventions

Problems with notation are especially severe in the area of electroacoustic transduction. Efforts have been made in this book to be consistent and to define quantities at their introduction. Although this does not solve the problem, it is hoped that it will help the student cope with it. The symbols are those conventionally used in electrical engineering textbooks or handbooks (8). There are a number of cases where the same symbol is used for different quantities. An attempt has been made to provide some sort of clarifying remark or definition in each case so that, together with the context in which the symbol is used, the risk of confusion should be very small.

Superscripts on piezoelectric and piezomagnetic constants are used to designate the field variables held constant during their measurement or specification. Subscripts generally have their customary meanings. A special problem exists in distinguishing between electrical and mechanical quantities. Here, as an example, a lower case m is used as a subscript to designate a mechanical quantity, such as mechanical resistance R_m, while an upper case subscript is used to designate an electrical quantity, such as motional impedance Z_M.

Since the piezoelectric and piezomagnetic constants relate first order tensors (electric and magnetic field vectors) to second order tensors (stresses and strains), the array of these coefficients is usually a 3×6 matrix. The convention used here is the normal one of using the first subscript for the electric or magnetic field component direction and the second for the stress or strain component in the shorthand notation. In computing the resulting effects, care must be exercised in carrying out the product operation. In some cases, the transpose matrix must be used in order to do this operation with the customary rules of matrix multiplication.

The complex exponential $\exp(j\omega t)$ has been used to designate simple harmonic time variation. In this convention, the phasor rotates counterclockwise in the complex plane. The student must always keep in mind that when it is necessary to calculate or measure a quantity that is represented by a phasor, only the real part is used.

1.6 Electromechanical Analogies

The following brief discussion of electromechanical analogies is provided to help insure that the student clearly understands the distinction between the two analogies commonly used in electroacoustic transduction. More thorough treatments are given by Olson (9), Mason (10), and Beranek (11).

The impedance analogy is used more frequently, and examples of its use can be found in refs. (11) and (12). Since this analogy is more convenient for electric field type transducers, it will be used in this book. The mobility analogy, sometimes called the inverse analogy, was first described by Firestone (13) and developed further by LeCorbeiller and Yeung (14). It is often more convenient for magnetic field type transducers. Tabs. 1.1 and 1.2 list the correspondence between mechanical and electrical quantities in these two analogies. In the construction of diagrams, it is often convenient to use the same symbol for corresponding electrical and mechanical quantities. To distinguish between them, a lower case m is often used to designate the mechanical quantity and an upper case subscript, if needed, is used for the electrical quantity.

Table 1.1

The Impedance Analogy

MECHANICAL QUANTITY	ELECTRICAL QUANTITY
Force F	Electromotive force V
Velocity u	Current I
Displacement $x = \int u\,dt$	Charge $q = \int I\,dt$
Mass M	Inductance L
Mechanical Resistance R_m	Resistance R
Compliance C_m	Capacitance C

Table 1.2

The Mobility Analogy

MECHANICAL QUANTITY	ELECTRICAL QUANTITY
Force F	Current I
Velocity u	Electromotive force V
Displacement x	
Impulse $\int F dt$	Charge q
Mass M	Capacitance C
Mechanical Resistance R_m	Conductance g
Compliance C_m	Inductance L

The Impedance Analogy

Most students are already acquainted with the use of the impedance analogy. The example often used to illustrate it, a simple harmonic mechanical oscillator, consists of a parallel combination of discrete lumped elements supported by a rigid boundary: a mass M, a spring C_m, and a viscous damper with a damping force proportional to the velocity, R_m. A simple harmonic driving force acts on the mass causing it to execute simple harmonic motion along the vertical direction. The system is illustrated by the sketch in Fig. 1.1a. The motion of the mass must be relative to an inertial frame of reference denoted by the dotted line in the figures. Note that the quantity common to all three elements is the velocity. The analogous electric circuit for this mechanical system using the impedance analogy is the series circuit consisting of a resistor R, an inductor L, and a capacitor C excited by a voltage source, as shown in Fig. 1.1b. Here, the quantity common to all three electrical elements is the current.

The differential equations of motion for the mechanical system and the electrical circuit have the same form. These equations are:

$$M\frac{du}{dt} + R_m u + \frac{\int u dt}{C_m} = F(t) \tag{1.1}$$

$$L\frac{dI}{dt} + RI + \frac{\int I dt}{C} = V(t). \tag{1.2}$$

Thus the driving point mechanical impedance for the mechanical system may be expressed in the same manner as the driving point electrical impedance of the analogous electrical circuit, one of the useful features of the electromechanical analogy.

The use of this analogy for the displacement–driven simple oscillator is now shown. The mechanical system, shown in Fig. 1.2a, consists of a series arrangement of a spring, a viscous damper, and a mass driven by a source of controlled velocity. The parameter common to all elements is the force. The electrical circuit shown in Fig. 1.2b is the electrical analogue of the system in Fig. 1.2a, and consists of a parallel arrangement of a resistor, a capacitor, and an inductor

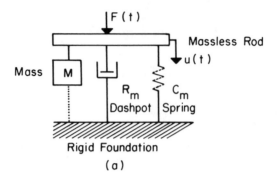

FIG. 1.1 Electromechanical analogies for a force–driven simple oscillator. (a) A simple one–dimensional mechanical system of elements having a common velocity. The rod is assumed to be constrained to prevent rotation. (b) A series electrical circuit analogous to (a) using the impedance analogy.

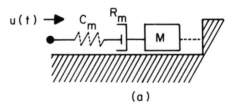

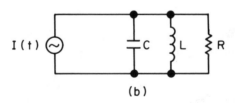

FIG. 1.2 Electromechanical analogies of a displacement–driven simple oscillator. (a) A simple one–dimensional mechanical system of elements having a common force. The system is driven at one end of the spring. The mass and damper slide without friction on the foundation. (b) A parallel electric circuit driven by a current generator, analogous to (a).

driven by a current generator. The voltage across each element is the same. It is easy to show that the differential equations for each of the systems are:

$$C_m \frac{dF}{dt} + \frac{F}{R_m} + \frac{\int F dt}{M} = u(t) \tag{1.3}$$

$$C \frac{dV}{dt} + \frac{V}{R} + \frac{\int V dt}{L} = I(t). \tag{1.4}$$

Thus, we continue to have a basis for the use of electrical methods for calculating driving point mechanical impedance and its behavior as a function of frequency.

Kirchhoff's voltage law, the sum of the voltage drops around a mesh must be zero, was applied in the first example. In the second example, Kirchhoff's current law, the sum of the currents flowing into a junction must be zero, was used. It is seen that the role of the nodes and meshes has been interchanged in these two examples even though the impedance analogy is employed in both. Force and voltage are the analogous intensive or "across" variables and velocity and current are the analogous extensive or "through" variables. Also, the analogue of mechanical elements in parallel is a series electrical combination and the analogue for mechanical elements in series is a parallel electrical circuit.

The Mobility Analogy

In the impedance analogy, force and voltage, the intensive or "across" variables, are analogous and the extensive or "through" variables, velocity and current, are analogous. This analogy can be used to correctly describe the behavior of both systems illustrated in Figs. 1.1 and 1.2. For the mobility analogy described in Tab. 1.2, the mechanical "across" and "through" variables are interchanged. That is, velocity is now the "across" variable and force is the "through" variable. This is a major departure from the usual philosophy and conception of electric circuit analogies. Often, one thinks of the source of emf as the cause and the current flow in the electrical circuit as the effect due to the emf. Accordingly, in the impedance analogy force may be conceived of as the cause and velocity as the effect. In the mobility analogy, velocity may be conceived of as the cause and the force as the effect. The behavior of a mechanical system can be correctly described by the analogous circuit.

In the mobility analogy, the roles of mass and compliance are reversed and the role of mechanical resistance is played by mechanical conductance. If these changes in the coefficients are made in Eq. (1.3), then the equation, which describes the behavior of the series mechanical elements, has the same form as Eq. (1.2), which describes the series electrical circuit. In the same manner, the mobility analogy permits the parallel mechanical system described by Eq. (1.1) to correspond to the parallel electrical circuit described by Eq. (1.4). That is, in the mobility analogy, a mechanical node corresponds to an electrical node and a mechanical loop corresponds to an electrical mesh. For mechanical vibration problems this often simplifies drawing equivalent networks, writing network equations, and calculations.

Using the spring as an example of the conventions appropriate to the mobility analogy, the force is the same throughout the spring and the positive direction for the "force through" the spring is consistent with the spring's becoming longer than its unstretched length. The "velocity difference across" the spring is the relative velocity of the two ends. The sign of the velocity must be consistent with the direction of force through the spring. This and corresponding interpretations for the new "across" and "through" variables in the case of a mass and a mechanical resistance are illustrated in Fig. 1.3.

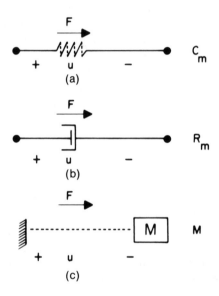

FIG. 1.3   Examples of interpretation of "across" and "through" variables in the mobility analogy. (a) A spring in tension. (b) A mechanical damper in tension. (c) A mass being accelerated to the right with respect to the inertial frame of reference.

References

1. Frederick V. Hunt, *Electroacoustics*, Harvard University Press: Cambridge, MA. Reprinted by the American Institute of Physics for the Acoustical Society of America.
2. Ivor V. Groves, Ed. *Acoustic Transducers*. Benchmark Papers in Acoustics/14. Hutchinson Ross: Stroudsburg, PA (1981).
3. Warren P. Mason, Electrical Wave Filters Employing Quartz Crystals as Elements. *Bell Sys. Tech. Jour.* **13** 405–452 (1934).
4. K.S. Van Dyke. *Phys. Rev.* **25** 895 (1929).
5. K.S. Van Dyke. The Piezoelectric Resonator and its Equivalent Network. *Proc. I.R.E.* **16** 742–764 (1928).

6. W.G. Cady, *Piezoelectricity*. Rev. Ed. Vol. 1. Dover: New York (1964).

7. Warren P. Mason. Piezoelectricity, Its History and Applications. *J. Acoust. Soc. Am.* **70** 1561–1566 (1981).

8. Donald G. Fink and H. Wayne Beatty. *Standard Handbook for Electrical Engineers*. 11th Ed. McGraw-Hill: New York (1978).

9. Harry F. Olson. *Dynamic Analogies*. Van Nostrand: New York (1943).

10. Warren P. Mason. *Electromechanical Transducers and Wave Filters*. 2nd Ed. Van Nostrand: New York (1948).

11. Leo L. Beranek. *Acoustics*. McGraw-Hill: New York (1954). Republished by the American Institute of Physics for the Acoustical Society of America.

12. Lawrence E. Kinsler, Austin R. Frey, Alan B. Coppens, and James V. Sanders. *Fundamentals of Acoustics*. 3rd Ed. Wiley: New York (1982). Ch. 1.

13. F.A. Firestone. A New Analogy Between Mechanical and Electrical Systems. *J. Acoust. Soc. Am.* **4** 249–267 (1933).

14. P. LeCorbeiller and Y. Yeung. Duality in Mechanics. *J. Acoust. Soc. Am.* **24** 643–648 (1952).

Problems

1.1.   Derive expressions for the driving point impedance for the mechanical and electrical circuits shown in Fig. 1.1 and show that the results are consistent with the impedance analogy.

1.2.(a) Make simple sketches of the way in which the real and imaginary parts of the input mechanical impedance of the system shown in Fig. 1.1a change with frequency.

(b)   Make a simple plot of mechanical reactance versus mechanical resistance with frequency as the parameter for the system of Fig. 1.1a.

1.3.(a) Derive an expression for the complex mechanical admittance for the system of Fig. 1.1a.

(b)   Make a simple sketch showing how mechanical susceptance b_m varies with mechanical conductance g_m with frequency as a parameter for the system of Fig. 1.1a.

(c)   Show analytically that the locus of points on a plot for the system of Fig. 1.1a forms a circle as frequency varies from zero to infinity.

1.4.   Show that the use of the mobility analogy causes the parallel mechanical combination of Fig. 1.1a to be analogous to the topologically similar parallel electrical circuit of Fig. 1.2b.

CHAPTER 2

EQUIVALENT ELECTRIC CIRCUITS FOR TRANSDUCERS

2.1 Four-Terminal Transducer Networks

The technical basis for electroacoustic transducers is the experimentally observed association between electrical and mechanical phenomena in certain systems. There is a unique functional relationship between the electrical and mechanical variables which characterize the systems. If the systems are simple enough to be described by two pairs of variables (that is, there is a single degree each of electrical and mechanical freedom), then only two equations are needed to relate these variables. In most textbooks on electroacoustics (e.g., Hunt (1)), it is assumed that a two-port, four-terminal device called the transducer produces the coupling between the electrical and mechanical variables. The device is characterized by two transduction coefficients, one indicating the electrical effects arising from or due to the mechanical forces or motion and the other the mechanical effects arising from or due to the electrical voltage or current. It will be seen that this approach applies generally to transducers, regardless of the details of the actual device.

Following Hunt, a schematic representation of such a device is given in Fig. 2.1a. The transduction coefficient T_{em} gives the electromotive force (emf) at the electrical terminals per unit of velocity in the mechanical terminal. Similarly, T_{me} represents the force acting at the mechanical terminal per unit of current in the electrical mesh. For steady state, simple harmonic conditions, the pair of equations relating the voltage V, the current I, the force F, and the velocity u have the canonical form:

$$V = Z_E I + T_{em} u$$

$$F = T_{me} I + Z_m u$$

$$(2.1)$$

where Z_E and Z_m represent, respectively, the input electrical impedance with the mechanical terminals blocked to restrain movement and the input mechanical impedance with the electrical terminals open-circuited.

That is, if the mechanical port is blocked so that the mechanical velocity is zero, then, from Eq. (2.1), the electrical impedance is:

$$Z_{IN} = \left.\frac{V}{I}\right|_{u=0} = Z_E.$$

If the electrical port is open-circuited so that the electrical current is zero, the

11

impedance presented to the mechanical port is, from Eq. (2.1):

$$Z_{in} = \frac{F}{u}\bigg|_{I=0} = Z_m.$$

If the force is set to zero, that is, if the mechanical terminals are allowed to be completely free to move, then the driving point electrical impedance is readily determined from Eq. (2.1) to be:

$$Z_{IN} = \frac{V}{I}\bigg|_{F=0} = Z_E - \frac{T_{em}T_{me}}{Z_m} \tag{2.2}$$

which is called the free electrical impedance. Similarly, a driving point

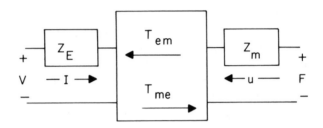

FIG. 2.1a   Schematic diagram of a four-terminal electromechanical transducer.

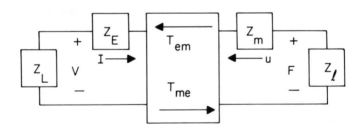

FIG. 2.1b   Schematic diagram of a four-terminal electromechanical transducer with both electrical and mechanical loads.

mechanical impedance can be computed for the case where the voltage is set to zero, that is, the electrical terminals are short–circuited:

$$Z_{in} = \frac{F}{u}\bigg|_{V=0} = Z_m - \frac{T_{em}T_{me}}{Z_E}. \tag{2.3}$$

This is called the short–circuit mechanical impedance.

Several features are to be seen in these last two equations. If either T_{em} or T_{me} were to vanish, the driving point impedances would be the usual electrical or mechanical impedances that exist in the absence of the transducing effect. Thus, we see the importance of bilateral coupling, since the additive terms in each equation arise from the product of the two transduction coefficients. It is also seen that the additive impedance terms are inversely proportional to the impedances in the opposing mesh and the transducer therefore acts as an impedance inverter. Earlier, it was shown that the driving point impedances for the cases where the velocity or current is zero are different from those in which the force or voltage is zero.

The additive term in Eq. (2.2) is usually called the motional impedance. It represents the portion of the electrical driving point impedance that arises from electromechanical coupling. The additive term in Eq. (2.3), which normally has no name, is clearly the portion of the driving point mechanical impedance arising from electromechanical coupling.

The utility of this notion of a motional impedance is not limited to the case of a zero applied force. Consider the system illustrated in Fig. 2.1b in which the electrical and mechanical terminals are loaded with impedances Z_L and Z_l, respectively. Eq. (2.1) may again be solved for the electrical and mechanical driving point impedances with the help of the equations:

$$Z_L = -V/I \tag{2.4a}$$

$$Z_l = -F/u. \tag{2.4b}$$

The result for the electrical driving point impedance in this case is readily determined to be:

$$Z_{IN} = Z_E - \frac{T_{em}T_{me}}{Z_m + Z_l} \tag{2.5}$$

and for the mechanical driving point impedance:

$$Z_{in} = Z_m - \frac{T_{em}T_{me}}{Z_E + Z_L}. \tag{2.6}$$

We now write the input electrical impedance as the sum of the blocked and motional impedances:

$$Z_{IN} = Z_E + Z_M. \tag{2.7}$$

From Eq. (2.5), the motional impedance for this case is:

$$Z_M = -\frac{T_{em}T_{me}}{Z_m + Z_l}. \tag{2.8}$$

The inverse transformation of mechanical impedance to the electrical side of the circuit has profound effects on how the electrical impedance changes with changes in mechanical loading or changes in frequency. For example, when the motional impedance is at a maximum, which corresponds approximately to the condition for electrical anti-resonance, the mechanical impedance appearing in the denominator of Eq. (2.8) is a minimum, corresponding to a mechanical resonance.

2.2 Reciprocity, Symmetry, and Realizability

The principle of reciprocity (*1,2*) provides a basis for using the methods of electric circuit analysis in describing and analyzing the behavior of electro-acoustic transducers since both electrical and mechanical systems obey this principle. Because relationships between mechanical variables and mechanical elements in the transducer are analogous to the relationships between electrical variables and electrical elements connected in a corresponding manner, it is possible to draw equivalent electrical circuits for mechanical and acoustical vibrating systems (*3*). The impedance analogy, which is used most in this book, designates an analogy between mechanical and electrical impedance. That is, the complex ratio of force to velocity is analogous to the complex ratio of voltage to current. This creates correspondences between mechanical mass and electrical inductance, mechanical compliance and electrical capacitance, and mechanical resistance and electrical resistance. These relationships are shown in Tab. 1.1. The mobility analogy, in which force and velocity are analogous to current and voltage, respectively, is convenient for some problems (see Tab. 1.2).

Two consequences of the principle of reciprocity make it important to the use and design of electroacoustic transducers. First, reciprocity leads to a very basic relationship (*4,5*) between the receiving sensitivity of a transducer and its transmitting response, which permits a method of absolute calibration of the transducer based on electrical measurements. Also, the directional pattern of a reversible transducer is the same whether it is used as a projector or a receiver, which will be discussed in more detail in Ch. 9.

An important question is whether the electrical–to–mechanical transduction mechanism also obeys the reciprocity principle. The answer for most transducers is yes. It will be demonstrated by two simple examples later in this chapter that transducers involving the interaction between electric fields and mechanical effects, so–called electric field type transducers, are indeed reciprocal devices, and that the so–called magnetic field type transducers which involve interactions between the magnetic fields arising from current flow and mechanical effects, are anti–reciprocal. This anti–reciprocity appears because of the conventions used to describe the forces due to current flowing in a conductor in a magnetic field and the induced emf arising from motion of a conductor in a magnetic field. The particular association of reciprocity and anti–reciprocity with these devices holds only for the impedance analogy. There are several methods for making the behavior of such elements become reciprocal (*1*), two of which will be described later.

The reciprocity principle is very general and a reciprocal relationship exists between variables in both mechanical and electrical systems that vibrate at small amplitudes. Rayleigh's statement (*2*) of the reciprocity theorem for mechanical systems may be paraphrased in the following way. Let:

$$F_1, F_2, \ldots, u_1, u_2, \ldots \quad \text{and} \quad F_1', F_2', \ldots, u_1', u_2', \ldots$$

be two sets of sinusoidally varying forces acting on a system and the corresponding velocities. If the array of coefficients in the equations of motion of the system is symmetrical, then:

$$F_1 u'_1 + F_2 u'_2 + \ldots = F'_1 u_1 + F'_2 u_2 + \ldots. \tag{2.9}$$

If all forces except F_1 and F_2 are zero, then:

$$F_1 u'_1 + F_2 u'_2 = F'_1 u_1 + F'_2 u_2. \tag{2.10}$$

If we let $F_2 = 0$ and $F'_1 = 0$, then:

$$F_1 u'_1 = F'_2 u_2$$

or   (2.11)

$$\frac{u_2}{F_1} = \frac{u'_1}{F'_2}.$$

Thus, in the first case, the relation between the response u_2 and the force F_1 when $F_2 = 0$ is the same as the relation between the response u'_1 and the force F'_2 in the second case, when $F_1 = 0$.

The principle of electrical reciprocity states that the ratio of the response transform to the excitation transform is invariant when the positions of the

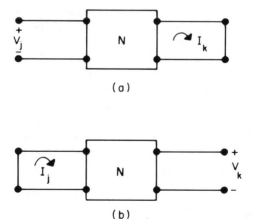

FIG. 2.2   Reciprocal network. (a) A source V_j produces a current I_k in another loop of network N. (b) A source V_k in the loop k produces a current I_j in the jth loop of the network.

excitation source and the response sensor are interchanged in the network (2,6). The relationships in a reciprocal network are illustrated by the two circuits in Fig. 2.2. In (a) the excitation is a generator located in loop j and the response is the current flowing in loop k. In (b) the generator is moved to the kth loop and the current is measured in the jth loop. If the network N is reciprocal, that is, if the transform impedance is symmetric, then the ratios of current to voltage will be identical for the two situations. That is:

$$\frac{I_k}{V_j} = \frac{I_j}{V_k}. \tag{2.12}$$

The similarity between Eq. (2.11) and Eq. (2.12) is apparent. The reciprocity principle also applies to distributed systems but in a more complicated form.

Thus, if the principle of reciprocity and all of its consequences are to be applicable to the entire transducer system, it is necessary for the matrix of coefficients relating the electrical and mechanical variables to be symmetrical. If this is the case, then the commonly used theorems of electrical circuit theory, such as Thévenin's theorem, Kirchhoff's laws, etc., will apply. Applying this condition to the networks of Fig. 2.1 requires that:

$$T_{em} = T_{me}. \tag{2.13}$$

At times, the transducer designer may only be concerned with the analysis or determination of the response of a given assembly of electrical and mechanical elements for a specified excitation. At other times the design objective is a transducer that will have a specified response to this excitation. For example, electric circuit synthesis methods may be useful in solving the problem: Given a desired excitation and response, design a network symbolizing the transducer which will give the specified response. In such a case, it is important for the designer to avoid placing requirements on the response that may not be physically realizable. The conditions for the physical realizability of an electric network that is equivalent to a mechanical system are similar to those for the realizability of any electrical circuit (7). Hunt (1) demonstrates a sufficient condition of realizability for a simple case.

The second consequence of reciprocity, mentioned earlier, may be stated in the following way. Consider a system in which M_H is the open–circuit receiving sensitivity of a transducer measured in open–circuit voltage per unit of acoustic pressure, and S_T is the free field transmitting current response measured in acoustic pressure at a range r from its acoustic center per unit of current flow into the transducer. Then, according to the reciprocity theorem, the free field reciprocity parameter J is given by:

$$J = \frac{M_H}{S_T} = \frac{2r\lambda}{\rho c} \tag{2.14}$$

where λ is the acoustic wavelength and ρc is the specific acoustic impedance of the fluid in which the sound is measured. For details of the development and proof of this result, the student should consult refs. (4), (5), and (8). Bobber (9) describes methods for using this result in the calibration of transducers by free field techniques and techniques in which the sound field is generated in an enclosure, such as a cavity or tube.

2.3 An Elementary Electrostatic Transducer

This section and the next treat two very simple elementary electromechanical transducers. One has an electric field transducing mechanism and the other a magnetic field mechanism. The purpose is to illustrate the physical methods which may be used to determine quantitative relationships between electrical and mechanical variables and to show that one mechanism behaves in a reciprocal manner while the other is anti–symmetrical.

Consider a parallel plate capacitor in which one electrode is rigidly fixed and the other is thin and capable of motion. The arrangement is sketched in Fig. 2.3. The area of the electrodes is A, the space between them, which is a vacuum, has an equilibrium thickness d, that is assumed to be very small

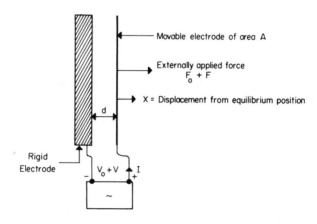

FIG. 2.3   An elementary parallel plate electrostatic transducer.

compared to the transverse dimensions of the electrodes. A voltage having a steady component V_0 and a sinusoidally varying component V is applied to the capacitor. A sinusoidally varying current I is assumed to flow. An externally applied force also consisting of a steady component F_0 and a time varying component F acts on the movable electrode. It is assumed that the electrode executes a sinusoidally varying displacement x and has a corresponding velocity of motion u in the same direction.

Elementary expressions for the force between the electrodes due to electrostatic effects F_e, the capacitance C, and the charge on the electrodes q are:

$$F_e = - \frac{q^2}{2\epsilon_0 A}$$

$$C = \frac{\epsilon_0 A}{d + x}$$

$$q = C(V_0 + V)$$

(2.15)

where ϵ_0 is the dielectric permittivity of a vacuum.

The negative sign in the expression for F_e indicates that the force is always one of attraction and thus acts in the direction opposite to that chosen for positive placement. If it is assumed that the movable electrode has a mechanical impedance Z_m consisting of a mass M, a mechanical resistance R_m, and a compliance C_m, then the equation of motion is:

$$F_0 + F + F_e = Z_m u. \tag{2.16}$$

A corresponding equation for the electrical mesh can be written as:

$$V_0 + V = ZI \tag{2.17}$$

where it is assumed that the device has an electrical impedance Z consisting of an inductance L, a resistance R, and a capacitance C.

The existence of a steady polarizing voltage, required for proper functioning of the electrostatic transducer, creates a steady electrostatic force between the electrodes that must be countered by a steady external force component in order to maintain the equilibrium electrode spacing. This, in addition to the nonlinear relationships shown above, makes it more convenient and instructive to write the circuit equations as differential equations. Following Hunt (1), the differential equation for the electrical mesh is:

$$V_0 + V = L \frac{d^2q}{dt^2} + R \frac{dq}{dt} + \frac{q(d + x)}{\epsilon_0 A} \tag{2.18}$$

and for the mechanical mesh is:

$$F_0 + F = M \frac{d^2x}{dt^2} + R_m \frac{dx}{dt} + \frac{x}{C_m} + \frac{q^2}{2\epsilon_0 A}. \tag{2.19}$$

These are clearly nonlinear differential equations. However, they can be "linearized" by assuming that the charge consists of a steady component q_0 and a sinusoidally varying part q_1. Both x and q_1 are assumed to be small enough compared to d and q_0, respectively, that second–order small quantities, involving the square of q_1 or the products of q_1 and x, may be neglected. Thus, the nonlinear terms in Eqs. (2.18) and (2.19) can be rewritten:

$$\frac{q(d + x)}{\epsilon_0 A} \simeq \frac{q_0 d}{\epsilon_0 A} + \frac{q_1 d}{\epsilon_0 A} + \frac{q_0 x}{\epsilon_0 A} = \frac{q_0}{C_0} + \frac{q_1}{C_0} + \frac{q_0 x}{\epsilon_0 A} \tag{2.20}$$

and

$$\frac{q^2}{2\epsilon_0 A} \simeq \frac{q_0^2}{2\epsilon_0 A} + \frac{q_0 q_1}{\epsilon_0 A} \tag{2.21}$$

where $C_0 = \epsilon_0(A/d)$.

If we let:

$$F_0 = \frac{q_0^2}{2\epsilon_0 A} \tag{2.22a}$$

and

$$V_0 = \frac{q_0}{C_0} \qquad (2.22b)$$

then Eqs. (2.18) and (2.19) become, in their linearized form:

$$V = L\frac{d^2q_1}{dt^2} + R\frac{dq_1}{dt} + \frac{q_1}{C_0} + \frac{q_0 x}{\epsilon_0 A}$$

$$F = M\frac{d^2x}{dt^2} + R_m u + \frac{u}{j\omega C_m} + \frac{q_0 I}{j\omega\epsilon_0 A}.$$

Noting that:

$$I = \frac{dq_1}{dt} = j\omega q_1$$

and

$$u = \frac{dx}{dt} = j\omega x$$

the above equations can be written as:

$$V = j\omega L I + R I + \frac{I}{j\omega C_0} + \frac{q_0 u}{j\omega\epsilon_0 A}$$

$$F = j\omega M u + R_m u + \frac{u}{j\omega C_m} + \frac{q_0 I}{j\omega\epsilon_0 A}$$

or, in the canonical form:

$$V = Z_E I + \frac{q_0 u}{j\omega\epsilon_0 A} \qquad (2.23a)$$

$$F = \frac{q_0 I}{j\omega\epsilon_0 A} + Z_m u. \qquad (2.23b)$$

Thus, the form of Eq. (2.1) is obtained with:

$$T_{em} = T_{me} = \frac{q_0}{j\omega\epsilon_0 A} \qquad (2.24)$$

and the electrostatic transducer, described by a symmetrical transformation matrix, is a reciprocal transducer for the impedance analogy used here. It is also to be noted that the transduction coefficient can be written in terms of an electromechanical capacitance:

$$C_{em} = \frac{\epsilon_0 A}{q_0}$$

so that Eq. (2.24) becomes, using Eq. (2.22) and deleting the subscripts on T:

$$T = \frac{1}{j\omega C_{em}} = \frac{V_0}{j\omega d}. \tag{2.26}$$

Note that T varies inversely with frequency and is limited by the maximum attainable electric field strength in the capacitor.

2.4 An Elementary Electrodynamic Transducer

Consider a linear segment of a conductor of length ℓ oriented at right angles to a steady magnetic field of intensity **B**. An electrical voltage V is applied and a current I flows through the conductor. An externally applied mechanical force **F** acts at right angles to both the conductor and the magnetic field and the conductor moves with velocity **u** in the same direction. The arrangement is sketched in Fig. 2.4.

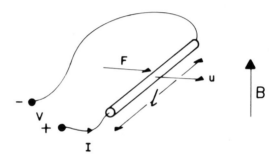

FIG. 2.4   An elementary electrodynamic transducer. The current carrying conductor of length ℓ is oriented perpendicularly to the magnetic field **B**. An externally applied force **F** acts perpendicularly to ℓ and **B**. The resulting velocity **u** is colinear with **F**.

That is:

$$V\big|_{u=0} = Z_E I$$
$$F\big|_{I=0} = Z_m u. \tag{2.27}$$

The interaction between the current flow and the magnetic field results in a force acting on the conductor F_{mag} given by Ampere's law:

$$\mathbf{F}_{\text{mag}} = I\ell \times \mathbf{B} \tag{2.28}$$

where the indicated operation is the vector product. For the orientations chosen in this case, this force has the value of $\ell B I$ and is oriented parallel to and in the same direction as the applied force **F**. Therefore:

$$F + \ell B I = Z_m u. \tag{2.29}$$

The motion of the conductor in the magnetic field also generates an electromotive force in the conductor that is, from Faraday's law of induction:

$$\mathbf{emf} = \ell u \times \mathbf{B}. \tag{2.30}$$

According to Lenz's law, the direction of the emf would tend to cause a current to flow that in interacting with the existing magnetic field would create a force opposing the motion. For the orientations chosen in Fig. 2.4, this emf has the magnitude of $B\ell u$ and opposes the applied voltage. Thus:

$$V - B\ell u = Z_E I \tag{2.31}$$

and, from Eqs. (2.29) and (2.30), we have the canonical relations:

$$V = Z_E I + B\ell u \tag{2.32a}$$

$$F = -B\ell I + Z_m u. \tag{2.32b}$$

Comparison of these results with Eq. (2.1) makes it clear that, for this mechanism:

$$T_{em} = B\ell$$
$$T_{me} = -B\ell. \tag{2.33}$$

The matrix of the transformation impedance function is anti-symmetric. Thus, according to impedance analogy used here in which voltage and force are analogous quantities and current and velocity are analogous, a transducer based on the above coupling mechanism would violate the principle of reciprocity.

2.5 Equivalent Circuits for Transducers

Reciprocal Transducers

An electrical circuit is called equivalent to another if identical relationships between the electrical variables are obtained when the ordinary circuit theorems such as Kirchhoff's laws are applied. Circuits for electromechanical transducers are equivalent if they yield the same relationships between variables when the theorems and the electromechanical analogies described in Ch. 1 are used. If the equations relating the variables, e.g., Eq. (2.1), are symmetrical, then the reciprocity conditions are satisfied and it is always possible (1) to find an electrical network that conforms or is equivalent to the equations relating the variables. Another way to describe an equivalent circuit is given by Cady:

The "equivalent network" of any electromechanical system is generally understood to mean an assemblage of R-, L- and C-values, each independent of
frequency, so interconnected that when the assemblage is substituted for the
actual system in any electric circuit its effect on the circuit will be the same as that
of the electromechanical system itself, at least over a certain range of frequency.[1]

In the following section, several examples of typical equivalent electrical
circuits for reciprocal transducers are described. One circuit will be examined
more closely and the admittance method for describing its behavior will be
presented.

It will be assumed that the transformation factors are symmetric and
$T_{em} = T_{me} = T$. Following Hunt(1), several examples of equivalent circuits
are shown in Fig. 2.5. It is a simple exercise to show that applying ordinary

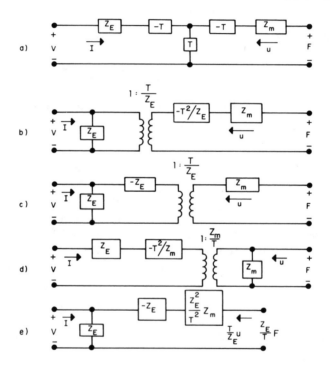

FIG. 2.5   Typical equivalent networks for four-terminal reciprocal transducers. Note that the turns ratios for
the idealized transformers have dimensions.

circuit analysis procedures to these circuits results in the relations given by Eq.
(2.1). The circuit of Fig. 2.5b uses the symbol for the ideal electrical transformer
in which the turns ratio has the dimensions of force to voltage or current to
velocity. In Fig. 2.5e, all mechanical elements and variables have been transformed so they have the dimensions of the corresponding electrical quantities.

---

[1] W.G. Cady. *Piezoelectricity.* Vol. 1, pg. 333. Dover, New York (1962).

Note that another difference in Fig. 2.5b is the placement of the blocked impedance in shunt with the electromechanical transformer. In many transducers for underwater sound, the transducing material is piezoelectric and the blocked impedance is a capacitance shunted by a very large leakage resistance. Because of this, it is often more convenient to compute the input electrical admittance. An equivalent circuit such as Fig. 2.5b places the blocked impedance in shunt with the motional impedance. This circuit will be discussed in detail in a later section, where it will be convenient to change notation and let the transformer turns ratio be designated by:

$$N = T/Z_E. \tag{2.34}$$

Coping with Anti-Reciprocal Transducers

It was pointed out earlier that a consequence of anti-symmetry in the transduction coefficients is that the transducer is anti-reciprocal and therefore the device as a whole will not obey the conventional laws of electric circuit theory, even though the electrical and mechanical parts separately do obey reciprocity. This does not mean that the canonical relations of the sort given in Eq. (2.1) in the analysis of an anti-reciprocal transducer cannot be used; in fact, the transducer's behavior can be described with perfectly valid equivalent electrical circuit elements. However, to do so involves a change in the electromechanical analogy from the impedance analogy to the mobility analogy described in Ch. 1.

A very simple step is required to change to the mobility analogy. Let the transformation factor $T_{em} = -T_{me} = T$, so Eq. (2.1) becomes:

$$V = Z_E I + Tu \tag{2.35a}$$

$$F = -TI + Z_m u. \tag{2.35b}$$

These are recast so that velocity becomes the dependent variable. A little algebra results in:

$$V = Z_E \left(1 + \frac{T^2}{Z_E Z_m} \right) I + \frac{T}{Z_m} F \tag{2.36a}$$

$$u = \frac{T}{Z_m} I + \frac{1}{Z_m} F. \tag{2.36b}$$

Thus, we have achieved a system that has a symmetrical array of coefficients and, therefore, obeys the principle of reciprocity. We have made velocity effectively an "across" variable, since it is now analogous to voltage, and force a "through" variable, analogous to current. The conventions for the mobility analogy are described in the previous chapter. Several networks that give these equations, and are therefore equivalent, are shown in Fig. 2.6.

Hunt (1) developed another rule for stating the correct direction of the force

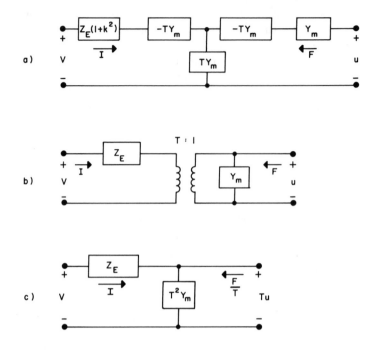

FIG. 2.6   Typical equivalent networks for an anti-symmetric transducer.

due to the interaction between the current flowing in a conductor and a fixed magnetic field and the direction of the emf induced in a conductor moving in a magnetic field which still preserves the formal symmetry necessary for reciprocity. He introduced the spatial operator $\bar{\mathbf{k}}$, which is used in expressions for the force and induced emf, as:

$$\mathbf{F} = B\ell\bar{\mathbf{k}}\mathbf{I} \qquad \text{and} \qquad \text{emf} = B\ell\bar{\mathbf{k}}\mathbf{u}.$$

The operator rotates the positive direction of the vector which follows it, $+I$ or $+u$, by 90 degrees counterclockwise in the direction of the vector which precedes it, B, in order to determine the positive direction of F or emf. Another property of this operator is that it does not commute with the imaginary time operator j. That is, $j\bar{\mathbf{k}} = -\bar{\mathbf{k}}j$. The role of $\bar{\mathbf{k}}$ is illustrated in Fig. 2.7. Hunt (1) states that this approach permits the full use of electric circuit analysis for systems that mix symmetrical and anti-symmetrical coupling mechanisms in the same transducer, which ordinarily would violate the reciprocity theorem (11). We will not need to use this method in this book.

It is worthwhile from a historical viewpoint to note that Tellegen (12) introduced a passive, anti-reciprocal circuit element, which he called a gyrator, in order to account for physical situations where reciprocity does not hold.

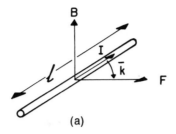

(a)

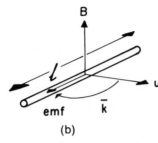

(b)

FIG. 2.7 Schematic illustration of the role of the spatial operator $\bar{\mathbf{k}}$ in determining directions of the force and induced emf due to interactions with a magnetic field. In (a), the force is due to the interaction between the current in the conductor and the B field. In (b), the direction of emf is determined from the velocity of motion and the B field. The $\bar{\mathbf{k}}$ operator rotates the direction of I or u by 90° counterclockwise around the positive direction of B (After Hunt (1)).

The voltage and current relations for the gyrator are:

$$V_1 = \mp r I_2 \tag{2.37}$$

$$V_2 = \pm r I_1 \tag{2.38}$$

where r is called the gyration resistance. In matrix form, these become:

$$\begin{bmatrix} V_1 \\ V_2 \end{bmatrix} = \begin{bmatrix} 0 & \mp r \\ \pm r & 0 \end{bmatrix} \begin{bmatrix} I_1 \\ I_2 \end{bmatrix} \tag{2.39}$$

where the choice of signs depends on the direction in which the phase reversal occurs. Its behavior as an impedance invertor is illustrated by the analysis of Fig. 2.8 in which the gyrator is terminated by a resistor R. Using the relation of Eq. (2.37) and the additional relation:

$$V_2 = -R I_2. \tag{2.40}$$

it is seen that the input electrical impedance is given by:

$$Z_{IN} = \frac{V_1}{I_1} = \frac{r^2}{R} = r^2 G \tag{2.41}$$

where $G = 1/R$. The similarity to the behavior of the anti–reciprocal transducer is clear.

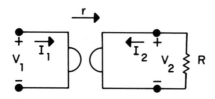

FIG. 2.8   Schematic representation of an ideal gyrator loaded with a resistor R (*13*).

2.6 Admittance and Impedance Analysis

Impedance and admittance analysis, so useful in the study of electrical circuits, is also very important in examining the behavior of electroacoustic transducers. This can take the form of calculating or measuring the magnitudes of Y or Z or the values of the real and imaginary parts of Y or Z and then plotting these results as a function of frequency. It is often useful to plot the real and imaginary parts of Y or Z in the complex plane using frequency as a parameter. For the purpose of illustrating these methods, it will be assumed

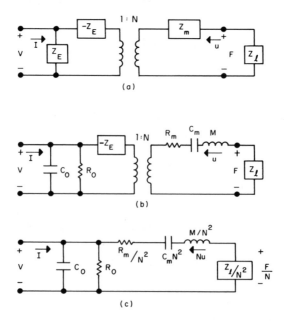

FIG. 2.9   Typical equivalent circuits for a simple piezoelectric transducer. In (c), all mechanical elements have been transformed into electrical units. The effects of $-Z_E$ are ignored.

that the transducer is constructed using an ideal piezoelectric material and that the mechanical system has reasonably small losses so that a distinct resonance will be exhibited. In this case the change in the values of the blocked impedance elements R_0 and $1/\omega C_0$ in the neighborhood of mechanical resonance is relatively small. It will be shown later that the mechanical impedance of a transducer can be represented in the neighborhood of the mechanical resonance as a mechanical resistance, a compliance, and a mass connected in parallel.

An equivalent circuit that is often useful for the case of a reciprocal piezoelectric transducer is shown in Fig. 2.9a. The mechanical terminals may be connected to a mechanical load that is, in general, a complex quantity. In Fig. 2.9c, all elements are in electrical units. The input electrical admittance is:

$$Y_{IN} = \frac{I}{V} = Y_E + \frac{N^2}{Z_m + Z_l} \tag{2.42}$$

or

$$Y_{IN} = Y_E + Y_M \tag{2.43}$$

where Y_M, the motional admittance, is the part of the input electrical admittance due to the motion of the mechanical system. The values of the terms which determine the admittance are given by:

$$Y_E = \frac{1}{R_0} + j\omega C_0 \tag{2.44a}$$

$$Z_m = R_m + j\left(\omega M - \frac{1}{\omega C_m}\right) \tag{2.44b}$$

$$Z_l = R_l + jX_l. \tag{2.44c}$$

First consider the case where the force is zero. That is, the mechanical terminals are not loaded and are free. The input electrical admittance becomes:

$$Y_{IN}\big|_{F=0} = \frac{1}{R_0} + j\omega C_0 + \frac{N^2}{R_m + j\left(\omega M - \frac{1}{\omega C_m}\right)} \tag{2.45}$$

and the motional admittance can be written as:

$$Y_M = \frac{N^2 R_m}{|Z_m|^2} - jN^2 \frac{\omega M - \frac{1}{\omega C_m}}{|Z_m|^2}. \tag{2.46}$$

Assuming that the square of the turns ratio of the electromechanical transformer is real, the real and imaginary parts of the input admittance for unloaded mechanical terminals are:

$$g = \frac{1}{R_0} + \frac{N^2 R_m}{|Z_m|^2}$$

$$b = \omega C_0 - N^2 \frac{\omega M - \dfrac{1}{\omega C_m}}{|Z_m|^2}. \tag{2.47}$$

As the frequency increases from a value slightly below the level of mechanical resonance, defined for the unloaded case by:

$$\omega_s^2 = \frac{1}{M C_m} \tag{2.48}$$

inspection of Eq. (2.47) shows that the mechanical impedance is stiffness–controlled and the susceptance increases with frequency while the conductance changes very little. Near resonance, both b and g change rapidly with frequency. At the mechanical resonance frequency, g goes through its maximum value while the motional contribution to b goes to zero. As the frequency increases above ω_s, the susceptance and the conductance decrease somewhat. Thus, the locus of points of the motional admittance plotted in the complex plane with frequency as a parameter forms a circle for the case of a series resonant mechanical system.

When the transducer is loaded by the mechanical impedance Z_l, the complex input admittance is:

$$Y_{IN} = \frac{1}{R_0} + j\omega C_0 + \frac{N^2}{R_m + R_l + j\left(\omega M - \dfrac{1}{\omega C_m} + X_l\right)} \tag{2.49}$$

which has real and imaginary parts given by:

$$g = \frac{1}{R_0} + \frac{N^2(R_m + R_l)}{|Z_m + Z_l|^2} \tag{2.50a}$$

$$b = \omega C_0 - N^2 \frac{\omega M - \dfrac{1}{\omega C_m} + X_l}{|Z_m + Z_l|^2}. \tag{2.50b}$$

In this case, the frequency of mechanical resonance may change due to the existence of a reactive component in the load and the diameter of the motional admittance loop will be smaller than for the unloaded case. Martin (14) gives a more thorough development of the use of admittance measurements in the equivalent circuit analysis of a piezoelectric resonator, including means for estimating and reducing errors.

2.7 Analysis of a Simple Equivalent Circuit

A great deal of information about the characteristics of the mechanical parts of the transducer can be obtained from measurements at the electrical terminals.

In order to illustrate the use of electrical impedance and admittance analysis, a very simple equivalent electrical circuit for a piezoelectric–type transducer, valid only in the neighborhood of mechanical resonance, is now worked out as an example. It will be seen that although the admittance Y is the reciprocal of the impedance Z, the behavior of the two functions in the frequency domain is basically very different. In many cases of practical importance, the admittance function for a piezoelectric transducer is more easily interpreted. However, there are often circumstances that prohibit the measurement of Y and require that Z be measured. For these reasons, both methods of analysis are demonstrated.

In simplifying the equivalent circuit for Fig. 2.9c it is assumed that the blocked leakage conductance $1/R_0$ is small enough compared to the suscep-tance term ωC_0 that it may be neglected. The motional impedance is repre-sented by a series R–L–C circuit in shunt with the blocked capacitance, an approximation that is often valid in the neighborhood of a mechanical resonance. A schematic representation of this circuit is shown in Fig. 2.10a. Occasionally, the equivalent series network of the sort shown in Fig. 2.10b must be used.

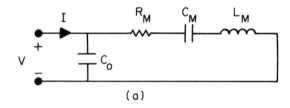

(a)

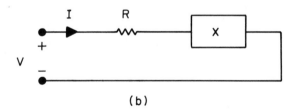

(b)

FIG. 2.10   A simplified equivalent circuit for a piezoelectric transducer valid in the neighborhood of mechani-cal resonance. (a) The series R–L–C elements form the motional parts of the impedance. C_0 is the blocked capacitance. (b) The form of an equivalent series circuit.

Graphical presentations of data on Y or Z are useful. Decisions about which functions are to be plotted or the format for plotting may be affected by several factors. For example, the characteristics of the instruments to be used may limit the available options or the information needed for a particular design problem may make one choice more useful than another. A method that will be used often here is to plot the real and imaginary parts of Y or Z in the complex plane with frequency as a parameter. This will give the so-called "admittance circles" or "impedance circles" in the neighborhood of the resonances. Plots of the real and imaginary parts of the admittance or impedance as a function of frequency are commonly used. Because the blocked impedance element is a capacitor electrically in parallel with the motional elements, it is more convenient and easier to interpret the data for piezoelectric transducers from admittance measurements. However, in some cases it may be much easier to measure impedance rather than admittance. Requirements for the driving amplifiers are often specified in terms of the electrical impedance of the applied load.

The input electrical admittance of the circuit can be written down upon inspection:

$$Y_{IN} = Y_E + Y_M = j\omega C_0 + \cfrac{1}{R_M + j\left(\omega L_M - \cfrac{1}{\omega C_M}\right)}. \tag{2.51}$$

The reciprocal of this function, the input electrical impedance, becomes a more complicated function of frequency. It is a straightforward process to determine the real and imaginary parts of the series circuit shown in Fig. 2.10b. In some cases, it may be more convenient to find another equivalent circuit of R-, L-, and C-elements from which the impedance is more easily calculated. The definitions of the critical frequencies and their relationships to specific points on the impedance and admittance circles plotted in the complex plane are given in Fig. 2.11. These are patterned after the definitions given in the IRE standards on piezoelectric crystal vibrators (15).

An example more typical of a piezoelectric projector designed to be used in water is similar to an example used by Miller (16). Values chosen by Miller for the circuit shown in Fig. 2.10a were:

$C_0 = 1.5$ nF $C_M = 0.5$ nF

$R_M = 3200$ ohms $L_M = 0.5$ H.

These give a frequency for mechanical resonance of about 10 kHz, a frequency of minimum admittance of about 11.5 kHz, a Q of about 10 in the neighborhood of resonance, and an electromechanical coupling factor of 0.5. In addition, results are presented for values of motional resistance of 1600 and 6400 ohms in order to demonstrate the effects of varying the acoustic loading.

Figs. 2.12a and 2.12b give plots of the magnitude and phase of the input admittance of the simple circuit as a function of frequency for three values of the resistance R_M. It is clear that for lower values of Q the changes in $|Y|$ and phase in the neighborhood of resonance occur more slowly with changes in frequency and the excursions of the admittance from the median value are smaller than for a higher Q. It is also clear from the graphs that for least values of Q the phase angle does not pass through zero and the definitions of electrical resonance and anti–resonance do not have their usual meanings.

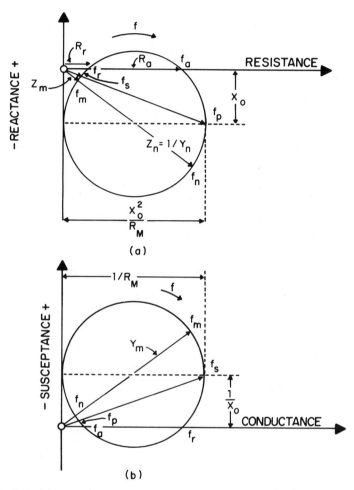

(a)

(b)

C_M = Motional capacitance	Characteristic frequencies:
L_M = Motional inductance	f_m = Frequency of maximum admittance and minimum impedance
R_M = Motional resistance	
C_0 = Blocked, shunt capacitance	f_s = Frequency of motional (series) resonance $= \dfrac{1}{2\pi \sqrt{L_M C_M}}$

f_r = Electrical resonance frequency, where the electrical reactance is zero

f_a = Electrical anti–resonance frequency (electrical reactance is zero)

f_p = Parallel resonance frequency $= \dfrac{1}{2\pi} \sqrt{\dfrac{1}{L_M} \dfrac{C_0 + C_M}{C_M C_0}}$

f_n = Frequency of minimum admittance and maximum impedance

FIG. 2.11   Vector impedance and admittance diagrams for a piezoelectric vibrator in the neighborhood of mechanical resonance. The leakage resistance R_0 is assumed to be infinite. (After (14)).

(a)

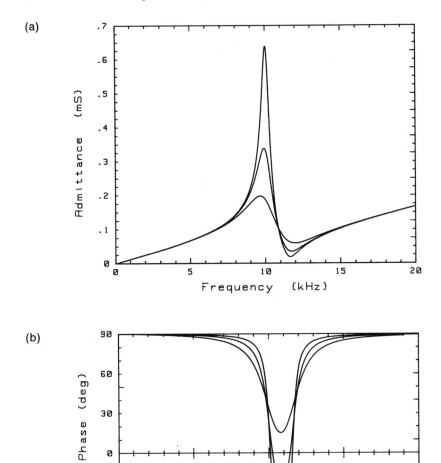

(b)

FIG. 2.12   (a) Plot of the admittance of the simple transducer circuit as a function of frequency for values of motional resistance of 1600, 3200, and 6400 ohms. (b) Plot of the phase of the admittance shown in (a).

Fig. 2.13 is a plot of the real and imaginary parts of the admittance as a function of frequency. It can also be seen from inspection of Fig. 2.12a and Eq. (2.51) that if the value of R is not too large (that is, if the Q is not too small), at low frequencies the asymptotic value of the electrical admittance corresponds to completely free mechanical terminals. Similarly, at high frequencies the electrical admittance approaches the clamped value. That is, at low frequencies:

$$Y_{IN} = j\omega(C_0 + C_M). \tag{2.52}$$

At high frequencies:

$$Y_{IN} = j\omega C_0. \tag{2.53}$$

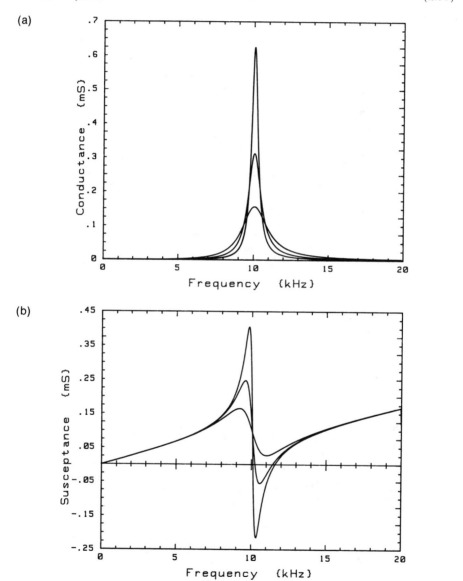

FIG. 2.13 Plot of the conductance (a) and susceptance (b) of the simple transducer circuit for motional resistances of 1600, 3200, and 6400 ohms.

Thus, the slopes of b versus f at low and high frequencies, which may be estimated directly from the plot, can be used to estimate values of the blocked capacitance and the motional capacitance. This is often practical in evaluating transducers if the frequencies of other mechanical resonances are not too close to the resonance under study.

(a)

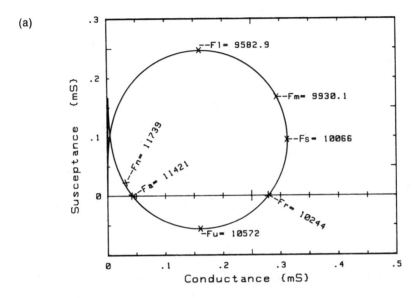

FIG. 2.14   Admittance circles for the simple transducer circuit with a motional resistance of 3200 ohms.

(b)

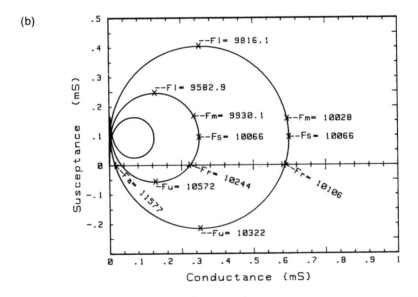

FIG. 2.15   Admittance circles for the simple circuit with motional resistances of 1600, 3200, and 6400 ohms.

Fig. 2.14 is a plot of the susceptance versus conductance with frequency as a parameter and values of critical frequencies annotated for the case where R_M is 3200 ohms. The effects of varying the load resistance on the admittance circles are shown in Fig. 2.15.

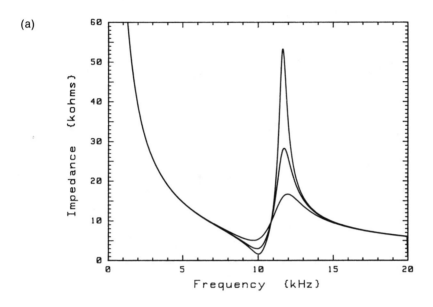

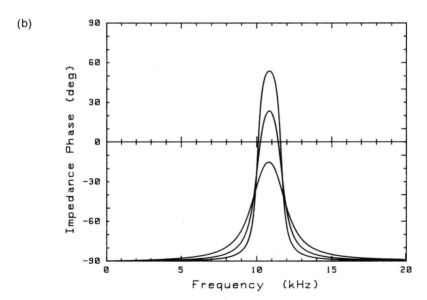

FIG. 2.16 Plot of the impedance (a) and its phase angle (b) for the simple transducer circuit with motional resistances of 1600, 3200, and 6400 ohms.

Figs. 2.16a and 2.16b show plots of the magnitude and phase angle of the input impedance for this circuit as a function of frequency for three values of the motional resistance. The resistance and reactance are similarly plotted in Figs. 2.17a and 2.17b. It is seen that these differ significantly in appearance from the plots of the admittance parameters. Finally, Fig. 2.18 shows the

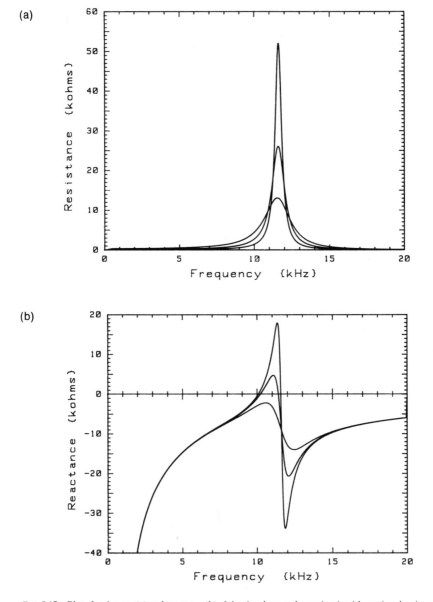

FIG. 2.17   Plot of resistance (a) and reactance (b) of the simple transducer circuit with motional resistances of 1600, 3200, and 6400 ohms.

vector impedance plotted in the complex plane with frequency as a parameter. Again, three different values of the motional resistance were used. The contrast in the appearance of the impedance and admittance circles is clear.

Values of several parameters for this circuit are given in Tab. 2.1. Small differences between the tabulated critical frequencies and those shown as annotations in the figures are due to interpolation errors in the computer programs that produced the curves.

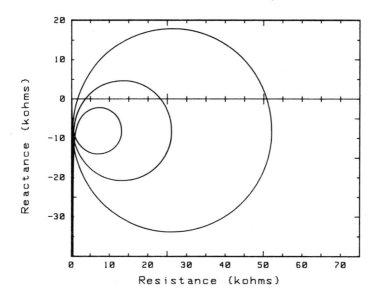

FIG. 2.18   Impedance circles for the simple circuit with motional resistances of 1600, 3200, and 6400 ohms.

Table 2.1

Parameters for the Simple Transducer Equivalent Circuit

PARAMETER		PARAMETER VALUES FOR MOTIONAL RESISTANCES OF:		
		1600 ohms	3200 ohms	6400 ohms
f_s	Motional resonance frequency (Hz)	10,066	10,066	10,066
	Conductance at f_s mS	0.625	0.313	0.156
	Susceptance at f_s mS	0.095	0.095	0.095
f_ℓ	Lower half power frequency (Hz)	9,816	9,568	9,098
f_u	Upper half power frequency (Hz)	10,321	10,588	11,136
f_r	Electrical resonance frequency (Hz)	10,103	10,244	—
f_a	Anti-resonance frequency (Hz)	11,577	11,421	—
f_m	Frequency for maximum Y (Hz)	10,028	9,930	9,657
f_n	Frequency for minimum Y (Hz)	11,655	11,739	11,900
Q	(approximate)	20	10	5

2.8 Electroacoustic Efficiency

Measurements of Y_M made with the transducer loaded and unloaded permit the determination of the electroacoustic efficiency of the transducer at resonance. This is of interest in transducers for use in water. Because of the large difference between the acoustic impedance of air and water, the unloaded measurements can be made with the transducer in air, in most cases. The subscripts A and W are used to indicate measurements made in air and water, respectively.

The motional admittances under these two conditions can be written, first for the unloaded condition:

$$Y_M = \frac{N^2}{R_m + j\left(\omega M - \frac{1}{\omega C_m}\right)}. \tag{2.54}$$

Then, for the transducer loaded by the radiation impedance of water:

$$Y_M = \frac{N^2}{R_m + R_l + j\left(\omega M - \frac{1}{\omega C_m}\right)}. \tag{2.55}$$

The diameters of the motional admittance circles for the two cases are:

$$D_A = \frac{N^2}{R_m} = \frac{1}{R_M} \tag{2.56}$$

$$D_W = \frac{N^2}{R_m + R_l} = \frac{1}{R_M + R_L}. \tag{2.57}$$

From these, it is seen that:

$$R_M = \frac{1}{D_A}$$
$$R_L = \frac{1}{D_W} - \frac{1}{D_A}. \tag{2.58}$$

Determination of the diameter of the motional admittance circles is illustrated schematically in Fig. 2.19. Here, the input admittance circles for the two conditions of acoustic loading are plotted on the same graph. It is assumed that the blocked capacitance and conductance do not change with acoustic loading or with frequency in the neighborhood of the mechanical resonance frequency.

The electroacoustic efficiency is defined as the ratio of the acoustic power delivered at the load resistance to the total electrical power input to the electrical terminals. The power delivered to the load, W_L, is given by:

$$W_L = I_L^2 R_L \tag{2.59}$$

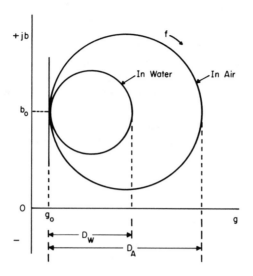

FIG. 2.19   Schematic illustration of the determination of the diameters of the motional admittance circles of a simple transducer from measurements made with the transducer in air and water.

where I_L is the current flowing in the load resistance, given by:

$$I_L = \frac{V}{R_M + R_L} \tag{2.60}$$

The input electrical power at mechanical resonance is:

$$W_I = I^2 R_I = V^2 \left(\frac{1}{R_0} + \frac{1}{R_M + R_L} \right). \tag{2.61}$$

Thus, the electroacoustic efficiency at resonance is given by:

$$\eta = \frac{W_L}{W_I} \tag{2.62}$$

or:

$$\eta = \frac{V^2 R_L/(R_M + R_L)^2}{V^2 \left(\dfrac{1}{R_0} + \dfrac{1}{R_M + R_L} \right)} \tag{2.63}$$

or:

$$\eta = \frac{D_W (D_A - D_W)}{D_A (g_0 + D_W)} \tag{2.64}$$

where $g_0 = 1/R_0$.

2.9 The Electromechanical Coupling Factor

It is often useful to describe the transducing phenomenon in a material or in the transducer in terms of the electromechanical coupling factor or coefficient, which is based on how much of the input electrical and mechanical energy is transformed. If the total work done at the electrical and mechanical terminals is calculated, it is possible to specify separately the work done on the blocked electrical impedance, work done on the open–circuit mechanical impedance, and the work transformed from one form to the other. Designating these as W_E, W_m, and W_{Mut}, respectively, the total work done in the time interval Δt is given by:

$$W = \int_{\Delta t} VI\,dt + \int_{\Delta t} Fu\,dt. \tag{2.65}$$

In the following, it will be assumed that the transformation factors are symmetrical, that $T_{em} = T_{me} = T$, and that there is no dissipation of energy. It is convenient to assume that the electrical and mechanical variables are simple harmonic functions of time. Then:

$$W = W_E + W_m + 2W_{Mut}. \tag{2.66}$$

Using Eq. (2.1) results in:

$$W = \int_{\Delta t}(Z_E I^2 + TuI)\,dt + \int_{\Delta t}(TIu + Z_m u^2)\,dt$$

$$\tag{2.67}$$

$$W = \frac{Z_E I_0^2 \Delta t}{2} + 2T\int_{\Delta t} Iu\,dt + \frac{Z_m u_0^2 \Delta t}{2}$$

where I_0 and u_0 represent the amplitudes of the current and velocity, respectively. Each term in Eq. (2.67) is associated with the corresponding term in Eq. (2.18). Following Berlincourt (10), we define the electromechanical coupling factor or coefficient as the ratio of the mutual energy to the geometric mean of W_E and W_m. Thus:

$$k = \frac{W_{Mut}}{(W_E W_m)^{1/2}}. \tag{2.68}$$

If the current and velocity are in phase, W_{Mut} is given by:

$$W_{Mut} = \frac{TI_0 u_0 \Delta t}{2}$$

and the electromechanical coupling factor is given by:

$$k = \frac{T}{(Z_E Z_m)^{1/2}}. \tag{2.69}$$

An inspection of the terms in Eqs. (2.2) and (2.3) shows that the difference between the blocked and free electrical driving point impedances and the difference between the open- and short-circuited mechanical driving point impedances is determined by the square of the electromechanical coupling factor. Thus, Eq. (2.2) becomes:

$$Z_{IN} = Z_E \left(1 - \frac{T^2}{Z_m Z_E}\right) = Z_E(1 - k^2) \tag{2.70}$$

and Eq. (2.3) becomes:

$$Z_{in} = Z_m \left(1 - \frac{T^2}{Z_m Z_E}\right) = Z_m(1 - k^2). \tag{2.71}$$

Similarly, it may be noted that the coefficient of the current in Eq. (2.36a) can also be expressed in terms of the electromechanical coupling coefficient. If we let $Y_m = 1/Z_m$, the canonical equations for the anti-symmetric transducer become:

$$V = Z_E (1 + k^2) I + T Y_m F \tag{2.72}$$

$$u = T Y_m I + Y_m F. \tag{2.73}$$

In the case where a transducer receives energy from only one of its ports, either electrical or mechanical, the electromechanical coupling coefficient can be defined and calculated more simply as:

$$k^2 = \text{(energy transduced)}/\text{(total energy input)}. \tag{2.74}$$

This can be illustrated by the following simple example. Consider the equivalent network shown in Fig. 2.10 and assume that the frequency of operation is low enough that the motional inductive reactance is small compared to the motional capacitive reactance and the dissipation in the motional resistance is small. In this case the equivalent network consists of two capacitors in parallel, C_0 and C_M, so the maximum energy stored in the complete transducer when an alternating voltage of amplitude V is applied is:

$$\frac{(C_0 + C_M)V^2}{2}$$

and the maximum energy transduced is:

$$\frac{C_M V^2}{2}.$$

Then, the electromechanical coupling coefficient is given by:

$$k^2 = \frac{C_M}{C_0 + C_M}. \tag{2.75}$$

It can be shown that for the network shown in Fig. 2.10 the coupling factor can be calculated from the measured frequencies of resonance and anti-resonance:

$$k^2 = \frac{f_p^2 - f_s^2}{f_p^2}. \tag{2.76}$$

Thus, it appears as if k^2 is a transduction efficiency. In a sense, it is. However, it is a characteristic of the mechanism with all dissipative processes ignored. In considering electroacoustic conversion efficiency, a number of other factors in the transducer design must also be taken into account.

The electromechanical coupling factor is often used as a figure of merit for transducers and transducing materials. Later, the symbol k will have subscripts to denote the coupling factor for the particular mode of operation of the electrically active material of the transducer. It should be noted that although one may calculate a value for the quantity k and numerical values of k are often tabulated, the effect of this quantity on transducer behavior is always measured by its square.

References

1. Frederick V. Hunt. *Electroacoustics*. Harvard University Press: Cambridge, MA (1954). Reprinted by the Acoustical Society of America (1982).
2. Lord Rayleigh. *Theory of Sound*. Vol. 1, Sec. 108–110. Dover: New York (1945).
3. Harry F. Olson. *Dynamical Analogies*. D. Van Nostrand: New York (1943).
4. Leslie L. Foldy and Henry Primakoff. A General Theory of Passive Linear Electroacoustic Transducers and the Electroacoustic Reciprocity Theorem I. *J. Acoust. Soc. Am.* 17 109–120 (1945).
5. Henry Primakoff and Leslie L. Foldy. A General Theory of Passive Linear Electroacoustic Transducers and the Electroacoustic Reciprocity Theorem. II. *J. Acoust. Soc. Am.* 19 50–58 (1947).
6. M.E. Van Valkenburg. *Network Analysis*. 2nd Ed. Prentice Hall: New York (1964).
7. Franklin F. Kuo. *Network Analysis and Synthesis*. 2nd Ed. Wiley: New York (1966).
8. Lawrence E. Kinsler, Austin R. Frey, Alan B. Coppens, and James V. Sanders. *Fundamentals of Acoustics*. 3rd Ed. Wiley: New York (1982).
9. Robert J. Bobber. *Underwater Electroacoustic Measurements*. Naval Research Laboratory, Washington, D.C. (1970).
10. Don A. Berlincourt, Daniel R. Curran, and Hans Jaffe. Piezoelectric and Piezomagnetic Materials and Their Function in Transducers. Chapter 3 in *Physical Acoustics*. Vol. 1A. Warren P. Mason, Ed. Academic Press: New York (1964).
11. W.G. Cady. *Piezoelectricity*. Dover: New York (1962). Vol. One, Chapter 14.
12. E.M. McMillan. Violation of the Reciprocity Theorem in Linear Passive Electromechanical Systems. *J. Acoustic Soc. Am.* 18 344–347 (1946).
13. B.D.H. Tellegen. *The Gyrator, a New Network Element*. Philips Research Reports. Vol. 3. 81–101, Apr. 1948.
14. G.E. Martin. Determination of Equivalent Circuit Constants of Piezoelectric Resonators of Moderately Low Q by Absolute–Admittance Measurements. *J. Acoust. Soc. Am.* 26 413–420 (1954).

15. IRE Standards on Piezoelectric Crystals. *The Piezoelectric Vibrator: Definitions and Methods of Management.* (1957). Published by the IEEE, New York.
16. H.B. Miller. *Handbook for the Analysis of Piezoelectric Transducers.* Part 1, The Untuned Transducer. NUSC Tech. Doc. 6029, Sept. 1978. Naval Underwater Systems Center, New London, CT.

Problems

2.1. A simple mechanical oscillator consists of a mass M (a magnet) and a suspension consisting of a spring of stiffness k and a dashpot of damping coefficient r, which is supported on a foundation. The magnetic field B from the magnet and a coiled electrical conductor attached to the foundation are arranged so that the relative motion between them will generate an emf in the coil proportional to the relative velocity. (This is the essence of the moving coil velocity sensor often used in geophysical measurements.) Assume that the relative movement is excited by vertical motion of the foundation.

(a) Draw an equivalent electrical circuit for this system.

(b) Derive an expression for the open circuit sensitivty of this device as a velocity sensor of simple harmonic oscillations of the foundation.

(c) Show that the sensitivity is independent of frequency for the mass controlled regime. (Let $L =$ length of conductor.)

2.2. A magnetic field type transducer is described by the circuit shown below. Assume that the three shunt elements are due to motional coupling.

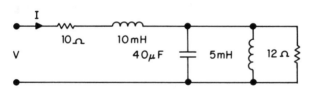

(a) Draw the locus of points for the complex motional impedance, determine the resonance frequency, the half-power frequencies, and the values of the real and imaginary parts of the motional impedance at these frequencies.

(b) Draw the locus of points for the complex input impedance.

(c) Find the electromechanical conversion efficiency at resonance and at the half-power frequencies, assuming that the 12 ohm shunt resistance represents the useful load.

CHAPTER 3

THE PIEZOELECTRIC AND PIEZOMAGNETIC EFFECTS

3.1 Properties of Ordinary Materials

Before the piezoelectric and piezomagnetic effects are discussed, the dielectric, magnetic, and elastic properties of ordinary materials—that is, materials that are neither piezoelectric nor piezomagnetic—will be briefly reviewed. A brief outline of a thermodynamic basis for the linear piezoelectric and piezomagnetic effects is then presented. From this, the relations are developed and many of the coefficients that are "constants" of the materials are defined. Examples of applications of the relations for piezoelectric materials are discussed for several simple configurations. Discussion of applications to the magnetostrictive effect is deferred until a later chapter. The notion of an electromechanical coupling coefficient is introduced and discussed. Refs. (1) through (6) provide a more detailed development of the theory.

Dielectric Properties

In an isotropic nonconducting material, the relationships between the electric field vector **E**, the electric displacement vector **D**, and the dielectric polarization vector **P** are given by:

$$\mathbf{D} = \epsilon\mathbf{E} \qquad \text{and} \qquad \mathbf{D} = \epsilon_0\mathbf{E} + \mathbf{P} \tag{3.1}$$

where ϵ is the dielectric permittivity or capacitivity and ϵ_0 is the capacitivity of a vacuum. In SI units, ϵ_0 has the value of 8.85×10^{-12} farads per meter. The dimensions of D and P are coulombs per square meter and those of E are volts per meter.

The capacitivity may also be expressed as:

$$\epsilon = \epsilon_0 + \frac{|\mathbf{P}|}{|\mathbf{E}|} = \epsilon_0 + \chi \tag{3.2}$$

where χ is called the electric susceptibility. In this convention, the susceptibility and capacitivity have the same dimensions.

In an aeolotropic medium, the vectors **D**, **E**, and **P** are not necessarily parallel to each other since values of the capacitivity may depend on the direction relative to the crystalline or other axes within the material. (In a piezoelectric material the elastic strain may also affect the values of the electric field parameters.) Therefore, the vector equations relating the field quantities must be written more carefully. The three components of the polarization vector **P** are related to the three components of the **E** vector by a three by three matrix

45

called the susceptibility tensor:

$$\mathbf{P}_m = \chi_{mn}\mathbf{E}_n \tag{3.3}$$

where m and n take values from 1 to 3 and the repeated index indicates a summation.

Also, the capacitivity is a tensor, with:

$$\epsilon_{mm} = \epsilon_0 + \chi_{mm}$$

$$\epsilon_{mn} = \chi_{mn} \tag{3.4}$$

where $m \neq n$.

For all crystalline classes except triclinic and monoclinic, the cross susceptibilities are zero. In cubic crystals, all three of the diagonal elements in the susceptibility matrix have the same value. Handbooks of physical data usually tabulate the dielectric property values only for the crystalline axes of the material. If values are needed for other directions, they must be computed using conventional transformation techniques for rotated coordinate axes (2).

Magnetic Properties

In a vacuum, the relationship between the magnetic flux density or magnetic induction $\mathbf{B}$ and the magnetizing force or magnetic field strength $\mathbf{H}$ is given by:

$$\mathbf{B} = \mu_0\mathbf{H} \tag{3.5}$$

where μ_0 is the magnetic permittivity or permeability of a vacuum. In SI units, μ_0 has the value of $4\pi \times 10^{-7}$ henrys per meter, $\mathbf{H}$ has the dimensions of amperes per meter, and the unit for $\mathbf{B}$ is the tesla, which has the dimensions of webers per square meter.

The permeability μ of other media may differ significantly from the permittivity of a vacuum and may also be a function of the magnetic field strength. The notion of a relative magnetic permeability is often used:

$$\mu_r = \frac{\mu}{\mu_0}.$$

In most materials of interest, the properties are not isotropic and the value of the permeability is dependent upon direction. Therefore, the relation must be written:

$$B_m = \mu_{mn}H_n. \tag{3.6}$$

The repeated index indicates a summation and both m and n range from 1 to 3. In most magnetostrictive materials, there is complete symmetry about the axis determined by the imposed magnetic field or the magnetic polarization.

Elastic Properties

Definition of stress

The stress vector **T** is the force per unit area acting on a surface. It may be resolved into components along the three coordinate directions. In addition, the components may also depend upon the orientation of the surface upon which **T** acts. If an elementary parallelopiped as shown in Fig. 3.1 is considered, the stresses on all six surfaces must be taken into account, which would appear to require the specification of eighteen components. However, in the limit as the volume of the parallelopiped diminishes to zero, conditions of equilibrium require that the state of stress at a point be specified by a symmetrical 3 × 3 matrix, thus requiring only six components. This array of components behaves as a tensor.

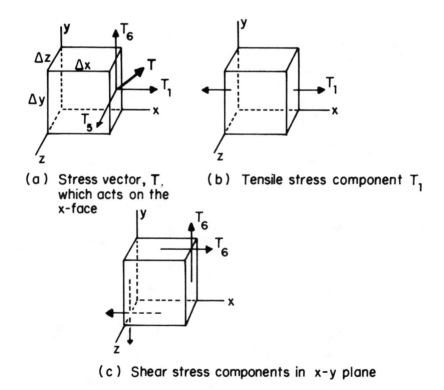

(a) Stress vector, **T**, which acts on the x-face

(b) Tensile stress component T_1

(c) Shear stress components in x-y plane

FIG. 3.1   Examples of positive stress components acting on faces of a parallelopiped, using the shorthand notation.

Let the coordinate axes be x_1, x_2, x_3. The components of the stress tensor are:

$$[T_{ij}] = \begin{bmatrix} T_{11} & T_{12} & T_{13} \\ T_{21} & T_{22} & T_{23} \\ T_{31} & T_{32} & T_{33} \end{bmatrix} \tag{3.7}$$

A shorthand notation is often used in engineering calculations in which:

$$\begin{aligned}
T_{11} &= T_1 & T_{23} &= T_{32} = T_4 \\
T_{22} &= T_2 & T_{13} &= T_{31} = T_5 \\
T_{33} &= T_3 & T_{12} &= T_{21} = T_6.
\end{aligned} \tag{3.8}$$

The components are illustrated in Fig. 3.1. For example, the component T_5 represents the force per unit area acting on the face that has its normal along the 1– or x–axis and directed along the 3– or z–axis. The stress components T_1, T_2, T_3 act in a direction normal to the respective coordinate faces and tend to cause tension or compression. For this reason they are called tensile or normal stresses. The components T_4, T_5, T_6 act in directions parallel to the respective faces. Since they tend to cause shearing, they are called shearing stresses. "Positive" stress is defined as stress that tends to cause a positive strain.

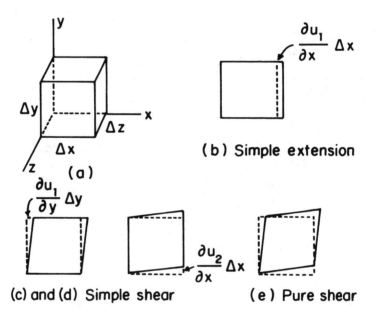

FIG. 3.2   Simple forms of strain.

Definition of strain

If a material is deformed slightly, the description of the deformation at a point can be given in terms of a strain tensor that has six independent components, defined in terms of the spatial derivatives of the displacement components. Letting x_1, x_2, x_3 be the coordinate axes and u_1, u_2, u_3 be the displacement components along these coordinate directions, respectively, the components for an infinitesimal strain are:

$$S_{11} = \frac{\partial u_1}{\partial x_1} \qquad S_{22} = \frac{\partial u_2}{\partial x_2} \qquad S_{33} = \frac{\partial u_3}{\partial x_3}$$

$$S_{21} = S_{12} = \frac{1}{2}\left(\frac{\partial u_2}{\partial x_1} + \frac{\partial u_1}{\partial x_2}\right)$$

$$S_{31} = S_{13} = \frac{1}{2}\left(\frac{\partial u_3}{\partial x_1} + \frac{\partial u_1}{\partial x_3}\right)$$

$$S_{32} = S_{23} = \frac{1}{2}\left(\frac{\partial u_3}{\partial x_2} + \frac{\partial u_2}{\partial x_3}\right).$$

(3.9)

The components S_{11}, S_{22}, S_{33} are the tensile strains and represent possible contributions to a change in volume. The remaining components are shearing strains and describe a change in shape but not a first order change in volume.

A shorthand notation that simplifies the indices is used in most engineering applications:

$$S_{11} = S_1 \qquad 2S_{32} = 2S_{23} = S_4$$
$$S_{22} = S_2 \qquad 2S_{13} = 2S_{31} = S_5$$
$$S_{33} = S_3 \qquad 2S_{12} = 2S_{21} = S_6.$$

(3.10)

The matrix is then:

$$[S_i] = \begin{bmatrix} S_1 & S_6 & S_5 \\ S_6 & S_2 & S_4 \\ S_5 & S_4 & S_3 \end{bmatrix}$$

(3.11)

Fig. 3.2 illustrates simple forms of extensional and shear strains.

Hooke's law

The relations between elastic variables may be based on energy principles. The simplest form of potential energy function in terms of strain is the quadratic:

$$W = \frac{1}{2} \sum_{pqrs} c_{pqrs} S_{pq} S_{rs}$$

(3.12)

where $\{c_{pqrs}\}$ is a fourth rank symmetric tensor. Conservation of energy leads to an expression for the stresses:

$$T_{pq} = \frac{\partial W}{\partial S_{pq}} = \sum_{r,s} c_{pqrs} S_{rs}.$$

(3.13)

This is a generalized form of Hooke's law and is from Cauchy. Shorthand notation simplifies the relationship to:

$$T_i = \sum_{j=1}^{6} c_{ij} S_j \qquad (3.14)$$

where the indices range from 1 to 6. The array $\{c_{ij}\}$ is a symmetrical six by six matrix, the components are called the elastic constants or stiffness constants and are, of course, properties of the material in which the stresses and strains exist.

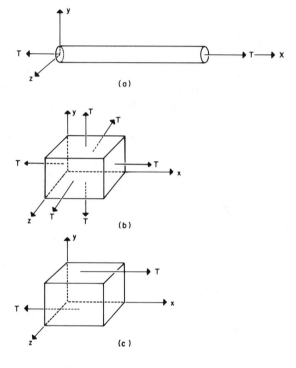

FIG. 3.3 Simple examples of stress. (a) Tensile stress in a long bar with unconstrained sides. (b) Uniform tensile stress in all directions. (c) Simple shearing stress in the x–y plane.

If the equations for stress are solved for the strain components, the result is a set of six equations:

$$S_i = \sum_{j=1}^{6} s_{ij} T_j. \qquad (3.15)$$

The array $\{s_{ij}\}$ is the (symmetrical) set of compliance coefficients or constants and is the inverse of the matrix of elastic stiffness constants.

For the most general anisotropic solid, there are twenty–one independent coefficients. If the solid is symmetrical about or with respect to a plane, the number of independent coefficients is thirteen. Symmetry about three mutually perpendicular planes gives nine independent coefficients. Cubic crystals have only three independent constants, an isotropic solid has only two, and an ideal fluid has only one. In a piezoelectric material, the values of the elastic coefficients also depend upon the electrical boundary conditions.

For quartz, as an example, there are six independent constants. The array is:

$$[c_{ij}] = \begin{bmatrix} c_{11} & c_{12} & c_{13} & c_{14} & 0 & 0 \\ c_{12} & c_{11} & c_{13} & -c_{14} & 0 & 0 \\ c_{13} & c_{13} & c_{33} & 0 & 0 & 0 \\ c_{14} & -c_{14} & 0 & c_{44} & 0 & 0 \\ 0 & 0 & 0 & 0 & c_{44} & c_{14} \\ 0 & 0 & 0 & 0 & c_{14} & c_{66} \end{bmatrix} \tag{3.16}$$

where $c_{66} = (1/2)(c_{11} - c_{12})$ and the piezoelectric properties of quartz have been ignored.

For an isotropic solid, the array of elastic constants is:

$$\begin{bmatrix} c_{11} & c_{12} & c_{12} & 0 & 0 & 0 \\ c_{12} & c_{11} & c_{12} & 0 & 0 & 0 \\ c_{12} & c_{12} & c_{11} & 0 & 0 & 0 \\ 0 & 0 & 0 & c_{44} & 0 & 0 \\ 0 & 0 & 0 & 0 & c_{44} & 0 \\ 0 & 0 & 0 & 0 & 0 & c_{44} \end{bmatrix} \tag{3.17}$$

It is sometimes convenient to write the elastic constants in terms of the Lamé constants λ and μ.

$$c_{12} = \lambda \qquad c_{44} = \mu \qquad c_{11} = \lambda + 2\mu. \tag{3.18}$$

It is easier to interpret the compliance constants than the elastic stiffness constants. For the case of an isotropic solid, Eq. (3.15) becomes:

$$\begin{aligned} S_1 &= s_{11}T_1 + s_{12}T_2 + s_{12}T_3 & S_4 &= s_{44}T_4 \\ S_2 &= s_{12}T_1 + s_{11}T_2 + s_{12}T_3 & S_5 &= s_{44}T_5 \\ S_3 &= s_{12}T_1 + s_{12}T_2 + s_{11}T_3 & S_6 &= s_{44}T_6 \end{aligned} \tag{3.19}$$

where we have used the fact that:

$$s_{11} = s_{22} = s_{33}$$

$$s_{13} = s_{31} = s_{23} = s_{32} = s_{12} = s_{21}$$

and

$$s_{44} = s_{55} = s_{66}$$

In order for the student to gain some insight into the physical significance of the elastic compliance coefficients, some simple examples of static stress and strain are now considered for a homogenous isotropic solid. First, assume that a long, thin cylindrical rod with its axis parallel to the x-axis is subjected to forces applied at the ends of the rod that cause a uniform tensile stress T along the bar, as shown in Fig. 3.3a. The side walls of the rod are assumed to be unconstrained. Thus, there is only one component of stress, $T_1 = T$. Eq. (3.19) then reduces to:

$$S_1 = s_{11}T \qquad S_4 = S_5 = S_6 = 0$$

$$S_2 = s_{12}T \tag{3.20}$$

$$S_3 = s_{12}T$$

Young's modulus is defined by the tensile stress–strain relation in the long bar, $Y = T_1/S_1$, and therefore we can make the association between Y and the reciprocal of s_{11}:

$$Y = \frac{1}{s_{11}}. \tag{3.21}$$

The ratio of the transverse tensile strain to the axial tensile strain defines Poisson's ratio:

$$\nu = -\frac{S_2}{S_1} = -\frac{s_{12}}{s_{11}}. \tag{3.22}$$

A little algebra gives Young's modulus and Poisson's ratio in terms of the Lamé constants:

$$Y = \frac{\mu(3\lambda + 2\mu)}{\lambda + \mu} \tag{3.23}$$

and

$$\nu = \frac{\lambda}{2(\lambda + \mu)}. \tag{3.24}$$

Assume that a rectangular parallelopiped oriented so that its sides are parallel to the coordinate axes is subjected to a uniform tensile stress T along each of the axes, as shown in Fig. 3.3b. The state of stress is:

$$T_1 = T_2 = T_3 = T$$

$$T_4 = T_5 = T_6 = 0$$

and Eq. (3.19) reduces to:

$$S_1 = S_2 = S_3 = (s_{11} + 2s_{12})T$$

$$S_4 = S_5 = S_6 = 0.$$

The bulk modulus K is defined as the ratio of the (homogenous) tensile stress to the cubical dilation, defined as the sum of the three principal strains:

$$\theta = S_1 + S_2 + S_3$$

so that:

$$K = \frac{1}{3(s_{11} + 2s_{12})}. \qquad (3.25a)$$

Using the relations between the compliance coefficients, Young's modulus, and Poisson's ratio, the bulk modulus is also given by:

$$K = \frac{Y}{3(1 - 2\nu)}. \qquad (3.25b)$$

If the rectangular parallelopiped is subjected to a shearing stress T in the x-y plane as shown in Fig. 3.3c, the only stress component is:

$$T_6 = T.$$

The only strain component resulting from this stress is:

$$S_6 = s_{44}T.$$

This configuration is normally used to define the shear modulus μ and we can thus associate the shear modulus with the reciprocal of s_{44}:

$$\mu = \frac{1}{s_{44}}. \qquad (3.26)$$

More thorough treatments of elastic properties of solids may be found in refs. (1), (3), and (5).

3.2 The Piezoelectric and Piezomagnetic Effects

The Thermodynamic Basis

The piezoelectric and piezomagnetic equations may be derived from thermodynamic potential functions. In the most general case, the thermal effects must also be included. The Gibbs function G can be used to illustrate this process (3,4):

$$G = U - S_jT_j - E_nD_n - H_nB_n - \sigma\theta \qquad (3.27)$$

where the repeated index indicates a summation, the values of j range from 1 to 6 and n from 1 to 3, U is the internal energy, σ is the entropy, and θ is the temperature. Using the first and second laws of thermodynamics:

$$dQ = \theta d\sigma \tag{3.28}$$

and

$$dU = dQ + T_j dS_j + E_n dD_n + H_n dB_n \tag{3.29}$$

the differential of Eq. (3.27) is:

$$dG = -S_j dT_j - D_n dE_n - B_n dH_n - \sigma d\theta. \tag{3.30}$$

So, if E, H, and θ are kept constant, we see that we can relate the strain to the stress derivative of the Gibbs function and, similarly, relate the electric displacement vector, the magnetic flux density, and the entropy to the appropriate derivatives of G:

$$S_i = -\left.\frac{\partial G}{\partial T_i}\right|_{E,H,\theta} \qquad D_m = -\left.\frac{\partial G}{\partial E_m}\right|_{H,T,\theta}$$

$$\tag{3.31}$$

$$B_m = -\left.\frac{\partial G}{\partial H_m}\right|_{E,T,\theta} \qquad \sigma = -\left.\frac{\partial G}{\partial \theta}\right|_{E,H,T}.$$

Since the strain is a function of T, E, H, and θ, the total differential for the components of the strain becomes:

$$dS_i = \left.\frac{\partial S_i}{\partial T_j}\right|_{E,H,\theta} dT_j + \left.\frac{\partial S_i}{\partial E_n}\right|_{H,\theta,T} dE_n$$

$$\tag{3.32a}$$

$$+ \left.\frac{\partial S_i}{\partial H_n}\right|_{E,\theta,T} dH_n + \left.\frac{\partial S_i}{\partial \theta}\right|_{T,E,H} d\theta.$$

Similarly, the differentials of the electric displacement, the magnetic flux density, and the entropy are, respectively:

$$dD_m = \left.\frac{\partial D_m}{\partial T_j}\right|_{E,H,\theta} dT_j + \left.\frac{\partial D_m}{\partial E_n}\right|_{T,H,\theta} dE_n$$

$$\tag{3.32b}$$

$$+ \left.\frac{\partial D_m}{\partial H_k}\right|_{E,\theta,T} dH_k + \left.\frac{\partial D_m}{\partial \theta}\right|_{T,E,H} d\theta$$

$$dB_m = \left.\frac{\partial B_m}{\partial T_j}\right|_{H,\theta,E} dT_j + \left.\frac{\partial B_m}{\partial H_n}\right|_{T,\theta,E} dH_n$$

$$\tag{3.32c}$$

$$+ \left.\frac{\partial B_m}{\partial \theta}\right|_{T,H,E} d\theta + \left.\frac{\partial B_m}{\partial E_n}\right|_{T,H,\theta} dE_n$$

$$d\sigma = \frac{\partial \sigma}{\partial T_j}\bigg|_{E,H,\theta} dT_j + \frac{\partial \sigma}{\partial E_n}\bigg|_{\theta H,T} dE_n$$

$$\text{(3.32d)}$$

$$+ \frac{\partial \sigma}{\partial H_n}\bigg|_{T,E,\theta} dH_n + \frac{\partial \sigma}{\partial \theta}\bigg|_{E,H,T} d\theta.$$

Since dG is a perfect differential, Eqs. (3.32a) through (3.32d) give the following relationships, which are defined as constants of the material.

Piezoelectric strain constant:

$$d_{mi}^{H,\theta} = \frac{\partial D_m}{\partial T_i} = \frac{\partial S_i}{\partial E_m} \qquad (3.33)$$

Piezomagnetic strain constant:

$$d_{mi}^{E,\theta} = \frac{\partial B_m}{\partial T_i} = \frac{\partial S_i}{\partial H_m} \qquad (3.34)$$

Pyroelectric constant:

$$p_m^{T,H} = \frac{\partial D_m}{\partial \theta} = \frac{\partial \sigma}{\partial E_m} \qquad (3.35)$$

Pyromagnetic constant:

$$i_m^{T,E} = \frac{\partial B_m}{\partial \theta} = \frac{\partial \sigma}{\partial H_m} \qquad (3.36)$$

Magnetodielectric constant:

$$m_{mn}^{T,\theta} = \frac{\partial D_m}{\partial H_n} = \frac{\partial B_n}{\partial E_m} \qquad (3.37)$$

Thermal expansion constant:

$$\alpha_i^{E,H} = \frac{\partial S_i}{\partial \theta} = \frac{\partial \sigma}{\partial T_i} \qquad (3.38)$$

Also, the following identifications may be made.

Elastic compliance constant:

$$s_{ij}^{E,H,\theta} = \frac{\partial S_i}{\partial T_j}\bigg|_{E,H,\theta} \qquad (3.39)$$

Dielectric constant:

$$\epsilon_{mn}^{T,H,\theta} = \frac{\partial D_m}{\partial E_n}\bigg|_{T,H,\theta} \qquad (3.40)$$

Magnetic permeability constant:

$$\mu_{mn}^{T,E,\theta} = \frac{\partial B_m}{\partial H_n}\bigg|_{T,E,\theta} \tag{3.41}$$

If ρ is the density and C is the heat capacity, then:

$$\frac{\partial \sigma}{\partial \theta}\bigg|_{E,H,T} = \frac{\rho C^{E,H,T}}{\theta}. \tag{3.42}$$

If the deviations of the field variables from their equilibrium values are assumed to be so small that the coefficients in Eqs. (3.29) through (3.32) are constant, then the integrals of these equations over the changes give the following results, where the definitions in Eqs. (3.33) through (3.42) have been used and the equilibrium value of each field variable has been chosen as zero:

$$S_i = s_{ij}^{E,H,\theta}T_j + d_{mi}^{H,\theta}E_m + d_{mi}^{E,\theta}H_m + \alpha_i^{E,H}d\theta \tag{3.43}$$

$$D_m = d_{mj}^{H,\theta}T_j + \epsilon_{mn}^{T,H,\theta}E_n + p_m^{T,H}d\theta + m_{mn}^{T,\theta}H_n \tag{3.44}$$

$$B_m = d_{mj}^{E,\theta}T_j + \mu_{mn}^{T,E,\theta}H_n + i_m^{T,E}d\theta + m_{mn}^{T,\theta}E_n \tag{3.45}$$

$$d\sigma = \alpha_j^{E,H}T_j + p_n^{H,T}E_n + i_n^{E,T}H_n + \frac{\rho C^{E,H,T}}{\theta}d\theta. \tag{3.46}$$

Again, the repeated index denotes summation.

In the most general case, Eq. (3.43) represents a set of six equations, Eq. (3.44) and Eq. (3.45) each represent a set of three equations, and Eq. (3.46) represents only one equation.

There also may be a small but finite difference between the isothermal and the adiabatic constants (5). In most acoustic applications, the adiabatic constants are appropriate. The adiabatic form of these equations may be derived from the thermodynamic function (4):

$$H = U - S_iT_i - E_mD_m - B_mH_m \tag{3.47}$$

for which:

$$dH_A = -S_idT_i - D_mdE_m - B_mdH_m + \theta d\sigma.$$

Berlincourt (4) gives the resulting equations, similar to Eqs. (3.43) to (3.46) as:

$$S_i = s_{ij}^{H,E,\sigma}T_j + d_{mi}^{H,\sigma}E_m + d_{mi}^{E,\sigma}H_m + \frac{\partial S_i}{\partial \sigma}\bigg|_{E,H}d\sigma \tag{3.48}$$

$$D_m = d_{mj}^{H,\sigma}T_j + \epsilon_{mn}^{T,H,\sigma}E_n + m_{mn}^{T,\sigma}H_n + \frac{\partial D_m}{\partial \sigma}\bigg|_{T,H}d\sigma \tag{3.49}$$

$$B_m = d_{mj}^{E,\sigma}T_j + \mu_{mn}^{T,E,\sigma}H_n + m_{mn}^{T,\sigma}E_n + \frac{\partial B_m}{\partial \sigma}\bigg|_{E,T}d\sigma \tag{3.50}$$

$$d\theta = \left.\frac{\partial\theta}{\partial T_j}\right|_{E,H} dT_j + \left.\frac{\partial\theta}{\partial E_n}\right|_{T,H} dE_n + \left.\frac{\partial\theta}{\partial H_n}\right|_{T,E} dH_n + \frac{\theta}{\rho C^{E,T,H}} d\sigma \tag{3.51}$$

where $C^{E,T,H}$ is a heat capacity.

Since dH_A is a perfect differential in this case, the following relationships exist:

$$\left.\frac{\partial S_i}{\partial\sigma}\right|_{E,H} = \left.\frac{\partial\theta}{\partial T_i}\right|_{E,H} \tag{3.52}$$

$$\left.\frac{\partial D_m}{\partial\sigma}\right|_{T,H} = \left.\frac{\partial\theta}{\partial E_m}\right|_{T,H} \tag{3.53}$$

$$\left.\frac{\partial B_m}{\partial\sigma}\right|_{T,E} = \left.\frac{\partial\theta}{\partial H_m}\right|_{T,E}. \tag{3.54}$$

Mason (3) shows that the difference between the adiabatic and isothermal coefficients is zero except for pyroelectric crystals. More thorough and extensive treatments of the phenomenological theory of the piezoelectric and piezomagnetic effects may be found in refs. (3) through (7).

For practical purposes, the magnetic field effects are negligible in most piezoelectric materials, and the dielectric effects are negligible in piezomagnetic materials. Some important piezoelectric materials are also pyroelectric so that terms involving temperature may be needed for certain problems. In the following section, the magnetic and pyroelectric coefficients are assumed to vanish so that only the effects of the elastic and electrical field interactions are considered.

The Piezoelectric Relations

If the magnetic and pyroelectric effects are ignored, the piezoelectric equations for the strain and electric displacement become:

$$S_i = s_{ij}^E T_j + d_{ni} E_n \tag{3.55a}$$

$$D_m = d_{mj} T_j + \epsilon_{mn}^T E_n \tag{3.55b}$$

or in matrix form:

$$S = s^E T + d_t E \tag{3.56a}$$

$$D = dT + \epsilon^T E \tag{3.56b}$$

where d_t stands for the transposed d matrix in which the rows and columns are interchanged.

The equations take the following forms when different variables are used as independent variables. It will be more convenient to use particular sets of independent variables for some problems.

When S and E are independent:

$$T = c^E S - e_t E \tag{3.57a}$$

$$D = eS + \epsilon^S E. \tag{3.57b}$$

When T and D are independent:

$$S = s^D T + g_t D \tag{3.58a}$$

$$E = -gT + \beta^T D. \tag{3.58b}$$

When S and D are independent:

$$T = c^D S - h_t D \tag{3.59a}$$

$$E = -hS + \beta^S D. \tag{3.59b}$$

The following definitions for the piezoelectric constants follow from Eqs. (3.28) through (3.36):

$$d = \left.\frac{\partial S}{\partial E}\right|_T = \left.\frac{\partial D}{\partial T}\right|_E \tag{3.60}$$

$$g = -\left.\frac{\partial E}{\partial T}\right|_D = \left.\frac{\partial S}{\partial D}\right|_T \tag{3.61}$$

$$e = -\left.\frac{\partial T}{\partial E}\right|_S = \left.\frac{\partial D}{\partial S}\right|_E \tag{3.62}$$

$$h = -\left.\frac{\partial T}{\partial D}\right|_S = -\left.\frac{\partial E}{\partial S}\right|_D. \tag{3.63}$$

The coefficients d and e are sometimes called the piezoelectric strain and stress constants, respectively.

There are a number of interrelationships between the piezoelectric constants:

$$d_{mi} = \epsilon_{nm}^T g_{ni} = e_{mj} s_{ji}^E \tag{3.64}$$

$$g_{mi} = \beta_{nm}^T d_{ni} = h_{mj} s_{ji}^D \tag{3.65}$$

$$e_{mi} = \epsilon_{nm}^S h_{ni} = d_{mj} c_{ji}^E \tag{3.66}$$

$$h_{mi} = \beta_{nm}^S e_{ni} = g_{mj} c_{ji}^D. \tag{3.67}$$

Also:

$$\{\beta_{mn}\} = \{\epsilon_{mn}\}^{-1} \tag{3.68}$$

and:

$$\{c_{ij}\} = \{s_{ij}\}^{-1} \tag{3.69}$$

where m and n range from 1 to 3 and i and j range from 1 to 6.

3.3 The Piezoelectric Coupling Factor

The piezoelectric coupling factor or coefficient is sometimes more useful for characterizing the capabilities of a transducer material in a high power projector than the piezoelectric stress or strain coefficients are. The piezoelectric coupling factor is defined as the ratio of the mutual elastic and dielectric energy density U_{Mut} to the geometric mean of the elastic strain energy density U_{Elas} and the dielectric energy density U_{Diel}:

$$k = \frac{U_{\text{Mut}}}{\sqrt{U_{\text{Elas}} \, U_{\text{Diel}}}}. \tag{3.70}$$

For a linear system, the total energy density is given by:

$$U = \frac{S_i T_i}{2} + \frac{D_m E_m}{2}. \tag{3.71}$$

Using the piezoelectric equations in which T and E are independent:

$$S_i = s_{ij}^E T_j + d_{ni} E_n \tag{3.55a}$$

$$D_m = d_{mj} T_j + \epsilon_{mn}^T E_n \tag{3.55b}$$

the equation for the energy density becomes:

$$U = \frac{T_i s_{ij}^E T_j}{2} + \frac{T_i d_{ni} E_n}{2} + \frac{E_n d_{ni} T_i}{2} + \frac{E_m \epsilon_{mn}^T E_n}{2} \tag{3.72}$$

or

$$U = U_{\text{Elas}} + 2U_{\text{Mut}} + U_{\text{Diel}}. \tag{3.73}$$

Thus, the piezoelectric coupling factor is an electromechanical factor, the measure of how much of the energy from one form or the other is converted by the transducing mechanism, as discussed in Ch. 2 for the case of the four–terminal equivalent network. The actual computation of these sums becomes complicated in all except the most simple cases. Often approximations may be used which ease the difficulties.

An example is now worked out for a very simple case. Consider a piezoelectric material for which the only non–zero elastic and electrical field variables are the z–components. The set, Eq. (3.55), in which T and E are the independent variables, reduces to one pair of equations:

$$S_3 = s_{33}^E T_3 + d_{33} E_3$$
$$D_3 = d_{33} T_3 + \epsilon_{33}^T E_3. \tag{3.74}$$

The elements of the energy densities are given by Eq. (3.72):

$$U_{\text{Mut}} = \frac{d_{33} T_3 E_3}{2}$$

$$U_{\text{Elas}} = \frac{s_{33}^E T_3^2}{2} \tag{3.75}$$

$$U_{\text{Diel}} = \frac{\epsilon_{33}^T E_3^2}{2}.$$

From Eq. (3.70), the electromechanical coupling factor is calculated and the subscripts indicate that the value for the particular set of elastic and electric field components is:

$$k_{33} = \frac{d_{33}}{\left(s_{33}^E \epsilon_{33}^T\right)^{1/2}}. \tag{3.76}$$

The k calculated in this manner assumes that the elastic and electric field variables are uniform throughout the material. Therefore, this value of k is what would be found in quasistatic conditions. It represents a characteristic of the material and is the maximum value that can be achieved. It will be shown later that the value of k will be smaller for other cases, e.g., in a resonant vibrator bar where the energy densities are not uniform throughout the piezoelectric material.

It should be noted that the definition of energy density, Eqs. (3.72) and (3.73), does not give correct results for the e and g piezoelectric constants since they appear with positive and negative signs in the piezoelectric equations. For these cases, the absolute values must be taken.

3.4 Elastic Waves in Solids

The preceding sections have shown the relations between static stresses and strains in several cases of simple geometry. These results are also valid for calculating the elastic stiffness of an element in a transducer for low–frequency dynamic cases. However, in sonar transducers the frequency of operation is often high enough that the dimensions of at least some of its parts are comparable to the wavelength of the elastic waves that can propagate in the medium. For this reason, it is worthwhile to review some of the results for the simplest types of waves which can propagate in transducer materials.

The anisotropic characteristics of many solids also cause a directional dependence of the speed of propagation of longitudinal and transverse waves. Although it is true that in some highly anisotropic solids it is not possible to have pure longitudinal or pure shear waves, in most cases of interest in sonar transducers little error is caused by the assumption of pure longitudinal waves along the axes of symmetry in the piezoelectric material. In most sonar transducers, the wave motion of primary interest is longitudinal or extensional. In some cases, the possibility or even the desirability of coupling between extensional wave motion and transverse wave motion is important and must be considered.

The results summarized here are equations for the speed of propagation of the simplest types of waves in an isotropic solid. An introduction to the theory of waves in bars and plates is provided in Kinsler *et al.* (8). A thorough treatment of general wave theory in solids may be found in Auld (1) and Mason (2).

The speed of propagation of infinite, plane compressional waves in a bulk solid is given by:

$$c_l = \left(\frac{Y(1 - \nu)}{\rho(1 + \nu)(1 - 2\nu)} \right)^{1/2}. \tag{3.77}$$

Here elastic boundary conditions are such that the strains perpendicular to the direction of propagation are zero.

Infinite plane shear waves in the bulk travel with the speed:

$$c_t = \left(\frac{\mu}{\rho} \right)^{1/2} = \left(\frac{Y}{2\rho(1 + \nu)} \right)^{1/2}. \tag{3.78}$$

The ratio of these wave speeds is determined by Poisson's ratio:

$$\frac{c_\ell}{c_t} = \left(\frac{2(1 - \nu)}{1 - 2\nu} \right)^{1/2}. \tag{3.79}$$

Extensional waves in a long bar or in a plate are affected by the same elastic boundary conditions used in developing the static stress–strain relations used earlier. For the long bar extensional waves, the speed of propagation is:

$$c_{E(\text{rod})} = \left(\frac{Y}{\rho} \right)^{1/2}. \tag{3.80}$$

Extensional waves in a thin plate travel at the speed:

$$c_{E(\text{plate})} = \left(\frac{Y}{\rho(1 - \nu^2)} \right)^{1/2}. \tag{3.81}$$

Flexural waves in rods and plates travel at speeds significantly less than the speeds for extensional waves and generally increase with an increase in frequency. At low frequencies, where the transverse dimensions of the rod or plate are small compared to the flexural wavelength, the flexural wave speed varies as the square root of the frequency.

In a thin rod at low frequencies:

$$c_{F(\text{rod})} = \left(\frac{Y\kappa^2}{\rho}\right)^{1/4}\omega^{1/2} \tag{3.82}$$

where κ is the radius of gyration of the cross sectional area of the rod, Y is Young's modulus, and ρ is the mass density. For a rod of circular cross section of radius a:

$$\kappa^2 = a^2/4$$

and for a rectangular rod of dimensions b and h, the radius of gyration for oscillations parallel to h is:

$$\kappa^2 = h^2/12.$$

In a thin plate of thickness h, the low frequency flexural wave speed is:

$$c_{F(\text{plate})} = \left(\frac{Yh^2}{12(1-\nu^2)\rho}\right)^{1/4}\omega^{1/2} \tag{3.83}$$

where ν is Poisson's ratio.

References

1. B.A. Auld. *Acoustic Fields and Waves in Solids*. Vol. I. Wiley: New York (1973).
2. Warren P. Mason. *Piezoelectric Crystals and Their Application to Ultrasonics*. D. Van Nostrand Co: New York (1950).
3. Warren P. Mason. *Crystal Physics of Interaction Processes*. Academic Press: New York (1966).
4. Don A. Berlincourt, Daniel R. Curran, and Hans Jaffe. Piezoelectric and Piezomagnetic Materials and Their Function in Transducers. Chapter 3 in *Physical Acoustics*, Vol. 1A. Warren P. Mason, Ed. Academic Press: New York (1964).
5. J.F. Nye. *Physical Properties of Crystals*. Oxford: London (1957).
6. Walter Guyton Cady. *Piezoelectricity*. Vols. I and II. Dover: New York (1964).
7. J. Grindlay. *An Introduction to the Phenomenological Theory of Ferroelectricity*. Pergamon Press Ltd. (Oxford): London (1970).
8. Lawrence E. Kinsler, Austin R. Frey, Alan B. Coppens, and James V. Sanders. *Fundamentals of Acoustics*. 3rd Ed. Wiley: New York (1982).

Problems

3.1. Using the basic definition of the piezoelectric coupling factor, Eq. (3.70), and the basic piezoelectric equations, show that the static values of the coupling factor for piezoelectric ceramics are:

(a) $\quad k_{31}^2 = \dfrac{d_{31}^2}{\epsilon_{33}^T s_{11}^E}$

when the only stress is along the x-direction and the electrical field is in the z-direction.

(b) $\quad k_{33}^2 = \dfrac{d_{33}^2}{\epsilon_{33}^T s_{33}^E}$

when the strain, stress, and electrical field components are along the z-axis.

3.2. A piezoelectric ceramic bar of length l, width w, and thickness t is cemented between a mass M and a foundation. The length dimension is oriented vertically. The mass is cemented to the top of the bar. The electrodes are on the width (z) faces of the bar.

(a) Draw an equivalent electrical circuit for this system.

(b) Using the equivalent electrical circuit, develop expressions for this device's low frequency sensitivity to simple harmonic acceleration and velocity of the foundation in the vertical direction in $V/m/sec^2$ and in $V/m/sec$, respectively.

CHAPTER 4

PROPERTIES OF COMMONLY USED PIEZOELECTRIC MATERIALS

4.1 Introduction

Many crystalline solids are piezoelectric. The effect arises because of asymmetries in the crystal structure that create an electric dipole moment in the crystal lattice which is sensitive to both elastic strain and applied electric field. Of the thirty-two crystal classes, twenty have the type of asymmetry that can give an elastic–electrical interaction. Important examples in underwater acoustics are quartz, Rochelle salt, ammonium dihydrogen phosphate, lithium sulfate, and tourmaline.

Some crystalline materials are also ferroelectric. Spontaneous electric polarization takes place and changes as the temperature changes, in a manner somewhat analogous to the magnetic polarization that occurs in ferromagnetic materials. There is also a Curie temperature above which the material is no longer ferroelectric or piezoelectric. Rochelle salt and barium titanate are examples of these materials.

One of the earliest uses of the piezoelectric effect in sonar was by Langevin (1), who used quartz in a composite vibrator. Because of its relatively low electromechanical coupling coefficient, quartz has rarely been used since then for sonar projectors, although it is still a very important piezoelectric material. It is very useful for electric filters in communications devices and as a projector and receiver in high frequency ultrasonics because of its excellent electrical and mechanical properties. Since the elastic moduli along some directions in the crystal have temperature coefficients of opposite signs, it is possible to construct vibrators oriented along particular directions with resonance frequencies that are independent of temperature under normal operating conditions. This, combined with the very high mechanical Q, makes precise frequency control of oscillators possible.

Rochelle salt, an extremely active piezoelectric material, was used a great deal in sonar projectors and hydrophones in the early years of underwater acoustics. It was often used in phonograph pickups and microphones. Its sensitivity to moisture and variations in temperature reduced its usefulness in sonar applications as better materials became available. It is still used in one type of sonic depth sensor. Another water soluble crystal, ammonium dihydrogen phosphate (ADP), which has less temperature sensitivity, was used as a replacement for Rochelle salt in a number of sonar transducers in the 1940's.

Discovery of the ferroelectric and electrostrictive properties of the ceramic barium titanate (2) in the 1940's resulted in many new sonar projector and hydrophone designs during the 1950's and 1960's. It also stimulated the search for new and more active ceramic compositions. For a number of reasons, single crystal barium titanate has not been employed in sonar transducers. Instead, sintered polycrystalline ceramics are used. These ceramics are polarized by the imposition of large electric fields while they are cooled from temperatures near or above the Curie temperature. Under these conditions, electrostrictive ferroelectric ceramics become piezoelectric.

Much effort has gone into the development of other ferroelectric polycrystalline ceramics that have piezoelectric properties superior to those of barium titanate, such as lead zirconate-lead titanate mixtures. Other ferroelectric crystals that have desirable properties, such as lithium niobate, lithium tantalate, bismuth–sodium niobate, and bismuth–potassium niobate, have been discovered (2). So far, these have not been used in sonar transducers to any significant extent.

Because many of these ceramics have exceptionally high electromechanical coupling coefficients and because the ceramic compositions can be fabricated with properties appropriate to a particular application, their use as transducing materials in sonar projectors and hydrophones is almost universal, displacing virtually all other piezoelectric and magnetostrictive materials. In the past several years, development of porous ceramics and flexible ceramic composite materials has created the potential for additional applications and improved the choices for a best material for a given design.

Other piezoelectric materials have been and continue to be useful in particular applications. Lithium sulfate and tourmaline are useful for hydrophones because of a significant volume coefficient of piezoelectricity. Tourmaline has been used quite often in hydrophones designed for shock and blast measurements. Recently developed piezoelectric polymers such as polyvinylidene fluoride (PVDF) appear to have a great deal of potential for use as hydrophones in hull–mounted arrays.

In the following sections, brief descriptions of the piezoelectric properties of the more important materials used in sonar are given. Typical values of the pertinent parameters are provided in tables. These descriptions and tabulated data are noticeably less complete than one finds in many other writings on piezoelectric materials and their applications, and comprise less information than the transducer designer needs to have available. However, it should be sufficient to introduce the student to some of the properties of these materials and to provide a basis for some simple design exercises.

Data on some of the pertinent properties of electrically inactive materials important to the design and construction of underwater sound transducers are included in a later chapter.

4.2 Properties of Quartz

Although quartz is no longer used in sonar transducers, some information about this crystal is included because of its historical importance and its

continued usefulness in frequency control applications. Alpha–quartz is a trigonal crystal with class 32 symmetry. The matrix of its elastic and piezoelectric constants is shown in the following arrays (4,5,6).
The matrix of the elastic compliance coefficients:

$$
\begin{bmatrix}
s_{11} & s_{12} & s_{13} & s_{14} & 0 & 0 \\
s_{12} & s_{11} & s_{13} & -s_{14} & 0 & 0 \\
s_{13} & s_{13} & s_{33} & 0 & 0 & 0 \\
s_{14} & -s_{14} & 0 & s_{44} & 0 & 0 \\
0 & 0 & 0 & 0 & s_{44} & 2s_{14} \\
0 & 0 & 0 & 0 & 2s_{14} & s_{66}
\end{bmatrix}
$$

The dielectric constants matrix:

$$
\begin{bmatrix}
\epsilon_1 & 0 & 0 \\
0 & \epsilon_1 & 0 \\
0 & 0 & \epsilon_3
\end{bmatrix}
$$

The piezoelectric constants matrix:

$$
\begin{bmatrix}
d_{11} & -d_{11} & 0 & d_{14} & 0 & 0 \\
0 & 0 & 0 & 0 & -d_{14} & -2d_{11} \\
0 & 0 & 0 & 0 & 0 & 0
\end{bmatrix}
$$

Numerical values of some of the constants are given in Tab. 4.1.

Using stress and electric field as the independent variables, Eq. (3.56) becomes, for quartz, the following:

$$S_1 = s_{11}^E T_1 + s_{12}^E T_2 + s_{13}^E T_3 + s_{14}^E T_4 + d_{11}E_1$$

$$S_2 = s_{12}^E T_1 + s_{11}^E T_2 + s_{13}^E T_3 - s_{14}^E T_4 - d_{11}E_1$$

$$S_3 = s_{13}^E T_1 + s_{13}^E T_2 + s_{33}^E T_3$$

$$S_4 = s_{14}^E T_1 - s_{14}^E T_2 + s_{44}^E T_4 + d_{14}E_1$$

$$S_5 = s_{44}^E T_5 + 2s_{14}^E T_6 - d_{14}E_2 \tag{4.1}$$

$$S_6 = 2s_{14}^E T_5 + 2(s_{11}^E - s_{12}^E)T_6 - 2d_{11}E_2$$

$$D_1 = d_{11}T_1 - d_{12}T_2 + d_{14}T_4 + \epsilon_1^T E_1$$

$$D_2 = -d_{14}T_5 - 2d_{11}T_6 + \epsilon_1^T E_2$$

$$D_3 = \epsilon_3^T E_3.$$

Table 4.1

Properties[1] of α-Quartz at 25 °C

$\epsilon_{11}^T/\epsilon_0$	4.52
$\epsilon_{33}^T/\epsilon_0$	4.68
d_{11}	2.31×10^{-12} C/N
d_{14}	0.727
s_{11}^E	12.77×10^{-12} m^2/N
s_{12}^E	-1.79
s_{13}^E	-1.22
s_{33}^E	9.60
s_{44}^E	20.04
s_{66}^E	29.12
s_{14}^E	4.50
c_{11} [2]	86.8×10^9 N/m^2
c_{12}	7.04
c_{13}	11.91
c_{33}	105.75
c_{44}	58.20
$[c_{66}]$	39.88
c_{14}	-18.04
ρ	2648.50 kg/m^3

[1] From Berlincourt, Curran, and Jaffe (22)
[2] From Landolt–Bornstein Tables

The electrical–elastic interaction for a few special cases are of interest. Consider a thin quartz plate cut so that its faces are perpendicular to the x–crystalline axis, its length is along the y-axis, and its width is along the z–axis. If electrodes are placed so that an applied field in the x–direction is E_1, then, assuming that the stress along the z–axis is negligible and all shear stresses are zero, Eq. (4.1) becomes:

$$S_1 = s_{11}^E T_1 + s_{12}^E T_2 + d_{11}E_1$$

$$S_2 = s_{12}^E T_1 + s_{11}^E T_2 - d_{11}E_1$$

$$S_3 = s_{13}^E T_1 + s_{13}^E T_2$$

$$S_4 = s_{14}^E T_1 - s_{14}^E T_2 + d_{14}E_1 \qquad (4.2)$$

$$S_5 = S_6 = 0$$

$$D_1 = d_{11}T_1 - d_{12}T_2 + \epsilon_{11}^T E_1$$

$$D_2 = D_3 = 0.$$

If elastic waves are excited by the impressed electric field and are assumed to travel in the x- and y-directions in this x-cut plate (the thickness and length directions in this example), then, in general, stresses T_1 and T_2 will not be zero. We see from an inspection of Eq. (4.2) that longitudinal strains will be generated along all three coordinate directions. The strain S_3 is due only to the Poisson's ratio effect. A shearing strain or face shear will be generated in the x-y face that will distort the plate's rectangular shape into a rhombohedron. It is possible to choose an orientation of the length direction of the plate, relative to the crystalline axes, which will reduce the face shear coupling to zero (4, 5).

If an elastic wave is transmitted into the plate because of coupling with waves in another medium, a surface charge will be generated on the electrodes and an emf will be generated at the terminals of the electrodes. Thus, the quartz plate may serve as a receiver of elastic waves and will convert some of the elastic wave energy into electrical energy.

If the frequency of the generated wave is appropriate, thickness resonances can be excited, which makes such a plate a useful sound source or receiver for waves in liquids and solids. The damping effects of coupling to a solid medium may make the waves unobservable in the length direction and the face–shear mode of vibration. For more details of such uses of quartz, the reader is referred to Mason (4) and Cady (5). Piezoelectric data for the x-cut thickness vibrator are provided in Tab. 4.9.

4.3 Piezoelectric Ceramics

For a number of practical reasons, single crystals of barium titanate and other heavy metal oxide mixtures have not been used as transducers for underwater sound. The materials used are ceramics, which are polycrystalline materials. However, they are ferroelectric and strongly electrostrictive so that when polarized, they behave, at least approximately, as piezoelectric materials.

It is worthwhile to quote here a definition of a ceramic. Although it appears to have been made with some humorous intent, it contains much truth. Ceramics are

> . . . minerals of inconstant composition and doubtful purity . . . exposed to immeasurable heat long enough to carry unknown reactions partly to completion, forming heterogeneous, non–stoichiometric materials . . .[1]

The piezoelectric ceramic materials described in this section are indeed quite variable in their properties. It is difficult to control properties from one batch to the next. There are significant differences between materials made to the same nominal specifications by different manufacturers. Their properties are not linear functions of electrical and mechanical stress. Aging effects cause the properties to change with time. In spite of these difficulties, the materials have certain symmetries which make their properties describable, approxi-

---

[1] S.W. Bradstreet. *Bull. Am. Cer. Soc.* 37 510 (1958).

mately at least, as if a sample of the material were a single piezoelectric crystal with the axis of symmetry along the direction of polarization. The elastic matrix has the following form:

$$
\begin{bmatrix}
s_{11} & s_{12} & s_{13} & 0 & 0 & 0 \\
s_{12} & s_{11} & s_{13} & 0 & 0 & 0 \\
s_{13} & s_{13} & s_{33} & 0 & 0 & 0 \\
0 & 0 & 0 & s_{44} & 0 & 0 \\
0 & 0 & 0 & 0 & s_{44} & 0 \\
0 & 0 & 0 & 0 & 0 & 2(s_{11} - s_{12})
\end{bmatrix}
\tag{4.3}
$$

The dielectric constant matrix has the form:

$$
\begin{bmatrix}
\epsilon_1 & 0 & 0 \\
0 & \epsilon_1 & 0 \\
0 & 0 & \epsilon_3
\end{bmatrix}
\tag{4.4}
$$

The convention used in describing the properties of piezoelectric ceramics is to define the z–axis as the poled axis. Since there is complete symmetry about this axis, $d_{31} = d_{32}$ and the array of piezoelectric constants becomes:

$$
\begin{bmatrix}
0 & 0 & 0 & 0 & d_{15} & 0 \\
0 & 0 & 0 & d_{15} & 0 & 0 \\
d_{31} & d_{31} & d_{33} & 0 & 0 & 0
\end{bmatrix}
\tag{4.5}
$$

Using stress and electric field as the independent variables, Eq. (3.56) of Ch. 3 becomes the following, which relates T and E to S and D:

$$S_1 = s_{11}^E T_1 + s_{12}^E T_2 + s_{13}^E T_3 + d_{31} E_3$$

$$S_2 = s_{12}^E T_1 + s_{11}^E T_2 + s_{13}^E T_3 + d_{31} E_3$$

$$S_3 = s_{13}^E T_1 + s_{13}^E T_2 + s_{33}^E T_3 + d_{33} E_3$$

$$S_4 = s_{44}^E T_4 + d_{15} E_2$$

$$S_5 = s_{44}^E T_5 + d_{15} E_1 \tag{4.6}$$

$$S_6 = s_{66}^E T_6$$

$$D_1 = \epsilon_1^T E_1 + d_{15} T_5$$

$$D_2 = \epsilon_1^T E_2 + d_{15} T_4$$

$$D_3 = \epsilon_3^T E_3 + d_{31}(T_1 + T_2) + d_{33} T_3.$$

A discussion of the electrical–elastic interaction for a few special cases is instructive. Consider a rectangular parallelopiped that has been poled along one of its rectangular axes and has completely free sides. That is, all stresses are zero. If an electric field E_3 is applied, Eq. (4.6) becomes:

$$S_1 = S_2 = d_{31}E_3 \qquad D_3 = \epsilon_3^T E_3$$

$$S_3 = d_{33}E_3$$

$$(4.7)$$

with zero values for all other S and D components.

Thus, longitudinal strains are induced along each of the axes of the parallelopiped. As may be noted from the values of the piezoelectric coefficients in Tab. 4.3, the sign of d_{31} is negative, so that the strains in the x- and y-directions of the parallelopiped will be opposite in sign to those along the z-direction. The electrical behavior appears to be the same as for any ordinary dielectric. That is, the effective dielectric constant is for zero stress.

If conducting electrodes on the z-faces are removed and an electric field is applied in one of the transverse directions—again with no externally applied mechanical force—the result is a shearing strain in the plane of the transverse direction. For example, if the only electric field component is E_1, the shear occurs in the plane perpendicular to the y-axis.

For E_1, only:

$$S_1 = S_2 = S_3 = S_4 = S_6 = 0$$

and:

$$S_5 = d_{15}E_1$$

$$D_1 = \epsilon_1^T E_1$$

$$(4.8)$$

and:

$$D_2 = D_3 = 0.$$

For E_2, only, the only non–zero strain is S_4, with:

$$S_4 = d_{15}E_2$$

$$D_2 = \epsilon_1^T E_2.$$

$$(4.9)$$

Properties of Some Commonly Used Piezoelectric Ceramics

The technology of barium titanate and lead zirconate–titanate ceramics has been relatively stable for a number of years. In the past several years, there has been very little development of new ceramic compositions but a great deal of

Table 4.2(a)

Small Signal Properties of Military Standard Sonar Ceramic Types (7). It should be noted that these refer to tests conducted on a thin ring near the first resonance in the hoop mode.

PROPERTY		I — 10 day value Min	I — Max	I — Aging[1] Rate	II — 10 day value Min	II — Max	II — Aging Rate	III — 10 day value Min	III — Max	III — Aging Rate	IV — 10 day value Min	IV — Max	IV — Aging Rate
						MATERIAL TYPES							
Dielectric constant (Relative)	K_{33}^T	1100	1400	-6%	1575	1875	-1.5%	950	1150	-5%	1100	1400	-2%
Dielectric loss tangent	tan δ	—	0.004	—	—	0.02	—	—	0.004	—	—	0.008	—
Piezoelectric[2] coupling factor (effective)	k_{eff}	0.31	0.36	-2.5%	0.32	0.38	-0.3%	0.27	0.33	-2%	0.145	0.20	-2%
Frequency[3] Constant (Hz-m)	N_1	1500	1750	+2.5%	1300	1550	+2.5%	1550	1880	+1.0%	2200	2500	+0.5%
Density kg/cm³	ρ	7550	—	—	7600	—	—	7350	—	—	5550	—	—
Mechanical[4] quality factor	Q_m	500	—	—	—	—	—	800	—	—	400	—	—
Percent change in K_{33}^T 0° to 50°C		—	7	—	—	30	—	—	7	—	—	6	—

NOTES:

[1] The aging rate is the maximum permitted change (percent) in properties in the period 10 to 100 days after poling.

[2] The effective coupling factor is defined by $k_{eff}^2 = \dfrac{f_n^2 - f_m^2}{f_n^2}$ where f_n is frequency of minimum admittance and f_m the frequency of maximum admittance to be measured at fields ≥ 0.1 V/cm.

[3] The frequency constant N_1 defined as $N_1 = \dfrac{2\pi D_{\text{mean}}}{2}$ where D_{mean} is the mean diameter.

[4] The mechanical quality factor Q_m defined by $Q_m = \dfrac{1}{2\pi f_m Z_m C^T k_{eff}^2}$ where C^T is the small signal capacity measured at 1 kHz and Z_m is the minimum impedance measured at f_m.

Values for the mechanical quality factor and the change in K_{33}^T with temperature are not 10 day values but shall be measured at approximately 100 days.

work on new applications, refining production techniques (*3*), and quality control. Therefore, the values of the physical properties of commonly used ceramics given in the tables in this section have not changed greatly for a number of years.

In the process of procuring sonar transducers for the Navy, problems of making comparisons between the products of different ceramic and transducer manufacturers and problems in obtaining reproducibility of transducer characteristics from one production run to the next led to the development in 1970 of a military specification for transducer ceramics (*7*), known as MIL–STD–1376(SHIPS). This classifies ceramics into four basic types:

Classification. The ceramic shall be of the following types:
Type I — Hard lead zirconate–titanate with a Curie temperature equal to or greater than 310°C.
Type II — Soft lead zirconate–titanate with a Curie temperature equal to or greater than 330°C.
Type III — Very hard lead zirconate–titanate with a Curie temperature equal to or greater than 290°C.
Type IV — Barium titanate with nominal additives of 5 percent calcium titanate and 0.5 percent cobalt carbonate as necessary to obtain a Curie temperature equal to or greater than 100°C (*7*).

The words "hard" and "soft" refer to the relative difficulty or ease of depolarization of the ceramic. This standard also specifies limits on some of the more critical physical properties, presented in Tab. 4.2, and the procedures for making the tests. At this time, studies are being conducted with the objective of updating this military standard.

Table 4.2(b)

Large Signal Dielectric Properties of Standard Sonar Ceramic Types[1]

PROPERTY		MATERIAL TYPE					
		I		II	III	IV	
Applied electric field KV/cm (rms)	E	2	4	Not applicable	4.0	1.5	3.0
Max. change in K_{33}^T (%) above small signal value	ΔK_{33}^T	5	18	Not applicable	4.0	6.0	12
Max. loss tangent	$\tan \delta$	0.02	0.04	Not applicable	0.01	0.015	0.03

[1] Data from (*7*).

Table 4.3

Properties of Navy Type Ceramics. Values are typical for low signal levels at 25°C and are taken from catalogs and other references for products made by Vernitron, Inc. Dielectric constants are values at 1 kHz.

		NAVY TYPE			
		I	II	III	IV
		VERNITRON TYPE			
		PZT 4*	PZT 5A*	PZT 8*	CERAMIC B*
Parameter	Units				
k_p†		(-)0.58	(-)0.60	(-)0.50	(-)0.33
k_{31}		(-)0.334	(-)0.344	(-)0.296	(-)0.194
k_{33}		0.70	0.705	0.62	0.48
k_{15}		0.71	0.685	—	0.48
k_t‡		0.513	0.486	—	0.384
$\epsilon_{33}^T/\epsilon_0$		1300	1700	1000	1200
$\epsilon_{33}^S/\epsilon_0$		635	830	600	910
$\epsilon_{11}^T/\epsilon_0$		1475	1730	—	1300
$\epsilon_{11}^S/\epsilon_0$		730	916	—	1000
d_{31}	10^{-12} C/N	-123	-171	-93	-58
d_{33}		289	374	218	149
d_{15}		496	584	—	242
d_h		43	32	32	33
e_{31}	C/m^2	-5.2	-5.4	—	-3.1
e_{33}		15.1	15.8	—	13.5
e_{15}		12.7	12.3	—	10.9
g_{31}	10^{-3} Vm/N	-11.1	-11.4	-10.5	-5.5
g_{33}		26.1	24.8	24.5	14.1
g_{15}		39.4	38.2	—	21.0
h_{31}	10^8 V/m	-9.2	-7.3	—	-3.8
h_{33}		26.8	21.5	—	16.7
h_{15}		19.7	15.2	—	12.3
s_{11}^E	10^{-12} m^2/N	12.3	16.4	11.1	8.6
s_{12}^E		-4.05	-5.74	-3.7	-2.6
s_{13}^E		-5.31	-7.22	-4.8	-2.7
s_{33}^E		15.5	18.8	13.9	9.1
s_{44}^E		39.0	47.5	—	22.2
s_{66}		32.7	44.3	29.6	22.4
s_{11}^D		10.9	14.4	10.1	8.3
s_{12}^D		-5.42	-7.71	-4.5	-2.9
s_{13}^D		-2.10	-2.98	-2.5	-1.9
s_{33}^D		7.9	9.46	8.5	7.0
s_{44}^D		19.3	25.2	—	17.1

Table 4.3 (continued)

Properties of Navy Type Ceramics.

		NAVY TYPE			
		I	II	III	IV
		VERNITRON TYPE			
		PZT 4*	PZT 5A*	PZT 8*	CERAMIC B*
Parameter	Units				
c_{11}^E	10^{10} N/m^2	13.9	12.1	—	15.8
c_{12}^E		7.78	7.54	—	6.9
c_{13}^E		7.43	7.52	—	6.75
c_{33}^E		11.5	11.1	—	15.0
c_{44}^E		2.56	2.11	—	4.5
c_{66}		3.06	2.26	—	4.5
c_{11}^D		14.5	12.6	—	15.9
c_{12}^D		8.39	8.09	—	7.0
c_{13}^D		6.09	6.52	—	6.2
c_{33}^D		15.9	14.7	—	17.7
c_{44}^D		5.18	3.97	—	5.85
Density	kg/m^3	7500	7750	7600	5550
Q (mech)		500	75	1000	400
tan δ		0.004	0.02	0.004	0.006
Curie Temp.	°C	328	365	300	115

* Trademarks of Vernitron, Inc.

† k_p is the planar coupling factor, relating transverse coupling in a disk or plate.

‡ k_t is the thickness coupling factor, relating parallel coupling in a disk or plate.

Characterization of the piezoelectric ceramics is very complex because of the nonlinearities of their properties. The piezoelectric, dielectric, and elastic parameters may be listed but the designer must consider the nonlinearities, the temperature variations, and the problems of achieving reproducibility as well. The tables of data given here are typical of the four types defined in this specification. Tab. 4.3 is taken from a manufacturer's catalog and gives a consistent set of values typical of these basic types. The values that may be found in a particular specimen may vary as much as ten percent from published values. Other compositions having different properties are available from a number of ceramic manufacturers. An indication of the wide variety of shapes and sizes of commercially available piezoelectric ceramics is shown in Fig. 4.1.

FIG. 4.1   An illustration of the wide variety of available sizes and shapes of piezoelectric ceramic elements. Included in this photograph are plates, bars, rings (both radially and circumferentially polarized), spheres, and small composite vibrators. Used with permission of the Edo Western Corp.

The properties of piezoelectric ceramics also change with time, temperature, elastic stress, and electric field. Fig. 4.2 provides data on typical variability of some of the piezoelectric properties with uniaxial stress and Tab. 4.2 provides limits on the high field values of the parameters of Navy type ceramics.

Because electric fields and mechanical stress tend to induce nonlinearities and cause depolarization of the "soft" ceramic types, type II ceramic is most often used for acoustic sensors, such as hydrophones or accelerometers. Types I and III, being harder and more resistant to depolarization, are used primarily for high powered projectors.

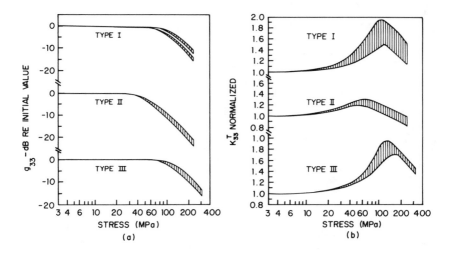

FIG. 4.2   Comparison of compressive stress along the poled axis of three Navy type ceramics. (a) Effect on g_{33}. (b) Effect on relative dielectric constant K_{33}^T. The shaded areas indicate the variability found among products from different manufacturers (From Browder and Meeks (18)).

4.4 Other Piezoelectric Materials

In addition to the piezoelectric ceramics just described, there are a number of other piezoelectric materials which are useful or have the potential of becoming useful in transducers for underwater sound. Some of the pertinent properties of several of these materials will now be described. How they are used or may be used is also indicated. References are provided to sources of more detailed information.

The choice of a piezoelectric material for a particular application will, of course, be based on parameters which will depend upon the application. In some cases, the electromechanical coupling coefficient is of primary importance; in other cases, other parameters are more signficant. For most of the materials listed in this section, the primary application is in hydrophones. It is pointed out in Ch. 8 that the product of the two piezoelectric strain coefficients, g and d, is a very useful measure of "goodness" per unit volume of a piezoelectric material when minimization of hydrophone internal noise is a major design criterion. Therefore, the tables of data will sometimes include only these coefficients or their product. A comparison of the hydrostatic or volume piezoelectric constants is given in Tab. 4.10.

Lithium Sulfate ($LiSO_4 \cdot H_2O$)
Lithium sulfate has long been useful and continues to be used for hydrophones. The major advantage is that it has a relatively large hydrostatic piezoelectric stress coefficient. Its acoustic and piezoelectric properties are

Table 4.4

Piezoelectric Parameters for Lithium Sulfate[1]
(in units of 10^{-12} C/N)

d_{14}	0.8
d_{25}	–5.0
d_{36}	–4.2
d_{16}	–2.0
d_{34}	–2.1
d_{21}	–3.6
d_{22}	18.3
d_{23}	1.7
ϵ_{11}/ϵ_0	5.6
ϵ_{22}/ϵ_0	10.3
ϵ_{33}/ϵ_0	6.5
ϵ_{13}/ϵ_0	0.07

[1] Data from Landolt-Bornstein tables

listed in Tab. 4.4. Data for the commonly used y–cut are given in Tab. 4.9. The open–circuit sensitivity to hydrostatic pressure is proportional to:

$$\frac{d_{21} + d_{22} + d_{23}}{\epsilon_{22}^T}.$$

Mason (*4*) provides additional data on this material.

Table 4.5

Piezoelectric Parameters for Tourmaline[1]

d_{15}	–3.63	(10^{-12} C/N)
d_{22}	–0.333	
d_{33}	–1.83	
d_{31}	–0.342	
e_{15}	–238	(10^{-3} C/m^2)
e_{22}	–52	
e_{33}	–326	
e_{31}	–170	
$\epsilon_{11}^T/\epsilon_0$	8.2	
$\epsilon_{22}^T/\epsilon_0$	8.2	
$\epsilon_{33}^T/\epsilon_0$	7.5	

[1] Data from Mason (*23*)

Tourmaline

The piezoelectric properties of tourmaline are presented in Tab. 4.5. Because the d_{31} and d_{33} elements in the piezoelectric constant matrix have the same sign, the two contributions are additive when the crystal is exposed to a homogeneous acoustic pressure. Thus, the open-circuit sensitivity to hydro-static pressure is proportional to:

$$\frac{d_{31} + d_{33}}{\epsilon_{33}^T}.$$

Tourmaline has been used for many years in the calibration of hydrostatic pressure devices and in the measurement of pressures associated with blast waves. In blast wave pressure measurements, the hydrophone sometimes consists of one, but usually several, small thin z-cut disks with electrodes on the z-faces, cemented together and connected electrically in parallel. Mason (4) provides additional information.

Table 4.6

Piezoelectric Properties of Lead Metaniobate[1]

k_p	(-) 0.7
k_{31}	(-) 0.045
k_{33}	0.38
$\epsilon_{33}^T/\epsilon_0$	225
d_{33}	8.5×10^{-12} C/N
d_{31}	$\sim -9 \times 10^{-12}$
g_{33}	42.5×10^{-3} Vm/N
g_{31}	$\sim -4.5 \times 10^{-3}$
s_{33}^E	25.4×10^{-12} m^2/N
s_{33}^D	21.8
Q	11
Tan δ	~ 0.01
ρ	6000 kg/m^3
Curie Temp.	570°C

[1] Data from Berlincourt, Curran, and Jaffe (22)

Rochelle Salt and Ammonium Dihydrogen Phosphate (ADP)

It was stated earlier that these two crystals played important roles in the early sonar transducers. Although these materials have been almost completely supplanted by newer and better piezoelectric materials, they are of historic interest. Rochelle salt is probably one of the most active naturally occuring piezoelectric materials. This extraordinarily large sensitivity made it useful in transducers. The fact that its Curie temperature is near room temperature makes its properties very sensitive to temperature in many applications and the x-cut form was often not used for this reason. Several cuts for various purposes can be used. Another reason for its decline in utility is that this material is affected by the relative humidity and must be protected from the atmosphere. ADP was used most often in the form of a 45 degree z-cut expander bar. Piezoelectric data for commonly used cuts of these two materials are presented in Tab. 4.9. Mason (4) and Berlincourt (8) provide additional information on these crystals.

Lead Metaniobate ($PbNb_2O_6$)

Lead metaniobate is a unique piezoelectric ceramic. It has a very high Curie temperature, a low permittivity, a reasonable value for the coupling coefficients k_t and k_{33}, and a low mechanical Q. The hydrostatic piezoelectric strain constant is rather large compared to that for the PZT ceramics, making this a material of potential use in deep submergence hydrophones. Also, a figure of goodness for hydrophone use where hydrophone noise is a limiting factor is the product of d and g. In this material, the product gd is almost ten times larger than in Navy ceramic type I. Some data on this material are given in Tab. 4.6. Other niobates have been found that have high Q and relatively low temperature drifts, but they have not been used for underwater sound transducers. Jaffe and Berlincourt (9) provide additional information.

Table 4.7

Piezoelectric Properties of Antimony Sulfur Iodide at 0°C[1]

$\epsilon_{33}^T/\epsilon_0$	2000
$\epsilon_{33}^S/\epsilon_0$	550
k_t	0.87
k_{33}	k_t
$|k_p|$	< 0.1
d_{33}	1300×10^{-12} C/N
$|d_{31}|$	$< 150 \times 10^{-12}$ C/N
d_n	1000×10^{-12}
e_{33}	13 C/m^2
c_{33}^D	4×10^{10} N/m^2
c_{33}^E	1×10^{10}
ρ	5250 kg/m^3

[1] Data from Jaffe and Berlincourt (9)

Antimony Sulfur Iodide (SbSI)

The piezoelectric properties of this compound have been known for some time. This material has a hydrostatic piezoelectric strain constant g_h much larger than that of the traditional piezoelectric ceramics. However, so far it has not been used in practical sonar transducers because its Curie temperature is 22°C. Above this temperature, its piezoelectric activity disappears. Studies have been conducted on the use of ion substitution techniques to change its properties and increase its potential usefulness. Experiments have been carried out at the Naval Research Laboratory (10) on oxygen–modified SbSI. This process not only increases the g-value but raises the Curie temperature. An optimum concentration of oxygen seems to be between four and eight percent. The Curie temperature was raised to 34°C for SBS$_{0.96}$O$_{0.04}$I. In order for this material to be a viable candidate for underwater acoustic applications, the Curie temperature needs to be in the neighborhood of 50°C. Some approximate values of the parameters for this material are given in

Tab. 4.7. Comparisons of its hydrostatic piezoelectric constants with those of other materials are shown in Tab. 4.10.

Lead Titanate ($PbTiO_3$)

Pure or nearly pure $PbTiO_3$ is a ferroelectric and piezoelectric material (2). It has not been used in transducers because of its tendency to crack and crumble upon cooling from temperatures used in its firing and its lower resistivity at elevated temperatures. Alloying with other materials helps to improve the properties. Recent developments by Japanese (11) and French (12) piezoelectric materials manufacturers indicate that $PbTiO_3$–based ceramics have a large piezoelectric coupling in the 33 mode and a much smaller piezoelectric coupling in the 31 mode. The result is a large value for the hydrostatic piezoelectric contant g_h. If this type of material were to become available in commercial quantities, it could lead to the construction of a simple hydrophone, such as a disk, with reasonable sensitivity over a wide frequency range. Such a configuration should also be insensitive to effects of hydrostatic pressure. The relatively low dielectric permittivity of this material may be a handicap in matching to a low noise preamplifier.

Composite Ceramics

The properties of the conventional lead zirconate–lead titanate types of ceramics are rather well optimized for current applications and little improvement can be expected in their properties (3). There have been considerable efforts devoted to the development of new composite configurations of the ceramic with other nonactive materials in order to improve their properties and to enhance their utility for specific tasks or environments. These materials are known variously as composite ceramics or porous ceramics. When the nonactive component is a flexible material, the composition is often called flexible ceramic. The parameter improvement generally sought in the development of these materials is a decrease in d_{31} and an increase in d_{33}, so that the hydrostatic piezoelectric constant is increased. It is also desirable to keep the relative dielectric constant small so that the product of the hydrostatic values of d and g is as large as possible. The application of greatest interest for these materials is for hydrophones operating in a hydrostatic mode.

The properties of a structure composed of two components or phases are determined in part by the degree of connectivity between the parts of each phase. The objective is to reduce the coupling of the transverse piezoelectric constant to the E field or the D field when the material is subjected to a hydrostatic or homogeneous acoustic pressure. There are many possible arrangements for two–phase composites. Examples include ceramic particles imbedded in plastic or rubber, a ceramic sponge filled with plastic, a ladder structure of ceramic with the voids filled by a fluid or plastic, or foamed, perforated, or honeycomb ceramic.

These materials are the subject of considerable research at the present time. There are now commercially available piezoelectric rubber compounds in both sheet and coaxial cable form with electrodes of a conductive rubber. Some indications of the merits of this form of material are shown in the comparisons in Tab. 4.10. There are some obvious underwater acoustic applications to linear and planar arrays. For additional information, see refs. (13) and (14).

Piezoelectric Polymers

It has been known for many years that many organic materials exhibit some piezoelectric properties. In 1969, Kawai (15) discovered that there were large, useful piezoelectric pyroelectric effects in the polymer polyvinylidene fluoride (PVDF or PVF$_2$). The compound PVDF (16) is a semicrystalline polymer with the chains composed of about 2,000 monomers, $-CF_2CH_2-$, which has a significant dipole moment. The molecular weight is about 10^5. These chains are imbedded in a mixture of crystals and amorphous phases, the latter behaving as a super-cooled liquid. The chains have a length of about 50 μm and the dimensions of the crystal regions are typically of the order of 0.01 μm thick $\times$ 0.1 μm long. The chains extend through both crystal and amorphous regions.

Four crystalline forms have been identified and the arrangements are dependent on production processes. The piezoelectric properties are enhanced by mechanical stretching of the sheet material in one or two directions and by electrical polarization. The piezoelectric effect in the poled material may be due to differences in the dielectric constants and the elastic constants of the crystalline and amorphous phases and to the intrinsic electrical dipole moment of the crystalline regions. The consensus is that this last effect is the dominant one.

The array of piezoelectric coefficients in material that has been poled but not stretched is:

$$\begin{bmatrix} 0 & 0 & 0 & 0 & d_{15} & 0 \\ 0 & 0 & 0 & d_{15} & 0 & 0 \\ d_{31} & d_{31} & d_{33} & 0 & 0 & 0 \end{bmatrix}$$

When the material is mechanically stretched along one axis in the sheet and then polarized, it becomes:

$$\begin{bmatrix} 0 & 0 & 0 & 0 & d_{15} & 0 \\ 0 & 0 & 0 & d_{24} & 0 & 0 \\ d_{31} & d_{32} & d_{33} & 0 & 0 & 0 \end{bmatrix}$$

The material is normally provided in sheet form with electrodes on the surfaces. It has both transverse and parallel piezoelectric effects. Two thicknesses are commercially available: thin, about 30 μm, and thick, about 0.5 mm. It is also available in so-called voided form in which the material is filled with a large number of gas-filled microbubbles. Some piezoelectric data are given in Tab. 4.8.

Table 4.8

Piezoelectric Coefficients of a PVDF Sample at Room Temperature[1]

Sample was stretched and poled with a relatively high field.

d_{31}	17.9	10^{-12} C/N
d_{32}	0.9	
d_{33}	-27.1	
d_{3h}	8.3	
k_{31}	0.103	
k_{33}	0.126	
s_{11}	2.6	10^{-13} m^2/N

[1] Data from Sessler (*16*)

Table 4.9

Properties of Commonly Used Cuts of Piezoelectric Crystals[1]

MATERIAL AND CUT	VIBRATION MODE/FIELD	k	d 10^{-12} C/N	e C/m^2	ϵ/ϵ_0	c m/s	ρ kg/m^3
Quartz – x	Thickness	0.1	2.3	0.17	4.6	5700	2650
ADP – 45°Z	Longitudinal				$\epsilon_{33}^T/\epsilon_0$		
	Transverse Field	0.28	24	0.30	15.3	3250	1800
LiSO$_4$·H$_2$O – Y	Thickness				$\epsilon_{22}^S/\epsilon_0$		
	Parallel Field	0.30	16.3	0.66	9	5470	2060
Rochelle Salt at 30°C							
45° – X	Longitudinal				$\epsilon_{11}^T/\epsilon_0$		
	Transverse Field	0.65	275	3.0	350	3100	1770
45° – Y	Longitudinal				$\epsilon_{22}^T/\epsilon_0$		
	Transverse Field	0.32	30	0.16	9.4	2340	1770

[1] Data from Berlincourt (*8*).

The piezoelectric constants of PVDF are significantly smaller than those of the PZT ceramics, and the material cannot be used at temperatures much above 80 °C because of the poor thermal stability of some of its properties. However, PDVF has the advantages of flexibility, toughness, and low density. It has a good acoustic impedance match with water, is available in large sheets, and is relatively low in cost. It is also different from other piezoelectric materials in that one can obtain very large piezoelectric strains in it, due mostly to the fact that larger fields can be applied without depolarizing the material. Its properties do not change significantly with hydrostatic pressure (*17*).

The material has been used in a large variety of applications ranging from earphones and microphones to mechanical pressure detectors. There have been a number of applications in medical ultrasonics. A great deal of effort is

Table 4.10

Comparisons of the Hydrostatic Piezoelectric Properties of Various Materials.[1]

MATERIAL	$\epsilon_{33}^T/\epsilon_0$	g_h	d_h	$g_h d_h$	ρ
			UNITS		
		10^{-3} Vm/N	10^{-12} C/N	10^{-15} m^2/N	kg/m^3
PZT 4	1300	4	45	180	7500
PZT 5	1420	30	38	120	
PbNb$_2$O$_6$	225	27	60	1620	6000
LiSO$_4$·H$_2$O	10	148	14	1990	2060
SbSI (at 22°C)	1360	36	437	15730	5000
Porous PZT	230	55	105	5775	
PZT Epoxy				1290	2800
PZT Rubber				17300	2800
Epoxy/PZT				16500	5400
PZT Foam				13600	3200
PVDF	13	64	7	450	1800

[1] R. Ting, Private communication

being devoted to developing it for use in towed arrays and hull–mounted planar arrays. The details of the piezoelectric phenomena in this and related polymers are not completely understood and are still the subject of basic research. Ref. (16) provides more detailed information about its properties.

4.5 Nonlinearities and Aging of Piezoelectric Ceramics

The process of polarizing the lead zirconate–lead titanate ceramics is a highly nonlinear one (18). The strains imposed by the poling far exceed values that one expects in normal solids within the elastic limits. For example, in a type I ceramic, the dimensions along the poled direction increase by 0.5 percent and those in the transverse direction shrink by 0.23 percent. The volume change is an increase of 0.04 percent. The internal stresses required to generate these large strains are enormous. The process is also accompanied by the generation of microcracks within the ceramic. It should not then be surprising to find that the properties of the ceramic behave in a nonlinear fashion when the material is subjected to large electric fields under high drive conditions, when large dynamic strains occur during operation at mechanical resonance, or when large static stresses are used in pre–stressing the ceramic elements in a transducer.

One might also expect that high driving conditions would affect the aging process. Aging is the partial relieving of internal stress induced by the poling. This is done by domain wall motion in most ceramics. Some compositions, such as Navy type II, have lower aging rates due, it is believed, to the rapid stress relief that occurs immediately after poling. In these materials, the donor element additions make up about one percent of the lead vacancies in the crystal lattice and provide room for stress relief. Thus, processes that reduce the internal stresses also reduce the aging rate. Berlincourt (18) lists the most desirable of these processes as heat treatment and compressive stress applied parallel to the poled directions.

Superior aging characteristics can be achieved with ceramics having reasonably good high drive behavior but with sacrifices in electromechanical coupling coefficients and permittivity and in greater processing difficulty.

Effects of Stress

The physical parameters that are important in the design of piezoelectric materials in transducers change with imposed mechanical stress. The importance of these effects depends, of course, on the application and the environment in which the transducer is to operate. For example, if a hydrophone is designed for deep submergence in the ocean, then consideration of these effects will be much more important than in the design of one that will always be used at low hydrostatic pressures. Effects of stress on the properties of ceramics are complex and varied. In order to characterize the extent of these effects properly, more space would be required than is appropriate for this book. However, the student should be exposed to the general nature of these effects and to the types of changes which are observed in ceramic compositions presently used in transducers. For these reasons, the following paragraphs will give very brief and mostly descriptive characterizations of the effects of stress on piezoelectric materials of interest in underwater sound.

It should be expected that piezoelectric, dielectric, and elastic properties of these materials change with any changes in the crystalline lattice dimensions or domain structure whether caused by externally applied stresses, temperature, or electric field. It also should be expected that these effects will be larger in piezoelectric materials such as ceramics and piezoelectric polymers because of electrical polarization during the manufacturing process, and will also depend on the composition of the ceramic. It also reasonable to expect that the effects of imposed stresses will depend upon their dimensionality, i.e., whether the stress is one-, two- or three-dimensional, and the orientation of the stress relative to the poled direction in the material. For example, if the applied stress generates charges that aid polarization, the effects of this stress should be different from the effects caused by stress-induced changes that tend to depolarize the material.

The effects of hydrostatic pressure turn out to be relatively small. In their studies of a barium titanate ceramic and a lead zirconate-titanate composition similar to Navy type I, Nishi and Brown (19) found that the d constants and permittivity changed less than 7 percent with pressure up to 10,000 psi (70 MPa) and there was a small increase in the dielectric loss tangent with changes in the pressure given above. The effects were less in the barium titanate type material. They found that stress aging occurred at the highest pressure but that high field dielectric properties reached constant values after a few minutes.

When the stress is a unidirectional one, the effects generally are much larger than with hydrostatic stress. Studies conducted by Browder and Meeks (20) on ceramic types I, II, and III found the following effects:

a. The dielectric constant always increases with increasing stress up to a maximum value, then decreases with approximately the $-4/3$ power of the stress. The stress at the maximum value of dielectric constant depends upon the type, with the maximum stress point for type II being about half that for types I and III.

b. In the hard ceramics, types I and III, the dielectric loss tangent increases with stress up to a point and then decreases. Upon relieving the applied stress the loss tangent is larger than it was before the stress was applied. In type II material, the loss tangent decreases with increasing stress and does not indicate the permanent increase in value after removal of the stress as noted for the other types.

c. The piezoelectric constant g_{33} is relatively independent of applied stress up to a point that depends upon the type of ceramic. Above that stress, .the piezoelectric constant decreases at about the $-5/3$ power of the stress. The roll-off stress point for the type II material is about half that for types I and III.

d. The d constant is the product of the dielectric constant and the g constant. Type II material exhibited only a small increase in d_{33} with stress, but the other two types exhibited a noticeable peak. The constant d_{33} increases with stress up to a point, then decreases at about the -2 power of the stress.

e. Electrical or mechanical stress tends to depole the ceramic, especially type II.

For these reasons types I and III are used primarily as high powered projectors and type II is used for hydrophones. Deep submergence hydrophones are often made with a type I rather than a type II ceramic. Some graphical summaries of these effects observed by Browder and Meeks (20) are shown in Fig. 4.2.

Henriquez (21) conducted tests of various materials, configured as hydrophones, made at hydrostatic pressures as high as 16,000 psi (about 100 MPa). Sensitivities generally decrease as pressure increases. Those least affected by pressure were also the least acoustically sensitive as hydrophones.

References

1. Ivor Groves, Ed. *Acoustic Transducers*. Benchmark Papers in Acoustics, Vol. 14. Hutchinson Ross: Stroudsburg, PA (1981), pp 266–269.
2. Bernard Jaffe, William R. Cook, Jr., and Hans Jaffe. *Piezoelectric Ceramics*. Academic Press: New York (1971).

3. Don Berlincourt. Piezoelectric Ceramics: Characteristics and Applications. *J. Acoust. Soc. Am.* **70** 1586–1595 (1981).

4. Warren P. Mason. *Piezoelectric Crystals and Their Application to Ultrasonics.* Van Nostrand: New York (1950).

5. Walter Guyton Cady. *Piezoelectricity.* Vol. 1 Dover: New York (1964).

6. *IEEE Standard on Piezoelectricity.* IEEE Std 176–1978. Institute of Electrical and Electronic Engineers, Inc. New York.

7. Military Standard, *Piezoelectric Ceramics for Sonar Transducers,* MIL–STD–1376 (SHIPS) 21 Dec 1970. FSC 5845. U.S. Government Printing Office: 1974–713–151/3793, Washington, DC.

8. Don Berlincourt. Piezoelectric Crystals and Ceramics, Ch. 2 of *Ultrasonic Materials.* O.E. Mattiat, Ed. Plenum: New York (1971).

9. H. Jaffe and D.A. Berlincourt. Piezoelectric Transducer Materials. *Proc. I.E.E.E.* **53** 1372–1386 (1965).

10. Yariv Porat and Steven W. Meeks. The Predictions of a New Phenomenological Model for $SbS_xO_{1-x}I$. *Ferroelectrics* **38** 893–896 (1981).

11. A.J. Nepgen, *et al.* Evaluation of $PbTiO_3$–based Piezoelectric Ceramics for Hydrophone Applications, *J. Acoustic. Soc. Am.* **77** Supp. 1, 17(1), Spring 1985.

12. Dominque Odero. Private communication.

13. R.E. Newnham, D.P. Skinner and L.E. Cross. Connectivity and Piezoelectric-Pyroelectric Composites. *Mat. Res. Bull.* **13** 525–536 (1978).

14. R.C. Pohanka, R.W. Rice and P.L. Smith. *Advanced Ceramics and Composites for Underwater Acoustic and Engineering Applications.* NRL Memorandum Report 3854. Naval Research Laboratory, Washington, D.C. Oct. 1978.

15. H. Kawai. *Jpn. J. Appl. Phys.* **8** 975 (1969).

16. G.M. Sessler. Piezoelectricity in Polyvinylidene fluoride. *J. Acoust. Soc. Am.* **70** 1595–1608 (1981).

17. Steven W. Meeks and Robert Y. Ting. Effects of Static and Dynamic Stress on the Piezoelectric and Dielectric Properties of PVF_2. *J. Acoust. Soc. Am.* **74** 1681–1686, (1983).

18. D. Berlincourt. Comments on Papers Discussing Aging in Ceramics. In *Proceedings of the Workshop on Sonar Transducer Materials.* Naval Reserach Laboratory, Washington, D.C. Feb. 1976.

19. R.Y. Nishi and R.F. Brown. Behavior of Piezoceramic Projector Materials under Hydrostatic Pressure. *J. Acoust. Soc. Am.* **36** 1292–1296 (1964).

20. L.P. Browder and S.W. Meeks. *Effects of One-Dimensional Stress on MIL-STD-1376 Piezoelectric Ceramic Materials, Types I, II, and III.* NRL Report 8159, Oct 14, 1977. Naval Research Laboratory, Washington, DC.

21. T.A. Henriquez. Calibration at High Pressure of Piezoelectric Elements for Deep-Submergence Hydrophones. *J. Acoust. Soc. Am.* **46** 1251–1253 (1969).

Problems

4.1. A long piezoelectric ceramic bar of length l (y–direction), width w (x–direction) and thickness t (z–direction) is subjected to a static force F applied at the ends of the bar. Assume that the length is large compared to the lateral dimensions and that the poling is along the thickness direction.

(a) Calculate an expression for the potential difference between electrodes which must be applied in order for the longitudinal strain to be kept at zero when the force is applied.

(b) Are all the strains zero under these conditions? If so, explain why. If not, what values do these strains have?

4.2. A cylindrical tube of piezoelectric ceramic, polarized radially, has a length of 15 cm, inside diameter of 5 cm and wall thickness of 0.6 cm. Assume that the material is PZT–4 and that the published data are valid for DC. When a 100 V potential is applied to the electrodes on the inner and outer circumferential surfaces:

(a)   What changes should occur in length, mean diameter, and wall thickness if no forces are applied to the cylinder?

(b)   If the ends are constrained to prevent a change in length, what forces can be generated when the 100 V potential is applied?

4.3. A cubical block of piezoelectric material has a side length a and the sides are parallel to the crystalline axes. It is used as a hydrophone at frequencies such that its dimensions are small compared to the acoustic wavelength. First assume that the cube is exposed on all sides to the same acoustic pressure P. For the numerical calculations, let $a = 2$ cm.

(a)   For the case of a general type of piezoelectric material, what are the components of the stress and the components of the electric displacement vector, expressed in terms of P and the appropriate material properties?

(b)   If the material were lithium sulfate, which faces would be most appropriate for the application of electrodes? Explain.

(c)   What would be the open–circuit sensitivity of the hydrophone in part (b)?

(d)   If the material were PZT–5A with electrodes on the z–faces, what would be the open–circuit sensitivity?

(e)   If the ceramic of part (d) is configured so that only the electroded faces are exposed to the acoustic pressure and the other sides are mechanically free, what would be the open–circuit sensitivity?

(f)   Draw an equivalent electrical circuit for the device of part (e) which would be valid at low frequencies, showing values of the electrical elements.

4.4. A rectangular block of piezoelectric ceramic is to be used as a force sensor at low frequencies. Assume that the dimensions are L_x, L_y, and L_z and that the poled direction is along z. Derive expressions for the open–circuit sensitivity of this block in V/N for the following conditions:

(a)   Force is applied normally and uniformly to the z–faces and the electrodes where the voltage is measured are also on the z–faces.

(b)   Force is applied in the y direction, but tangentially to the z–face, causing shear in the y–z plane, and the electrodes are on the y-faces.

CHAPTER 5

SIMPLE PIEZOELECTRIC VIBRATORS

5.1 Basic Assumptions

This chapter will consider some of the modes of vibration of simple mechanical and electrical configurations of piezoelectric bars and plates and their representation by equivalent electrical circuits. This simple approach introduces the student to the principles of such analysis and provides a prototype for the analysis of more complicated vibrators. In most transducer designs of practical interest, the assumptions of simple mechanical and electrical boundary conditions are not valid, and in many cases internal losses and nonlinear effects are significant. For the time being, both internal losses and nonlinear effects are neglected.

The electrical and mechanical boundary conditions should be considered in choosing the appropriate piezoelectric equations and the appropriate coordinate system. In one- and two-dimensional problems, one can often assume either free or clamped boundaries at appropriate surfaces. The location of electrodes relative to the stresses or strains of interest determines whether E or D is constant.

In the equivalent circuits developed here, the parameters are determined in terms of applied mechanical forces and velocities. The exactness of the results is limited only by the assumptions made in the initial setup. In all cases, both mechanical and electrical losses are ignored and, depending on the situation, certain stresses or strains in the vibrator are assumed to be zero. For example, for the case of longitudinal vibrations in the long bar, it is assumed that there is no transverse stress. For thickness vibrations in the thin plate, the strains parallel to the face of the plate are assumed to be zero. In the case where the applied electric field is parallel to the vibrations of interest, the electric displacement $\mathbf{D}$ is assumed to be independent of position. For the transverse field case, the electric field $\mathbf{E}$ is spatially constant. Coordinates are those customarily used with piezoelectric ceramic elements in which the z–direction is arbitrarily defined as the direction of the poling. The applied electric field is chosen to be in this direction for all cases involving longitudinal or thickness vibrations. All shear stresses and strains are assumed to be zero. Examples that will be analyzed are:

   a. Ring vibrator with electric field transverse to the ring thickness
   b. Length expander bar with electric field perpendicular to its length
   c. Length expander bar with electric field parallel to the length
   d. Thickness vibrator with parallel field.

The procedure is to set up the piezoelectric equations, assume simple harmonic vibrations, and determine the electrical properties of the vibrator without any mechanical loading. An equivalent electrical circuit is then developed or verified for an arbitrary load. This approach, which follows methods developed by Mason (*1,2*), Berlincourt (*3*), and others, is perhaps somewhat more cumbersome then the Helmholtz integral method employed by Holland and EerNisse (*4*). However, in the author's view it has the advantage of illuminating the physical principles very well and is relatively simple for the one-dimensional problems analyzed here. The student or designer, when faced with a more realistic design problem in which the one-dimensional assumptions are not valid, will probably need more sophisticated models. Martin (*5*) has analyzed the effects of lateral dimensions on the longitudinal vibrations of cylindrical tubes. The use of finite-element methods in the analysis of transducers has become more practicable in recent years. An introduction to these methods is given by Becker *et al.* (*6*). Decarpigny (*7*) provides a thorough discussion of the application of finite-element methods to a wide variety of transducers. Even though these more realistic models are needed for precise calculation of transducer parameters, in many cases simple models of the sort used here will give correct order of magnitude results.

5.2 Ring Vibrator

The development of equations describing the coupling between electrical and mechanical variables is relatively simple for the radially symmetric vibrations of a thin piezoelectric ceramic ring. This is because the propagation of elastic waves in the ring is neglected and there are no spatially dependent elastic or electrical variables. The assumption that the width and thickness of the ring are small compared to its circumference permits stress to be neglected in the transverse directions so that the effective elastic modulus is Young's modulus. Polarization is assumed to be along the ring axis direction. The axial length is chosen as the ring thickness. The result would be the same if the ring were radially polarized and the symbols for width and thickness exchanged. All internal dissipation, electrical and mechanical, is neglected. These boundary conditions lead to the choice of stress and electric field as the most convenient independent variables. The first case studied will assume that no external mechanical forces act on the ring. This follows the methods of Berlincourt (*3*) and Camp (*8*).

Letting ζ be the radial displacement of the ring, the particle velocity is:

$$u = \frac{\partial \zeta}{\partial t}$$

and the circumferential strain is given by:

$$S_1 = \frac{\zeta}{a}$$

where a is the mean radius of the ring.

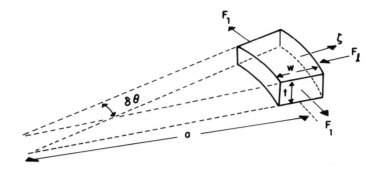

FIG. 5.1 A segment of a ring vibrator of piezoelectric ceramic. Polarization is in the thickness direction.

The equation of motion for the ring element, referring to Fig. 5.1, is seen to be:

$$\rho a \delta\theta w t \frac{\partial^2 \zeta}{\partial t^2} = - T_1 w t \delta\theta \tag{5.1}$$

where ρ is the density of the ring, w is the width, and t is the thickness. If the motion is uniform over the ring, the angle $\delta\theta$ can increase to 2π and, for the unloaded cases, Eq. (5.1) becomes:

$$M \frac{\partial^2 \zeta}{\partial t^2} = - 2\pi T_1 w t \tag{5.2}$$

where M is the mass of the ring, given by $M = 2\pi\rho a w t$.

The piezoelectric equations follow from Eq. (3.55):

$$S_1 = s_{11}^E T_1 + d_{31} E_3 \tag{5.3a}$$

$$D_3 = d_{31} T_1 + \epsilon_{33}^T E_3. \tag{5.3b}$$

The first of these may be solved for T_1:

$$T_1 = \frac{\zeta}{a s_{11}^E} - \frac{d_{31} E_3}{s_{11}^E} \tag{5.4}$$

which can be used with Eq. (5.2) to give:

$$M \frac{\partial^2 \zeta}{\partial t^2} + \frac{\zeta}{C_m} = \frac{2\pi w t d_{31}}{s_{11}^E} E_3. \tag{5.5}$$

The quantity C_m is the mechanical compliance, given by:

$$\frac{1}{C_m} = \frac{2\pi w t}{a s_{11}^E} \tag{5.6}$$

If simple harmonic excitation is assumed, a solution for the steady state displacement is:

$$\zeta = \frac{2\pi wtd_{31}}{j\omega s_{11}^{E}} \frac{1}{Z_m} E_0 e^{j\omega t} \tag{5.7}$$

where:

$$Z_m = j\left(\omega M - \frac{1}{\omega C_m}\right). \tag{5.8}$$

The surface charge q on the electrodes is determined by D_3, which is obtained from Eq. (5.3b):

$$q = 2\pi aw D_3$$

or

$$q = 2\pi aw\left[\frac{d_{31}}{s_{11}^{E}} \frac{\zeta}{a} + \epsilon_{33}^{T}\left(1 - \frac{d_{31}^2}{s_{11}^{E}\epsilon_{33}^{T}}\right) E_3\right]. \tag{5.9}$$

The electromechanical coupling coefficient for this mode is given by:

$$k_{31}^2 = \frac{d_{31}^2}{s_{11}^{E}\epsilon_{33}^{T}}. \tag{5.10}$$

The input current is the time derivative of q, so that the input electrical admittance is:

$$Y_I = \frac{I}{V} = \frac{\partial q}{\partial t} \frac{1}{E_3 t}$$

or

$$Y_I = j\omega \frac{2\pi aw}{t} \epsilon_{33}^{T}(1 - k_{31}^2) + \left(\frac{2\pi wd_{31}}{s_{11}^{E}}\right)^2 \frac{1}{Z_m}. \tag{5.11}$$

This may be rewritten as:

$$Y_I = j\omega C_0 + \frac{N^2}{Z_m} \tag{5.12}$$

or

$$Y_I = Y_E + Y_M \tag{5.13}$$

where Y_E is the blocked electrical admittance and Y_M is the motional admittance. Here:

$$C_0 = \frac{2\pi aw}{t} \epsilon_{33}^{T}(1 - k_{31}^2) \tag{5.14}$$

and

$$N = \frac{2\pi w d_{31}}{s_{11}^E}. \tag{5.15}$$

An equivalent electrical circuit is illustrated in Fig. 5.2, where the elements on the right side of the idealized transformer are the components of the mechanical impedance Z_m. The leakage resistance R_0 is assumed to be very large. Mechanical resonance occurs when Z_m becomes a minimum, or:

$$\omega_0 M - \frac{1}{\omega_0 C_m} = 0.$$

The mechanical resonance angular frequency is given by:

$$\omega_0 = (a^2 \rho s_{11}^E)^{-1/2}. \tag{5.16}$$

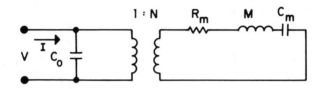

$$R_m = 0$$

$$M = 2\pi \rho a w t$$

$$C_m = \frac{a s_{11}^E}{2\pi w t}$$

$$N = \frac{2\pi w d_{31}}{s_{11}^E}$$

$$C_0 = \frac{2\pi a w}{t} \epsilon_{33}^T (1 - k_{31}^2)$$

$$k_{31}^2 = \frac{d_{31}^2}{s_{11}^E \epsilon_{33}^T}$$

FIG. 5.2 Equivalent network for the ring vibrator without loading. The leakage resistance R_0 is assumed to be infinite.

Noting that the speed of travel for longitudinal waves along the circumference of the ring is the same as that along a long bar, given by:

$$c_b^E = (\rho s_{11}^E)^{-1/2} \tag{5.17}$$

it is seen that the mechanical resonance occurs when the circumference of the ring is exactly one acoustic wavelength. The result is fortuitous since wave motion is not an essential assumption for the radially symmetric vibrations of the ring.

If external mechanical loading exists due to an acoustic pressure P acting uniformly on the exterior circumferential surface of the ring, the force due to the acoustic loading acting on a differential segment of the ring, shown in Fig. 5.1, is $F_l = -Pta\,\delta\theta$. The specific load impedance is given by:

$$z_l = r_l + jx_l = \frac{P}{u} \tag{5.18}$$

where $u = (\partial \zeta / \partial t)$.

The equation of motion must now include the forces exerted on the external surface of the ring. The additional term is:

$$z_l t a \delta \theta \, \frac{\partial \zeta}{\partial t}.$$

The end result has the same form as before with a redefinition of the mechanical impedance:

$$Z_m = 2\pi t a z_l + j \left(\omega M - \frac{1}{\omega C_m} \right). \tag{5.19}$$

5.3 Length Expander Bar with Perpendicular Field

Again following the development given by Berlincourt (3) for the analysis of the vibrations of a long piezoelectric bar, it will be assumed that the dominant motion is along the length of the bar. As indicated in Fig. 5.3, the electrodes are on the z–faces. It is assumed that the width w and thickness t are small with

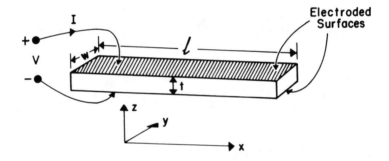

FIG. 5.3   Longitudinal piezoelectric vibrator bar with electric field transverse to the direction of the principal motion. Ends are free.

respect to length l. Since the electrodes form equipotential surfaces, E_3 is constant throughout the bar. Neglecting the fringing effects, E_1 and E_2 are zero. The tensile stresses in the y– and z–directions and all shear stresses are assumed to be zero. The choice of T and E as independent variables is for convenience since this choice leads to a simpler set of equations. Using Eq. (3.55), the piezoelectric equations for this case become:

$$S_1 = s_{11}^E T_1 + d_{31} E_3 \tag{5.20a}$$

$$D_3 = d_{31} T_1 + \epsilon_{33}^T E_3. \tag{5.20b}$$

It is assumed that simple harmonic longitudinal waves propagating along the x–direction have a displacement given by:

$$\xi = (A \sin kx + B \cos kx) e^{j\omega t} \tag{5.21}$$

where $k = \omega/c_b^E$ and c_b^E is the speed of propagation of longitudinal waves in the long bar at constant electric field, given by Eq. (5.17).

It is assumed that the electric field is sinusoidal in time, given by:

$$E_3 = E_0 e^{j\omega t}. \tag{5.22}$$

It is also assumed that the ends of the bar are mechanically free so that at each end, $x = 0$ and $x = \ell$, the forces are zero and, therefore, $T_1 = 0$ at these points. Applying these boundary conditions, the piezoelectric equations are now used to determine the constants A and B. Using:

$$S_1 = \frac{\partial \xi}{\partial x} = k(A \cos kx - B \sin kx)e^{j\omega t} \tag{5.23}$$

and $T_1 = 0$ at $x = 0$, Eq. (5.20a) is used to determine the amplitude:

$$A = \frac{d_{31}E_0}{k}. \tag{5.24}$$

Since $T_1 = 0$ at $x = \ell$, again Eq. (5.20a) with Eq. (5.22) are used to get:

$$B = -\frac{d_{31}E_0}{k \sin k\ell} + A \cot k\ell$$

or

$$B = -\frac{d_{31}E_0}{k} \tan \frac{k\ell}{2}. \tag{5.25}$$

Using Eqs. (5.23) through (5.25) in Eq. (5.20a) gives:

$$T_1 = \frac{S_1}{s_{11}^E} - \frac{d_{31}}{s_{11}^E} E_3$$

or

$$T_1 = \frac{d_{31}E_0}{s_{11}^E} \left(\cos kx + \tan \frac{k\ell}{2} \sin kx\right) e^{j\omega t} - \frac{d_{31}}{s_{11}^E} E_0 e^{j\omega t}. \tag{5.26}$$

Putting Eq. (5.26) into Eq. (5.20b):

$$D_3 = \left(\epsilon_{33}^T - \frac{d_{31}^2}{s_{11}^E}\right) E_0 e^{j\omega t} + \frac{d_{31}^2 E_0}{s_{11}^E} \left(\cos kx + \tan \frac{k\ell}{2} \sin kx\right) e^{j\omega t}. \tag{5.27}$$

The electromechanical coupling factor is:

$$k_{31}^2 = \frac{d_{31}^2}{s_{11}^E \epsilon_{33}^T} \tag{5.28}$$

and $\epsilon_{33}^T (1 - k_{31}^2)$ is the clamped capacitivity.

The current is given by integrating the time derivative of D_3 over the electrode area:

$$I = \int_0^w \int_0^\ell \frac{\partial D_3}{\partial t} \, dx \, dy \tag{5.29a}$$

or

$$I = j\omega w \ell \epsilon_{33}^T E_0 e^{j\omega t} \left[(1 - k_{31}^2) + \frac{k_{31}^2}{k\ell} \sin k\ell \left(1 + \tan^2 \frac{k\ell}{2} \right) \right]. \tag{5.29b}$$

It should be noted that the identities:

$$\frac{1 - \cos k\ell}{\sin k\ell} = \tan \frac{k\ell}{2}$$

and

$$\sin k\ell \left(1 + \tan^2 \frac{k\ell}{2} \right) = 2 \tan \frac{k\ell}{2}$$

have been used.

The potential difference between the electrodes is given by:

$$V = \int_0^t E_3 \, dz = E_3 t.$$

The electrical admittance $Y = I/V$ is then:

$$Y = j\omega \frac{w\ell}{t} \epsilon_{33}^T (1 - k_{31}^2) + j\omega \frac{w\ell}{t} \epsilon_{33}^T k_{31}^2 \frac{\tan (k\ell/2)}{(k\ell/2)}. \tag{5.30}$$

At low frequencies, $k\ell \ll 1$, so that:

$$\frac{\tan (k\ell/2)}{(k\ell/2)} \to 1$$

and

$$Y \to j\omega \frac{w\ell}{t} \epsilon_{33}^T = j\omega C_{\text{free}} \tag{5.31}$$

where C_{free} is the capacitance for the bar when no forces are applied. Thus, the free dielectric constant may be determined from low frequency measurements of the capacitance.

At resonance, $Y \to \infty$ since $k\ell/2 = \pi/2$. The resonance frequency is given by:

$$f_r = \frac{c_b^E}{2\ell}. \tag{5.32}$$

At anti-resonance, $Y \to 0$, or:

$$1 - k_{31}^2 + \frac{k_{31}^2 \tan (k\ell/2)}{k\ell/2} = 0$$

and the anti-resonance frequency $f_a = \omega_a/2\pi$ is determined from the roots of the equation:

$$\frac{\tan (\omega_a\ell/2c_b)}{(\omega_a\ell/2c_b)} = \frac{k_{31}^2 - 1}{k_{31}^2}. \tag{5.33}$$

Since c_b is related to ℓ and ω_r, this reduces to:

$$\frac{k_{31}^2 - 1}{k_{31}^2} = \frac{\tan (\pi\omega_a/2\omega_r)}{(\pi\omega_a/2\omega_r)}. \tag{5.34}$$

It is seen that the electromechanical coupling coefficient k_{31} can be determined from measurement of the unloaded resonance and anti-resonance frequencies of the vibrator.

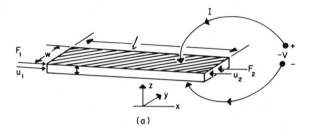

(a)

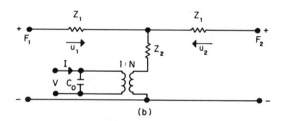

(b)

$$Z_1 = jZ_0 \tan \frac{k\ell}{2}$$

$$Z_2 = -j\frac{Z_0}{\sin (k\ell)}$$

$$Z_0 = \rho w t c_b^E$$

$$c_b^E = \frac{1}{\sqrt{\rho s_{11}^E}}$$

$$C_0 = \frac{w\ell}{t} \epsilon_{33}^T (1 - k_{31}^2)$$

$$k = \frac{\omega}{c_b^E}$$

$$k_{31}^2 = \frac{d_{31}^2}{s_{11}^E \epsilon_{33}^T}$$

$$N = \frac{w d_{31}}{s_{11}^E} = w \left(\frac{\epsilon_{33}^T}{s_{11}^E}\right)^{1/2} k_{31}$$

FIG. 5.4 (a) A longitudinal vibrator bar with arbitrary loading on the ends. (b) Equivalent network for the vibrator. Internal losses are neglected.

For the case of arbitrary forces applied to the bar ends, as shown in Fig. 5.4a, the new mechanical boundary conditions can be applied and a solution obtained. A six-terminal equivalent electrical circuit for the length expander bar with transverse field is presented in Fig. 5.4b. The additional terminals arise because there are two ends of the bar where forces may be applied. The values for the elements in the circuit are given by the relations shown in the legend for the figure. Units are mks.

In order to demonstrate the validity of this equivalent circuit, Eqs. (5.20) and (5.21) may be used again but now A and B must be found in terms of U_1 and U_2. The result is:

$$A = - \left(\frac{U_2}{j\omega \sin k\ell} + \frac{U_1}{j\omega} \cot k\ell \right) e^{-j\omega t}$$

$$B = \frac{U_1}{j\omega} e^{-j\omega t}.$$

(5.35)

Using $I = \int_0^\ell \int_0^w \frac{\partial D_3}{\partial t} \, dy \, dx$

and Eqs. (5.20) and (5.35) results in:

$$I = j\omega\ell w \left(\epsilon_{33}^T - \frac{d_{31}^2}{s_{11}^E} \right) E_0 e^{j\omega t} - \frac{d_{31}}{j\omega} w(\dot{U}_1 + \dot{U}_2)$$

(5.36)

where $\dot{U}_1$ and $\dot{U}_2$ are the time derivatives of U_1 and U_2. Then:

$$Y_I = \frac{I}{V} = \frac{I}{E_3 t}$$

or

$$Y_I = j\omega C_0 - \frac{d_{31}w}{V}(U_1 + U_2).$$

(5.37)

Applying the boundary conditions illustrated in Fig. 5.4a:

At $x = 0$, $T_1 = -\dfrac{F_1}{wt}$.

At $x = \ell$, $T_1 = -\dfrac{F_2}{wt}$.

Eqs. (5.20) and (5.35) can be combined to give:

$$F_1 = \frac{wtpc_b^E}{j} \left(\frac{U_2}{\sin k\ell} + U_1 \cot k\ell \right) + \frac{d_{31}w}{s_{11}^E} V$$

$$F_2 = \frac{wtpc_b^E}{j} (U_2 \cot k\ell + U_1 \cot k\ell \cos k\ell + U_1 \sin k\ell) + \frac{d_{31}w}{s_{11}^E} V.$$

Let $wtpc_b^E = z_0$ and $\dfrac{d_{31}w}{s_{11}^E} = N$. Using the identities:

$$\cot k\ell \cos k\ell + \sin k\ell = \frac{1}{\sin k\ell}$$

$$\tan \frac{k\ell}{2} = \frac{1 - \cos k\ell}{\sin k\ell}$$

results in:

$$F_1 = \frac{z_0}{j \sin k\ell} U_2 + \frac{z_0}{j \sin k\ell} U_1 + jz_0 \tan \frac{k\ell}{2} U_1 + N V \qquad (5.38a)$$

$$F_2 = \frac{z_0 U_1}{j \sin k\ell} + \frac{z_0}{j \sin k\ell} U_2 + jz_0 \tan \frac{k\ell}{2} U_2 + N V. \qquad (5.38b)$$

It may be seen that these results are consistent with the circuit in Fig. 5.4b.

5.4 Length Expander Bar with Parallel Field

The analysis of the longitudinal vibrations of a long bar with an electric field parallel to the length differs from the preceding case only in the electrical boundary conditions. This difference has a significant effect on mechanical behavior and the equivalent electrical circuit. A sketch of the bar is shown in

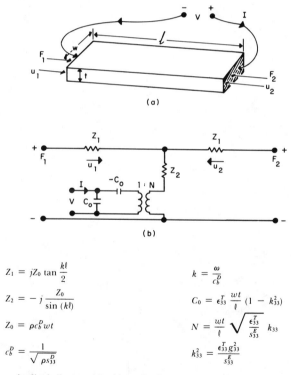

$$Z_1 = jZ_0 \tan \frac{k\ell}{2} \qquad\qquad k = \frac{\omega}{c_b^D}$$

$$Z_2 = -j \frac{Z_0}{\sin (k\ell)} \qquad\qquad C_0 = \epsilon_{33}^T \frac{wt}{\ell} (1 - k_{33}^2)$$

$$Z_0 = \rho c_b^D wt \qquad\qquad N = \frac{wt}{\ell} \sqrt{\frac{\epsilon_{33}^T}{s_{33}^E}} \, k_{33}$$

$$c_b^D = \frac{1}{\sqrt{\rho s_{33}^D}} \qquad\qquad k_{33}^2 = \frac{\epsilon_{33}^T g_{33}^2}{s_{33}^E}$$

FIG. 5.5   (a) Longitudinal vibrator with arbitrary loading on ends. Electric field is parallel to the longitudinal axis. (b) Equivalent network for the vibrator. Internal losses are neglected.

Fig. 5.5a. Again, it is assumed that the width and thickness of the bar are small compared to its length and that the only significant stress is along the length of the bar, which is now the z-direction. Neglecting fringing effects:

$$D_1 = D_2 = 0 \quad \text{and} \quad \frac{\partial D_3}{\partial z} = 0.$$

Therefore, D_3 is a constant. The most convenient choice for independent variables is D and T. The piezoelectric equations, from Eq. (3.58), are:

$$S_3 = s_{33}^D T_3 + g_{33} D_3 \tag{5.39a}$$

$$E_3 = -g_{33} T_3 + \beta_{33}^T D_3. \tag{5.39b}$$

The assumed simple harmonic displacement is:

$$\zeta = (A \sin kz + B \cos kz)e^{j\omega t}. \tag{5.40}$$

For the unloaded bar, applied forces are zero and the boundary condition at each end is $T_3 = 0$, which allows the values of A and B to be determined. Assuming that:

$$D_3 = D_0 e^{j\omega t}$$

we get:

$$A = \frac{g_{33}}{k} D_0$$

$$B = -\frac{g_{33}D_0}{k} \tan \frac{k\ell}{2}. \tag{5.41}$$

Using Eq. (5.39a) in the form:

$$T_3 = \frac{S_3}{s_{33}^D} - \frac{g_{33}}{s_{33}^D} D_3$$

Eq. (5.39b) becomes:

$$E_3 = -\frac{g_{33}}{s_{33}^D} S_3 + \left(\beta_{33}^T + \frac{g_{33}^2}{s_{33}^D}\right) D_3. \tag{5.42}$$

The potential difference between the electrodes is:

$$V = \int_0^\ell E_3 \, dz$$

which yields:

$$V = D_3 \left[\left(\beta_{33}^T + \frac{g_{33}^2}{s_{33}^D}\right) \ell - 2 \frac{g_{33}^2}{k s_{33}^D} \tan \frac{k\ell}{2}\right]. \tag{5.43}$$

The current is:

$$I = wt\dot{D}_3 = j\omega wt D_3.$$

In this case, the impedance rather than the admittance has the simpler form:

$$Z = \frac{V}{I} = \frac{1}{j\omega} \frac{\ell}{wt} \left[\left(\beta_{33}^T + \frac{g_{33}^2}{s_{33}^D} \right) - 2 \frac{g_{33}^2}{s_{33}^D} \frac{\tan(k\ell/2)}{(k\ell/2)} \right]. \tag{5.44}$$

Both Z and the motional impedance are maximum at anti–resonance, which occurs when $k\ell/2 = \pi/2$. The angular frequency at anti–resonance is then:

$$\omega_a = \pi \frac{c_b^D}{\ell}.$$

This frequency, which is also the frequency of maximum impedance, is:

$$f_a = f_p = \frac{c_b^D}{2\ell} = \frac{1}{2\ell \sqrt{\rho s_{33}^D}} = \frac{1}{2\ell \sqrt{\rho s_{33}^E (1 - k_{33}^2)}}. \tag{5.45}$$

The impedance is zero at the resonance frequency f_r, which is also the frequency of minimum impedance f_s, at which:

$$\beta_{33}^T \left(1 + \frac{g_{33}^2}{\beta_{33}^T s_{33}^D} \right) = \frac{g_{33}^2}{s_{33}^D} \frac{\tan(k\ell/2)}{k\ell/2}.$$

Using:

$$c_b = \frac{\omega_a \ell}{\pi}$$

the result is:

$$\frac{\tan(\pi\omega_r/2\omega_a)}{\pi\omega_r/2\omega_a} = \left(\frac{s_{33}^D \beta_{33}^T}{g_{33}^2} + 1 \right). \tag{5.46}$$

Thus, in this case the mechanical resonance occurs at the electrical anti–resonance. The electromechanical coupling factor k_{33} is given by:

$$k_{33}^2 = \frac{d_{33}^2}{s_{33}^E \epsilon_{33}^T} = \frac{\epsilon_{33}^T g_{33}^2}{s_{33}^E}. \tag{5.47}$$

Also:

$$s_{33}^D = s_{33}^E (1 - k_{33}^2)$$

so that:

$$\frac{\pi}{2} \frac{f_r}{f_a} \cot \left(\frac{\pi}{2} \frac{f_r}{f_a} \right) = k_{33}^2. \tag{5.48}$$

For an arbitrary loading, forces F_1 and F_2 are applied at each end and corresponding velocities U_1 and U_2 exist at these points, as shown in Fig. 5.5a. The boundary conditions are:

At $z = 0$, $\quad \dot{\zeta} = U_1$ and $F_1 = -wt\, T_3$

At $z = \ell$, $\quad \dot{\zeta} = U_2$ and $F_2 = -wt\, T_3$.

The constants A and B in Eq. (5.40) can be determined:

$$A = -\frac{1}{j\omega}\left(\frac{U_2}{\sin k\ell} + \frac{U_1}{\tan k\ell}\right) e^{-j\omega t}$$

(5.49)

$$B = \frac{1}{j\omega}\, U_1\, e^{-j\omega t}$$

and, using Eq. (5.39), the forces can be calculated:

$$F_1 = \frac{z_0^D}{j\tan k\ell}\, U_1 + \frac{z_0^D}{j\sin k\ell}\, U_2 + \frac{g_{33}}{j\omega s_{33}^D}\, I \tag{5.50a}$$

$$F_2 = \frac{z_0^D}{j\sin k\ell}\, U_1 + \frac{z_0^D}{j\tan k\ell}\, U_2 + \frac{g_{33}}{j\omega s_{33}^D}\, I \tag{5.50b}$$

where:

$$z_0^D = wt\rho c_b^D = wt\,\sqrt{\frac{\rho}{s_{33}^D}}$$

and $I = wt\dot{D}_3$. The voltage is:

$$V = \int_0^\ell E_3\, dz = \frac{g_{33}}{j\omega s_{33}^D}\, U_1 + \frac{g_{33}}{j\omega s_{33}^D}\, U_2 + \frac{I}{j\omega C_0}$$

where

$$C_0 = \frac{wt}{\beta_{33}^T \ell}\, (1 - k_{33}^2).$$

Ordinarily $V = -\int E_3\, dz$. However, the polarity is reversed here and positive V is chosen in the negative x_3 direction. A circuit equivalent to the preceding system is shown in Fig. 5.5b.

5.5 Thickness Vibrator

For the case of vibrations in the thickness directions in a thin plate, the mechanical boundary conditions differ from those for the longitudinal vibrations in a long bar. In a thin plate, the strains in the transverse directions are essentially zero. The electrical boundary conditions are similar to those for the expander bar with parallel field. The thickness direction is also the poled direction. For the analysis, it is assumed the width and length of the plate are large compared to the thickness and that the only non-zero strain is S_3. With the electrodes located as shown in Fig. 5.6a, it is seen that the only electric

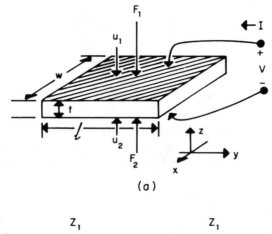

(a)

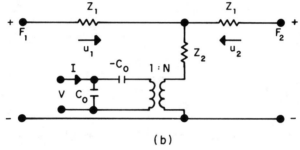

(b)

$$Z_1 = jZ_0 \tan \frac{kt}{2}$$

$$Z_2 = -j \frac{Z_0}{\sin(kt)}$$

$$Z_0 = \rho t w c_t^D$$

$$c_t^D = \sqrt{c_{33}^D/\rho}$$

$$k = \frac{\omega}{c_t^D}$$

$$C_0 = \frac{tw}{t} \epsilon_{33}^S$$

$$N = C_0 h_{33} = \frac{tw}{t} \sqrt{\frac{c_{33}^D}{\beta_{33}^S}} k_t$$

$$k_t^2 = \frac{h_{33}^2}{c_{33}^D} \epsilon_{33}^S$$

FIG. 5.6 (a) Thickness vibrator with arbitrary loading on its faces. (b) An equivalent network for this vibrator.

displacement component is D_3 and that it does not vary throughout the material. Therefore, the most convenient choice for independent variables is S and D. Using Eq. (3.59), the piezoelectric equations for this case become:

$$T_3 = c_{33}^D S_3 - h_{33} D_3 \tag{5.52a}$$

$$E_3 = -h_{33} S_3 + \beta_{33}^S D_3. \tag{5.52b}$$

The simple harmonic displacement is assumed to be:

$$\zeta = (A \sin kz + B \cos kz)e^{j\omega t} \tag{5.53}$$

where:

$$k = \frac{\omega}{c_t^D}$$

and

$$c_t^D = \sqrt{\frac{c_{33}^D}{\rho}} \; .$$

For the unloaded vibrator, one proceeds as before by evaluating A and B in terms of D_3. The resonances and anti-resonances and the impedance are similar in form to those for the expander bar with parallel field, except that the bulk sound speed is used.

For the free boundary case, since the applied forces are zero, the stress T_3 must be zero at $z = 0$ and $z = t$ (t is the plate thickness). Using Eqs. (5.52a) and (5.53), the constants A and B are:

$$A = \frac{h_{33} D_0}{k c_{33}^D}$$

and   (5.54)

$$B = -\frac{h_{33} D_0}{k c_{33}^D} \tan \frac{kt}{2}$$

where $D_3 = D_0 e^{j\omega t}$ has been assumed. Using these results, Eq. (5.52b) becomes:

$$E_3 = -\frac{h_{33}^2 D_0}{c_{33}^D} \left(\cos kz + \tan \frac{kt}{2} \sin kz \right) e^{j\omega t} + \beta_{33}^S D_0 e^{j\omega t}$$

and the strain becomes:

$$S_3 = k(A \cos kz - B \sin kz) e^{j\omega t}$$

or

$$S_3 = \frac{h_{33} D_0}{c_{33}^D} \left(\cos kz + \tan \frac{kt}{2} \sin kz \right) e^{j\omega t}.$$

The potential difference between electrodes is given by:

$$V = \int_0^t E_3 \, dz.$$

The current flow is given by:

$$I = \ell w \dot{D}.$$

Thus:

$$V = \left[\frac{h_{33}^2 D_0}{k c_{33}^D} \left(\sin kt + (1 - \cos kt) \tan \frac{kt}{2} \right) + \beta_{33}^S D_0 t \right] e^{j\omega t}.$$

The electrical impedance is:

$$Z = \frac{V}{I} = j\frac{t}{\omega\epsilon_{33}^S \ell w} - j\frac{h_{33}^2}{k\omega c_{33}^D \ell w}\left(\sin kt + (1 - \cos kt)\tan kt/2\right)$$

which reduces to:

$$Z = -\frac{j}{\omega C_0} - \frac{jk_t^2}{\omega C_0}\frac{\tan(kt/2)}{kt/2} \tag{5.55}$$

where the clamped capacitance is:

$$C_0 = \frac{\epsilon_{33}^S \ell w}{t} \tag{5.56}$$

and the electromechanical coupling factor for the thickness mode is given by:

$$k_t^2 = \frac{h_{33}^2}{\beta_{33}^S c_{33}^D} \tag{5.57}$$

where $\beta_{33}^S = 1/\epsilon_{33}^S$.

For an arbitrary loading in which forces F_1 and F_2 are applied uniformly over the faces, as shown in Fig. 5.6a, the equivalent circuit is as shown in Fig. 5.6b. A procedure that may be used to demonstrate the validity of this circuit is to solve for the constants A and B in terms of U_1 and U_2. The result is:

$$A = \frac{j}{\omega}\left(\frac{U_2 + U_1 \cos kt}{\sin kt}\right)e^{-j\omega t}$$

$$\tag{5.58}$$

$$B = \frac{U_1}{j\omega}e^{-j\omega t}.$$

The elastic boundary conditions are:

At $z = 0$, $\quad T_3 = \dfrac{F_1}{\ell w}$

At $z = t$, $\quad T_3 = -\dfrac{F_2}{\ell w}$.

Using these with Eq. (5.52) gives values for the forces F_1 and F_2 in terms of U_1, U_2, and I, which may be compared to equations for the equivalent circuit.

5.6 Equivalent Circuit of a Vibrator Near Resonance

It is often useful to describe the behavior of a vibrator's motional impedance in the neighborhood of resonance by an equivalent R–L–C series circuit. The equivalent circuit, which is valid only over a limited frequency range in the neighborhood of resonance, is obtained by the following procedure. The equivalent T–network for a longitudinal vibrator with free ends is shown in Fig. 5.7a. It is desired that constants be found for an R–L–C series network, as shown in Fig. 5.7b, which will change with frequency in the neighborhood of

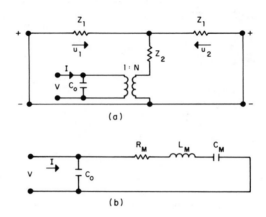

(a)

(b)

FIG. 5.7   (a) Equivalent network for a free longitudinal vibrator without damping. (b) Equivalent R–L–C netork for the vibrator valid in the neighborhood of resonance.

mechanical resonance in the same way as the motional impedance due to the T-network does.

The motional impedance is given by:

$$Z_M = \left(\frac{Z_0}{j \sin k\ell} + j \frac{Z_0}{2} \tan \frac{k\ell}{2} \right) N^{-2}. \tag{5.59}$$

Since damping has been neglected in this model, the resistance R_M in the circuit of Fig. 5.7b must be zero and the motional impedance must also be given by:

$$Z_M = j \left(\omega L_M - \frac{1}{\omega C_M} \right). \tag{5.60}$$

If the motional impedances determined by these two equations are to be equal and if their rates of change with frequency are also to be equal, then one can determine values of L_M and C_M that will make these two circuits equivalent. These turn out to be somewhat complicated functions of ω and ℓ. However, when $k\ell \simeq \pi$, some simplifying approximations can be made. The result is:

$$L_M \simeq \frac{1}{4} \frac{\rho w \ell t}{N^2} = \frac{M}{4N^2} \tag{5.61}$$

where M is the mass of the bar and:

$$C_M \simeq \frac{4N^2}{\pi^2 (wt/\ell s_{11}^E)} = N^2 \frac{4}{\pi^2} C_m \tag{5.62}$$

where C_m is the longitudinal compliance of a uniformly stressed thin bar.

5.7 Pressure Sensor

A thickness vibrator with parallel field is to be used as a pressure sensor. It is assumed that the same acoustic pressure is applied on both faces of the plate and that the sides of the plate are free of mechanical forces. Also, it is assumed that dimensions are small compared to acoustic wavelengths, i.e., the sound frequency is small compared to resonance frequencies.

The equivalent circuit for the vibrator is shown in Fig. 5.6. For low frequencies, $kt \ll 1$ so that $\sin kt \simeq kt$ and $\tan kt/2 \simeq kt/2$. Note that:

$$\frac{Z_0}{jkt} = \frac{\rho c_i^2 w\ell}{j\omega t} = \frac{c_{33}^D w\ell}{j\omega t} = \frac{1}{j\omega C_m}$$

where C_m is the compliance of the plate in compression. By inspection:

$$U = U_1 + U_2 = \frac{F}{(Z_1/2) + Z_2}$$

or

$$U \simeq -\frac{jPw\ell}{(Z_0 kt/4) - (Z_0/kt)}$$

or

$$U \simeq j\frac{Pw\ell}{Z_0} kt = jPw\ell\omega C_m. \tag{5.63}$$

Using the ideal transformer ratio N, the current in the electrical branch is NU and the voltage V appearing across the terminals is:

$$V = I\left(-\frac{j}{\omega C_0}\right) = NU\left(-\frac{j}{\omega C_0}\right) = N\frac{\omega Pw\ell C_m}{\omega C_0} = \frac{NPw\ell C_m}{C_0}. \tag{5.64}$$

The sensitivity is:

$$\frac{V}{P} = \frac{Nw\ell C_m}{C_0}.$$

Since C_m transforms into an electrical capacitance, the motional capacitance is:

$$C_M = N^2 C_m.$$

The open–circuit sensitivity is given by:

$$\frac{V}{P} = \frac{w\ell}{N}\frac{C_M}{C_0}. \tag{5.65}$$

References

1. Warren P. Mason. *Electromechanical Transducers and Wave Filters*. 2nd Ed. D. Van Nostrand: New York (1948).
2. Warren P. Mason. *Piezoelectric Crystals and Their Application to Ultrasonics*. D. Van Nostrand: New York (1950).

3. Don A. Berlincourt, Daniel R. Curran, and Hans Jaffe. Piezoelectric and Piezo-magnetic Materials and Their Function in Transducers. Chapter 3 in *Physical Acoustics*. Vol. 1A. Warren P. Mason, Ed. Academic Press: New York (1964).

4. Richard Holland and E.P. EerNisse.*Design of Resonant Piezoelectric Devices.* MIT Press: Cambridge, Massachusetts (1969).

5. G.E. Martin. Vibrations of Longitudinally Polarized Ferroelectric Cylindrical Tubes. *J. Acoust. Soc. Am.* 35 510–520 (1963).

6. Eric B. Becker, Graham F. Carey, and J. Trinsley Oden. *Finite Elements, An Introduction*. Vol. I. Prentice-Hall, Inc. Englewood Cliffs, NJ (1981).

7. Jean-Noel Decarpigny. Application de la Methode des Elements Finis a L'Etude de Transducteurs Piezoelectriques. Doctoral Thesis, L'Universite des Sciences et Techniques de Lille, France (May 1984).

8. Leon Camp. *Underwater Acoustics*. Wiley: New York (1970).

Problems

5.1. The equivalent T–network for the longitudinal vibrator bar with a transverse electric field is shown in Fig. 5.4. Show that the electrical input admittance for this network for the case when the forces F_1 and F_2 are zero reduces to Eq. (5.30), the result determined analytically for the vibrator with free ends.

5.2. Assume that the material in the vibrator in Prob. 5.1 is barium titanate and its dimensions are: $L = 8.5$ cm, $w = 1.9$ cm, $t = 1.3$ cm. Calculate the value of C_0 and, for the fundamental free bar resonance, the values of k_{31}^2, f_r, f_a, and N.

5.3. Calculate and compare the low–frequency force sensitivities of the transducer in Prob. 4.2 for each Navy type ceramic.

5.4. An electroacoustic transducer used as a hydrophone can be represented by the equivalent circuit shown in Fig. 5.4. The acoustic pressure is experienced at two points in the transducer, hence the need to consider two mechanical terminals.

(a)   Calculate an expression for the open–circuit sensitivity of the hydrophone in terms of the parameters shown in the figure.

(b)   If the electrical terminals are loaded with a cable having a capacitance C_i, what will be the sensitivity in terms of these parameters?

5.5. A Navy type I piezoelectric ceramic cylinder with radial polarization has at one end a rigid but massless circular cap of the same diameter as the cylinder. An alternating voltage is applied to the electrodes so that the half–wavelength resonant mode along the length is excited. The capped end is arranged so that it radiates plane waves of sound into a half space filled with water. The other end of the cylinder is free of loading. Let the length $L = 10$ cm, the outside radius $b = 2$ cm, and the inside radius $a = 1.5$ cm.

(a)   What would be the frequency of the half–wavelength resonance for the completely unloaded case? (Assume a long, thin cylinder.)

(b)   What would be the approximate frequency for the ring mode resonance? What assumptions are made?

(c)   Draw an equivalent electrical circuit for the half–wavelength resonance showing values for all elements.

(d)   If the radiation impedance presented to the cap at the half–wave resonance frequency is due to plane waves in water, what is the mechanical Q for the transducer, neglecting all other losses?

CHAPTER 6

COMPOSITE AND LOW FREQUENCY PROJECTORS

6.1 The Basic Problems

At this point, the student is already aware that most sonar projector transducers, particularly moderate- to low-frequency search sonars, consist of a large array of individual projector elemcnts. The student is also aware that the elements utilize a solid transducer material and operate at a frequency near mechanical resonance. In this chapter, some of the basic reasons for operating at resonance and for the choice of composite construction will be discussed. The word composite here implies that materials other than piezoelectrically or piezomagnetically active materials are a signficant part of the vibrating system. After discussing a typical moderate-frequency sonar projector element design and other design approaches, some of the consequences of size constraints for very low frequency underwater transducers are discussed. Finally, several types of very low frequency projector transducers are briefly described.

The typical search sonar projector element consists of a longitudinal vibrator housed so that one end of the vibrator is acoustically coupled to the water and the other end has as light an acoustic load as possible. Mechanical support for the vibrator must meet conflicting requirements. It must withstand hydrostatic pressure on the radiating face as well as other transient or steady mechanical loads and at the same time present a reasonably small mechanical impedance for the vibrational motions in order to reduce the power losses to the enclosure and the fluid within the enclosure.

A design objective for most sonar projectors is to achieve a large radiated sound power with as high an electroacoustic efficiency as possible, consistent with other design needs such as operating bandwidth. The acoustic power radiated into an infinite region of fluid by a projector is a function involving the product of the radiation resistance presented to the radiating surface of the projector, which is linearly proportional to the specific acoustic impedance of the fluid, and a term determined by the square of the velocity of motion of the surface. For some simple geometries when the surface dimensions are not large compared to the acoustic wavelength in the fluid, the expressions for the radiated power become relatively simple. An example is the case of the uniformly and sinusoidally driven plane piston of radius a located in a rigid baffle, radiating sound into an infinite half space filled with an ideal fluid of characteristic acoustic impedance $\rho_0 c$. The radiation impedance is given (1) by:

$$Z_r = \rho_0 c \pi a^2 \left(R_1(2ka) + j X_1(2ka) \right). \tag{6.1}$$

109

Here, $R_1(2ka)$ and $X_1(2ka)$ are the real and imaginary parts of the radiation impedance function and k is the wave number. If the velocity amplitude of the piston is U_0, the power radiated is given (2) by:

$$W = \frac{U_0^2 R_r}{2}. \tag{6.2}$$

Stated in terms of the volume velocity amplitude:

$$Q_0 = \pi a^2 U_0 \tag{6.3}$$

we have:

$$W_{\text{piston}} = \rho_0 c Q_0^2 \frac{R_1 (2ka)}{2\pi a^2}. \tag{6.4}$$

For large values of ka, i.e., at high frequencies or for large radiators, R_1 approaches the value of unity and X_1 approaches zero. At low frequencies, i.e., for values of ka less than unity, the approximate values of the resistance and reactance functions for the piston are given by:

$$R_1(2ka) \simeq \frac{(ka)^2}{2}$$

and $\tag{6.5}$

$$X_1(2ka) \simeq \frac{8ka}{3\pi}.$$

As a result, the low frequency value of the radiation Q, i.e., the ratio of radiation reactance to radiation resistance, becomes, for the piston:

$$Q_{\text{rad}} = \frac{16}{3\pi ka} \tag{6.6}$$

which decreases as ka increases.

When the dimensions of the radiator are small compared to the acoustic wavelength, the power output from the piston source, Eq. (6.4), becomes:

$$W_{\text{piston}} = \frac{\rho_0 c Q_0^2 k^2}{4\pi}. \tag{6.7}$$

A pulsating spherical source of radius a has a specific acoustic impedance at its surface (1) given by:

$$z = \rho_0 c \cos (\theta_a) \exp (j\theta_a)$$

where $\theta_a = \cot^{-1}(ka)$. The mechanical radiation impedance is the product of the specific acoustic impedance and surface area of the source. When this source radiates symmetrically into an infinite region, the power radiated is given by:

$$W_{\text{sphere}} = \frac{\rho_0 c Q_0^2 k^2}{8\pi}. \tag{6.8}$$

When ka becomes small, the specific acoustic impedance becomes:

$$z \simeq \rho_0 c\, ka(ka + j) \tag{6.9}$$

so that the radiation Q for the spherical source becomes:

$$Q_{\text{rad}} = \frac{1}{ka}. \tag{6.10}$$

The expression for the radiated acoustic power, Eq. (6.8), does not change form.

In many cases, the radiating faces of the sonar projector elements are small compared to the acoustic wavelength. It is seen from Eqs. (6.7) and (6.8) that for a given frequency and fluid medium, which sets the values of the propagation constant k and the specific acoustic impedance of the medium, the power output is a function of the volume velocity Q. Therefore, in order to obtain the largest power output possible, it is necessary to obtain as large a volume velocity as possible.

The large specific acoustic impedance of water makes it desirable to use a transducer that also has a large acoustic impedance. Hence, most sonar projectors use a solid transducer material. In order to obtain a large volume velocity using a solid transducer material, it is desirable for the mechanical system to be operated at resonance. At the frequencies often used in active sonar systems intended for use in long range search, the dimensions of a vibrator constructed of uniform cross section piezoelectric or piezomagnetic material become somewhat large. A composite construction is often used in order to reduce the overall length of a resonator for a given frequency of resonance. Masses of a different material are attached at the ends of the piezoelectric material making the vibrating system more like a pair of masses connected by a spring. This has two additional advantages: the stresses in the active material are more uniform, which makes the use of piezoelectric material more effective, and the mechanical Q is reduced.

Another method for increasing volume velocity for a given strain and obtaining a better impedance match between water and the active transducer material is to increase the area of the radiating face of the vibrator. This technique has led to frequent use of designs in which the radiating surface or head of the vibrator has a significantly larger area than the piezoelectric materials. The appearance is so much like a mushroom that the German word Tonpilz ("singing mushroom") is often used to describe it. Figs. 6.1 and 6.5 illustrate many of the features of construction of the composite piezoelectric ceramic longitudinal vibrator elements often used in moderate-frequency sonar projectors.

Once the sonar system specifications are set, many of the characteristics of the projector are determined. These include operating frequency, effective

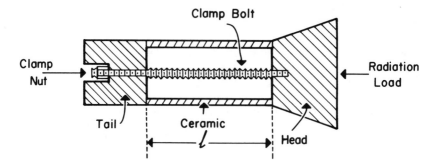

FIG. 6.1   Schematic cross section of a Tonpilz longitudinal vibrator (side view). The mechanical supports are not shown.

bandwidth, overall dimensions of the transducer, source level, and particle velocity at the transducer face. The transducer designer must then decide on the number of elements and design a structure that will operate at the desired frequency, provide the required velocity at its radiating face, and have the appropriate bandwidth and Q.

The number of elements will depend upon the overall dimensions. It is not feasible to discuss here all the technical and economic factors that must be considered. The Tonpilz design, in which the radiating area is larger than the active transducer material, provides a means for matching the relatively large specific acoustic impedance in most active transducer materials and water. The maximum area ratio is limited by the need to avoid spurious flexural resonance in the head of the projector. Thus, a compromise between the number of elements and area of radiating face must be reached. The designer then must arrive at dimensions which are consistent with the system and the desired mechanical resonance frequency, Q, bandwidth, and other requirements.

6.2 Requirements for a 5 kHz Projector Element

An example illustrating some of the considerations that the transducer element designer must take into account is the TR–208 transducer element used in the AN/SQS–23 sonar system. This projector consists of a cylindrical array of 432 elements arranged in 48 staves of 9 elements each. The sonar, which operates at a frequency of 5 kHz, has been used on surface ships of many different countries. McTaggert (2) lists some of the basic requirements placed on the transducer for these sonars:

a. *Design.* The transducer element must be a longitudinal resonator incorporating a lead zirconate–titanate ceramic (Navy type I) as the active material.

b. *Dimensions.* The element must be part of a cylindrical array of diameter 72 in and height 60 in. The center to center spacing of elements is to be about one–half wavelength (approximately 6 in).

c. *Cavitation threshold.* Full power continuous operation shall not cause cavitation at a water depth of 50 ft.

d. *Hydrostatic pressure.* Element must withstand repeated exposures to pressures of 50 pounds per square inch (psi) and be test-certified to a pressure of 100 psi.

e. *Resonance frequency.* The resonance frequency for a constant voltage input must be 5 kHz.

f. *Bandwidth.* Resonance shall be down no more than 3 dB from the resonance value at 4.5 and 5.5 kHz.

g. *Power handling.* The transducer element will be driven with an electrical power input of 500 watts, continuous operation.

h. *Efficiency.* Transducer efficiency at resonance must be greater than 50 percent at all operating temperatures.

i. *Impedance.* The transducer will be parallel tuned and transformed so that the impedance in the transmitting band is between 25 and 50 ohms.

j. *Receiving response.* The transducer will incorporate a solid state switching mechanism so that the transformer is not in the circuit in the receive mode. The transducer must receive efficiently over the band of 1 to 7 kHz.

k. *Voltage.* The voltage at the cable shall be less than 500 V rms at full power.

l. *Mechanical.* No metal hardware shall be exposed to sea water. Each transducer element shall weigh less than 10 lbs.

6.3 A 5 kHz Element of Simple Design

In this section a very simple mass-loaded piezoelectric ceramic vibrator element that meets some of the requirements of the preceding section will be discussed. Because of the simple construction and the procedure used in this example, the design is likely to be far from an optimum one. However, it may be useful to the student as an illustration of how the equivalent circuits can be used as a model for analysis and from which design choices may be made.

A radially polarized piezoelectric ceramic cylinder of length L_c is clamped between two metal elements in a manner similar to that shown in Fig. 6.1. One end, called the head, is coupled to a fluid into which sound is radiated. The other element is called the tail. The supports and container that provide mechanical isolation of the other end of the vibrator are not considered in this example. If it is assumed that the dimensions of all the elements with the possible exception of the ceramic are small compared to the acoustic wavelength in the material, then the circuit shown in Fig. 6.2 will give a reasonable approximation of the behavior of the vibrator near resonance.

In order to reach the design objectives, a number of interacting decisions must be made:

a. *Face Design.* The overall dimensions of the array and a desire to have the spacing between elements no larger than one half of the acoustic wavelength

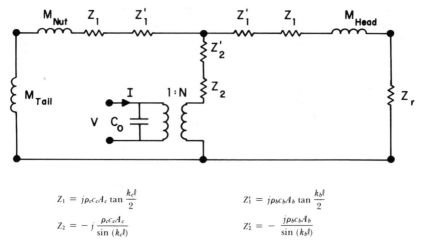

$$Z_1 = j\rho_c c_c A_c \tan\frac{k_c \ell}{2} \qquad\qquad Z_1' = j\rho_b c_b A_b \tan\frac{k_b \ell}{2}$$

$$Z_2 = -j\,\frac{\rho_c c_c A_c}{\sin(k_c \ell)} \qquad\qquad Z_2' = -\frac{j\rho_b c_b A_b}{\sin(k_b \ell)}$$

FIG. 6.2   Equivalent circuit for the Tonpilz vibrator of Fig. 6.1. The primed elements refer to the clamp bolt.

determines the number of elements and the maximum dimensions of the radiating face. For this example, the above considerations and the need to allow room for a protective coating on the face leads to a maximum diameter of about 14 cm (5 1/2 in). If flexural resonances in the face and head mass are to be avoided in the operating frequency range (up to 7 kHz for this example) the thickness of the head material must exceed a critical value. The calculation of flexural modes of vibration in a tapered head mass is difficult using the usual continuum wave theory. Availability of adequate computer facilities makes the use of finite–element methods for such analysis possible. In this example, as an approximation, the flexural resonance frequencies for a square plate with free edges is used to estimate a minimum plate thickness which has a fundamental resonance frequency above 7 kHz. In order to keep the head mass small, a low density metal of minimal thickness is desirable. Effects of head flexure on transducer performance has been studied by Butler et al. (3).

In order to assure that flexural resonances of the head mass will not be possible within the design operating frquency range, some means of estimation of the minimum length of the head mass is necessary. For the simple example discussed here, the complexities of calculating flexural resonances of a conically tapered head mass will be avoided by making the approximation that the head is a square aluminum plate of side a and thickness h with free edges. The frequency for the first symmetrical flexural mode in a thin, square plate with edges free and a node at its center is given by (4):

$$f_r = \frac{14.1}{2\pi a^2}\sqrt{\frac{Yh^2}{12\rho(1-\nu^2)}} \qquad\qquad (6.11)$$

where Y is Young's modulus, ν is Poisson's ratio, and ρ is the mass density. Taking $a = 14\,\text{cm}\,(5\,1/2\,\text{in})$ and $h = 2.5\,\text{cm}\,(1\,\text{in})$, the first flexural resonance frequency is about 4.5 kHz, clearly unsatisfactorily low. Doubling the thickness (length) of the head to 5 cm (2 in) also doubles the first resonance frequency, giving about 9 kHz, which would probably be acceptable. Thus, the minimum head length is about 5 cm (2 in).

b. *Cavitation Threshold.* The maximum possible surface intensity at the radiating surface is limited by the cavitation threshold. This is given by the approximate relation (5):

$$I_{max} = 0.3(1 + d/32)^2 \text{ watts/cm}^2 \tag{6.12}$$

where d is the depth in feet. For the area of the face and depth being considered here, the cavitation limited maximum power is about 300 watts. For a total power input of 500 watts and a conversion efficiency of about 50 percent, we see that cavitation should not be a limiting factor.

c. *Ceramic Assembly.* Considerations for the piezoelectric ceramic stack design include costs, size, electric field and power handling capability, and desired electromechanical coupling factor. Costs increase with thicker ceramics due to increased difficulty with polarization and reduced production yields. Choices for the assembly may be made from the following arrangements:

- Single cylindrical tube:
  - Axially polarized—with electrodes either on the ends or as a number of circumferential stripes parallel to ends.
  - Radially polarized—with electrodes on circumferential surfaces.
- Multiple rings.
- Solid rectangular block.
- Multiple rectangular plates in a stack, oriented with the plate thickness either along or perpendicular to the vibrator axis.

A factor affecting the choice of the ceramic stack design is the hydrostatic load that is imposed by depth of submergence. In most vibrator designs, support for the hydrostatic forces is transmitted through the ceramic. The compressive stress in the ceramic is also determined by the ratio of cross sections of the radiating face and the ceramic. Assuming an area ratio of the order of 16 and an operating depth of 15 m (50 ft) gives a compressive stress of only about 400 psi, which should be easily tolerated.

d. *Power Handling Capability.* The requirements of power output also influence the ceramic stack design. An approximate formula for the dynamic power density, given by Berlincourt (6) is:

$$\text{Power density} = \omega E^2 k^2 \epsilon_{33}^T Q_m. \tag{6.13}$$

For a Navy type III ceramic, the maximum usable electric field is about 2700 V/cm. Using $k_{33} = 0.5$, $\epsilon_{33}^T = 9 \times 10^{-9}$ F/m, $Q_m = 5$, a power density of about 14 watts/cm^3 is estimated. The volume of ceramic required to tolerate 500 watts then is about 40 cm^3. The minimum length of the ceramic to meet the power density requirements is about 4 cm (1 5/8 in).

In this example, the ceramic chosen is a radially polarized cylinder of Navy type III. An arbitrary choice of outside radius is 3 cm (1 1/5 in). In order to obtain the required cross sectional area of 12 cm², the inside radius must be about 2.25 cm (7/8 in).

   e. *Tail Mass.* In order to maximize the displacement of the radiating face for a given strain in the ceramic, the mechanical impedance presented by the tail mass M_T to the ceramic should be as large as possible. This would imply that M_T should be as large as possible. However, a large tail mass will obviously increase the total mass of the transducer and will also increase the effective mass reactance of the oscillator and thereby increase the Q. In this example, the tail mass is arbitrarily chosen to be three times the mass of the head. The configuration chosen is a cylinder of radius 5 cm (2 in). Steel is chosen as the material. For these conditions the following results are obtained:

$$M_H = 2.65 \text{ kg} \qquad M_T = 8 \text{ kg}$$

$$L_H = 5 \text{ cm } (2 \text{ in}) \qquad L_T = 13 \text{ cm } (5 \text{ 1/8 in}).$$

Comparing the tail length with the long bar acoustic wavelength in steel at 5 kHz (about one meter) shows that the assumption of a lumped mass is valid.

   Anticipating that the ceramic length will also be small compared to the acoustic wavelength, the ceramic cylinder is treated as a mechanical compliance coupled between the two masses:

$$C_m = \frac{L_c s_{11}^E}{A_c}. \tag{6.14}$$

Under these conditions, the resonance frequency of the assembly is given by:

$$f_r = \frac{1}{2\pi \sqrt{M'C_m}} \tag{6.15}$$

where M' is the effective mass:

$$M' = \frac{M_H M_T}{M_H + M_T}. \tag{6.16}$$

For the values chosen, $C_m = 5 \times 10^{-10}$ m/N. Using the elastic properties of this ceramic from Tab. 4.3, the ceramic length needed is $L_c = 5$ cm (2 in). It is seen that this length gives a ceramic volume that exceeds the 40 cm³ needed to meet power density requirements.

   f. *Clamp Bolt.* The purpose of the clamp bolt is to place the ceramic stack and all of its joints into compression so that the stress in the materials does not become positive during the positive strain parts of the dynamic cycle or during shock loading. The ceramic and the adhesive between the joints do not have great tensile strength. Inspection of the illustrations and the equivalent electrical circuit make it clear that the clamp bolt will have essentially the same velocities at its ends as the ceramic. The piezoelectrically generated motion of the ceramic is required to move the clamp rod as well as the head and tail masses and, therefore, it is desirable for the stiffness of the clamp bolt to be minimized. By using high strength steel for the bolt, a relatively small cross sectional area giving a smaller stiffness can be used and still provide sufficient compression in the ceramic with an adequate safety margin for the fatigue failure in the bolt. The maximum compressive stress in the ceramic is determined, at least in part, by the depoling effects of a compressive loading. This was described briefly in Ch. 4. Typical compressive loads in the ceramic stacks range between 2,000 and 5,000 psi.

g. *Adhesives.* In many cases, the adhesive used in the joints is a filled epoxy–type thermosetting resin. Joint thickness is controlled and an effective electrode contact is made with a thin metal foil, often an expanded metal, in the joint.

h. *Pressure Release System.* Some means must be provided to support the weight of the vibrator and other mechanical forces imposed by, say, impulsive loading, such as might occur from a nearby underwater explosion and changing hydrostatic pressure on the transducer face. The support should be designed to cause as little loss of acoustic energy as possible and should, therefore, be as resilient as possible, consistent with acceptable displacements due to static loading. For these reasons, a support as near as possible to a displacement node in the vibrator is desirable. One method for locating this support can be seen in Fig. 6.5. Other designs have also been successful.

i. *Shock Hardening.* The probability of damage to the ceramic caused by mechanical shock can be reduced by pre–stressing the ceramic. The use of the clamp bolt provides compressive pre–stressing of the ceramic along its axis. A technique for placing the ceramic in circumferential compression is to wrap the cylinder with a fiber material under tension. Glass fibers are often used in this manner.

j. *Mechanical Quality Factor.* The mechanical Q is determined by the ratio of the mass reactance to resistance. It is not realistic to compute its value for the simple element considered in this section. Generally, a low Q is desired in order to maintain an acceptable operating bandwidth. Typical values are in the range of 5 to 7. In order to obtain a high efficiency with a low Q, the designer must strive to minimize internal losses, make the radiation resistance as large as possible, and keep the mass reactance small.

k. *Electromechanical Coupling Factor.* In this simple design, the dimensions of the ceramic element are small compared to the acoustic wavelength so that the material is subjected to an essentially uniform dynamic stress. Therefore, the coupling factor of the device should be virtually the same as the ceramic coupling factor. In more complex designs, the effective electromechanical coupling coefficient must be calculated for the specific configuration using the basic definitions given in Ch. 3.

6.4 Segmented Piezoelectric Vibrators

In the example discussed earlier, a radially polarized piezoelectric ceramic element was used in the vibrator so that the coupling between the applied electric field and the direction of the dominant motion was transverse. It is known from the data in Ch. 4 that the electromechanical coupling factor for parallel coupling k_{33} is larger than the transverse coupling factor k_{31}. In order to utilize the 33 coupling in a moderately long vibrator and also avoid undesirably large potential differences that would be required if the electrodes were located at the ends of the ceramic, vibrators using 33 coupling are often constructed by stacking a number of identical smaller elements end to end and connecting the electrodes in parallel. With proper orientation of the poled directions in the elements, the piezoelectric strains add constructively. Martin (7) has developed a theory that permits the calculation of the equivalent T-network parameters for a segmented cylindrical vibrator in terms of the parameters for the individual element T-network.

If it is assumed that a set of n identical ring elements, each of length L and cross sectional area A, are stacked end to end and connected electrically in

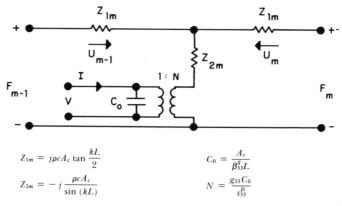

$$Z_{1m} = j\rho c A_c \tan \frac{kL}{2} \qquad C_0 = \frac{A_c}{\beta^S_{33} L}$$

$$Z_{2m} = -j \frac{\rho c A_c}{\sin (kL)} \qquad N = \frac{g_{33} C_0}{s^D_{33}}$$

FIG. 6.3 Approximate equivalent T-network for the mth element in the segmented longitudinal piezoelectric ceramic vibrator.

parallel, the vibrator ceramic has an overall length of nL. The equivalent T-network for the mth elemental segment is shown in Fig. 6.3. In this circuit, it is assumed that the elements are small in length compared to the longitudinal wavelength, i.e., $kL \ll \pi$ and the propagation constant $k = \omega/c$, where the appropriate longitudinal wave speed is at a constant E field. The forces F_m and F_{m-1} act on adjacent elements.

Relationships between the parameters of the network for the cascade and those of the element are not simple except for special cases. However, for the case where the length of the individual element is small compared to the acoustic wavelength and eight or more elements are used, Martin shows that the T-network shown in Fig. 6.4 is a good approximation for the segmented vibrator.

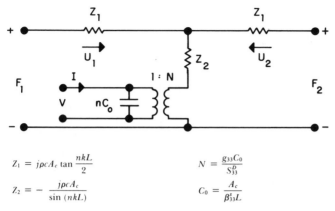

$$Z_1 = j\rho c A_c \tan \frac{nkL}{2} \qquad\qquad N = \frac{g_{33}C_0}{S_{33}^D}$$

$$Z_2 = -\frac{j\rho c A_c}{\sin(nkL)} \qquad\qquad C_0 = \frac{A_c}{\beta_{33}^s L}$$

FIG. 6.4 Approximate equivalent T-network for a segmented vibrator of n elements.

Fig. 6.5 is a photograph of a cut–away model of a Tonpilz transducer that uses a segmented piezoelectric ceramic stack operating in the parallel, or 33, mode. Other essential elements of the projector element are pointed out.

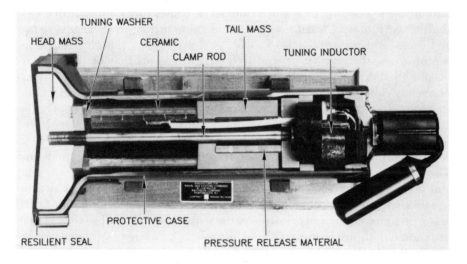

FIG. 6.5 Cut–away model of a Tonpilz vibrator that uses a segmented piezoelectric ceramic stack with parallel, or 33, coupling. Essential elements of the structure are indicated. The model is mounted on a wood base. The photograph was furnished through the courtesy of the U.S. Naval Sea Systems Command.

6.5 Design Adjustments

In order to maintain design source level, directivity, and beam patterns in a high–powered projector array, the performance parameters of the individual elements must be closely controlled during manufacture. An important source of variability in the parameters of the individual element is in the piezoelectric properties of the ceramic materials. A method that may be used to control element properties in some cases is to make small adjustments in dimensions of the ceramic elements or other parts of the vibrator after ceramic element fabrication but before final assembly of the stack. Benthien (8) has developed a set of design adjustment guidelines based on a simple one–dimensional model of the segmented longitudinal vibrator. This provides guidance for making changes in order to achieve a specified or base–line design objective in the electrical input impedance of the element and its resonance frequency. For example, the guideline permits computation of changes in the ceramic ring cross sectional area, or the thickness of a fiberglass washer clamped in the stack, or the addition of a capacitor in shunt with the blocked capacitance that will adjust to fit the design objective.

6.6 Other Design Procedures

It is clear from the examples just considered that although sonar system specifications will determine some of the projector element characteristics, the search for a proper combination of materials and their dimensions is a difficult task. Usually, there are a number of conflicting requirements. In a simple case it may be feasible and economical to utilize practical experience and a cut–and–try approach to arrive at a satisfactory design. In a more complex case the number of conflicting requirements may be too large to make a good design using this approach. For example, the system specifications may call for the primary resonance frequency, the mechanical Q, the electromechanical coupling factor, the input admittance at resonance, the position of the velocity node in the vibrator, the overall transducer length and weight, and perhaps the cost of the materials. A method that has been used to design Tonpilz transducer elements has been developed by McCammon and Thompson (9). It depends on the availability of a fairly large computer, the ability to write down the structure of the equivalent electrical network and the equations relating the circuit parameters to the design goals, and on being able to assign weights and priorities to the requirements and objectives. Their program is designed to minimize the differences between a calculated performance parameter and design objectives, subject to the assigned weights and priorities. Space does not permit further discussion of this method here.

6.7 Very Low Frequency Projectors

The effects of reducing the design operating frequency of a projector on the radiation impedance were discussed in an earlier section of this chapter. The effects on the dimensions of a longitudinal vibrator transducer of conventional design have been illustrated dramatically by Woollett (10). A typical 5 kHz projector is assumed to have a radiating face diameter of 0.12 m (about 0.4 wavelengths), a length of about 0.3 m (about one wavelength in water), an acoustic intensity at the radiating surface of one watt per cm², a peak displacement at the radiating face of 5.1 μm, a Q of about 5, and a weight of 12 kg. In scaling with frequency, linear dimensions are scaled in proportion to the acoustic wavelength. For a frequency of 100 Hz, the required dimensions are: diameter, 6 m; length, 15 m; weight, 1.5×10^6 kg; and peak displacement at the radiating face, 0.26 mm. Clearly, scaling to frequencies near 100 Hz leads to unacceptably large transducer dimensions, power outputs, and weights. For this reason, the designer must explore techniques for miniaturizing the projector for very low frequencies. The effect of some consequences of doing this will now be discussed.

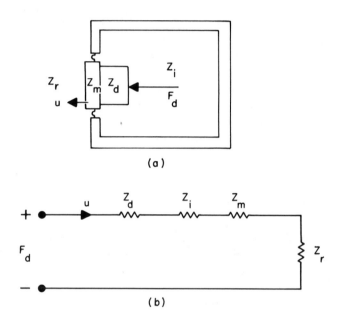

FIG. 6.6 Schematic diagram of a low frequency transducer. (a) Essential impedance in the transducer. (b) Equivalent circuit diagram of essential elements.

Fig. 6.6 illustrates schematically the essential impedances of a monopole type projector. The force F_d is the basic driving force for the transducer and Z_d is the intrinsic internal mechanical impedance of the driver. The impedance imposed on the transducer by the interior of the enclosure is Z_i. The impedance of the mechanical structure that radiates the sound is Z_m and Z_r is the radiation impedance. It was shown in Sec. 6.1 that for both piston and spherical sources at low frequencies the radiation resistance decreases as the frequency decreases. The radiation reactance also decreases, but more slowly than the resistance. A consequence of this is that the radiation Q increases at lower frequencies, as shown in Eq. (6.6). In order to lower the resonance frequency of a Tonpilz type structure either larger masses or a softer spring tying them together (or both) are required. Thus, it is seen that the velocity u

resulting from the driving force illustrated in Fig. 6.6 will be less if the reactive parts of the impedances in this circuit increase. We saw from Eqs.(6.7) and (6.8) that maintaining a given power output as the frequency decreased required a larger velocity.

Fortunately, for most low frequency active sonar transducers, the output power requirements are less severe than for systems that operate at moderate frequencies. Since the mechanical Q of the system is determined by the ratio of the total mass reactance in the circuit to the total resistance, the operating Q will increase and the effective bandwidth will diminish. Increasing internal damping in order to lower Q will normally be avoided because this will reduce electroacoustic conversion efficiency. It is clear that the mechanical reactances must be reduced. Not only will this reduce the mechanical Q, it will be easier to attain larger velocities. One technique for doing this is to use flexural motion of plates and shells which have a lower stiffness and a lower mechanical resonance frequency for the same overall dimensions of the structure. Other methods involve the use of a gas–filled enclosure as the stiffness element. The following provides descriptions of some approaches that have been used to solve this problem.

a. *Flexural Disk.* An example of a transducer which involves flexure is the bilaminar flexural plate transducer. The essential features of this device are illustrated in Fig. 6.7. Two piezoelectric ceramic plates are cemented together

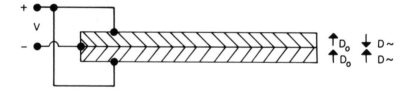

D_0 represents remanent electric displacement.

$D\sim$ represents alternating electric displacement.

FIG. 6.7   Side–on schematic of a basic bilaminar flexural disk transducer.

so that one electrode is common. The directions of the remanent polarizations in the two plates are reversed. The alternating fields create transverse strains in each disk but of opposite signs. The result is the excitation of flexure of the plate symmetrically about its center. The theory of the flexural plate transducer is given by Woollett (*11*). Of course, a single flexural plate transducer will not be an effective sound radiator unless radiation from one of the surfaces is prevented. In order to obtain a monopole radiator, flexural disk transducers are often operated in pairs, as illustrated schematically in Fig. 6.8. The orientations of the motions of the two disks must be in phase.

b. *Flextensional Transducer.* As indicated by the name, this device also utilizes flexure motion. The essential features of the flextensional transducer are illustrated schematically in Fig. 6.9. The longitudinal displacements induced by either piezoelectric or magnetostrictive effects in the vibrator bar

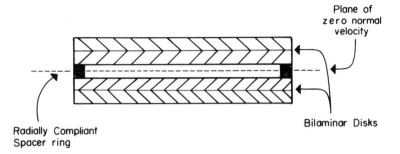

FIG. 6.8   Double bilaminar disk transducer.

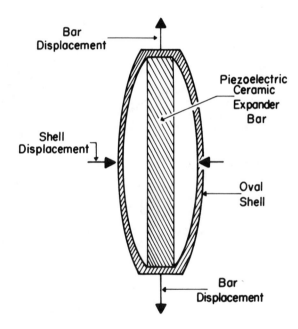

FIG. 6.9   Cross section of the basic components of a flextensional transducer (After Brigham and Glass (*14*)).

on the interior are coupled to the long ends of the oval–shaped shell. The resulting flexural motions of the sides of the shell create a net volume change for the oval body. There are several shapes which can be created from objects that have the cross section shown in the figure. One is an oval cylinder generated by extending the figure out of the plane of the sketch and capping it on both top and bottom. This is called a Class IV flextensional transducer and has been studied more thoroughly than other classes. More detailed information has been given by Royster (*12*) and Nelson and Royster (*13*). Brigham and Glass (*14*) describe the current status of the technology for this type of transducer.

c. *Flooded Ring.* Another structure that has been used at times for very low frequency projectors is a free-flooded cylindrical shell operated in the ring mode of vibration. Shells of piezoelectric ceramics have been used in recent years. Magnetostrictive scrolls have also been employed. The radiation from the interior of the ring opposes that from the exterior. However, a very important advantage of this form is that the need for a pressure release interior is avoided, so that the design is essentially unaffected by hydrostatic pressure.

d. *Resonant Bubble Transducer.* Sims (*15*) describes a low-frequency high-power transducer which employs a gas-filled bag as the principal mechanical stiffness element.

e. *Helmholtz Resonator.* The theory for design of a Helmholtz resonator for use as a low-frequency sound source in water is given by Woollett (*16*). The use of this device, some specific design parameters and their effects on the acoustic performance are addressed by Henriquez and Young (17).

FIG. 6.10   A segmented spherical transducer built from individual piezoelectric ceramic plates. Typical uses are in high power, low frequency, broad bandwidth operations when omnidirectional radiation is desired. The photograph was provided through the courtesy of Channel Industries.

f. *Mechanical Transducer.* Wilcox (*18*) has developed a novel sound source which operates in the range of 1 – 50 Hz. It employs a variable speed electric motor inside a rectangular box that causes periodic movement of pistons set into the wall of the box using a system of levers and rockers.

g. *Hydroacoustic Projector.* Bouyoucos (*19*) has described low–frequency high–power projectors that employ hydraulic fluid at high pressure to force flexural vibrations of a metal plate. The hydraulic fluid flow is controlled by a shuttle valve operated by a piezoelectric ceramic stack.

h. *Spherical Shell Transducer.* Employment of a spherical shell of piezo-electric ceramic is another method for obtaining a low resonance frequency with a reasonable value of Q. An example of such a design is shown in Fig. 6.10. Here, triangular–shaped ceramic plates that have been polarized in the thickness direction are cemented together into a quasispherical shape. A spherical source is nondirectional, of course, unless some means for blocking part of the radiation is employed. The unit shown in the photograph has a diameter of 30 in. The manufacturer claims that the usable frequency range is from 0.5 to 2.0 kHz with a minimum efficiency of 75 percent.

References

1. L.E. Kinsler, A.R. Frey, A.B. Coppens, and J.V. Sanders. *Fundamentals of Acoustics.* 3rd Ed. Wiley: New York (1982).
2. B.E. McTaggart. Design of Sound Receivers and Sources. Unpublished notes used in a short course on principles and design of sonar transducers, given in San Diego, May 1981 by the Catholic University of America.
3. J.L. Butler, et al. Radiating Head Flexure and Its Effect on Transducer Performance. *J. Acoust. Soc. Am.* **70** 500–503 (1981).
4. *Mechanical Engineers' Handbook.* 6th Ed. T. Baumeister, Ed. McGraw–Hill: New York (1958), p 5–108.
5. R.J. Urick. *Principles of Underwater Sound.* 2nd Ed. McGraw–Hill: New York (1975), p 70.
6. D.A. Berlincourt, D.R. Curran, and H. Jaffe. Piezoelectric and Piezomagnetic Materials and Their Function in Transducers. Ch. 3 in *Physical Acoustics.* Vol. IA. Warren P. Mason, Ed. Academic Press: New York (1964). p 250.
7. G.E. Martin, On the Theory of Segmented Electromechanical Systems, *J. Acoust. Soc. Am.* **36** 1366–1370 (1964).
8. G. Benthein. Design Adjustment Guidelines. Unpublished notes. (ca 1983).
9. D.F. McCammon and W. Thomson, Jr. The Design of Tonpilz Piezoelectric Transducers Using Nonlinear Goal Programming. *J. Acoust. Soc. Am.* **68** 754–757 (1980).
10. R.S. Woollett. Basic Problems Caused by Depth and Size Constraints in Low–Frequency Underwater Transducers. *J. Acoust. Soc. Am.* **68** 1031–1037 (1980).
11. R.S. Woollett. *Theory of the Piezoelectric Flexural Disk Transducer with Applications to Underwater Sound.* USL Research Report No. 490. U.S. Navy Underwater Sound Laboratory. New London, CT. Dec. 1960.
12. L.H. Royster. Flextensional Underwater Acoustics Transducer. *J. Acoust. Soc. Am.* **45** 671 (1969).

13. R.A. Nelson and L.H. Royster. Development of a Mathematical Model for the Class V Flextensional Underwater Acoustic Transducer. *J. Acoust. Soc. Am.* **49** 1609 (1971).

14. G. Brigham and B. Glass. Present Status in Flextensional Transducer Technology. *J. Acoust. Soc. Am.* **68** 1046–1052 (1980).

15. C.C.Sims. Bubble Transducer for Radiating High–Power Low–Frequency Sound in Water. *J. Acoust. Soc. Am.* **32** 1305–1308 (1960).

16. R.S. Woollett. *Underwater Helmholtz Resonator Transducers: General Design Principles.* NUSC Technical Report 5633. Naval Underseas Systems Center, New London, CT. July 1977.

17. T.A. Henriquez and A.M. Young. The Helmholtz Resonator as a High–Power Deep–Submergence Source for Frequencies Below 500 Hz. *J. Acoust. Soc. Am.* **67** 1555–1558 (1980).

18. H.A. Wilcox. *Non–Resonant Acoustic Projector Project.* NUSC TR579. Naval Ocean Systems Center, San Diego, CA June 1980.

19. J.V. Bouyoucos. Hydroacoustic Transduction. *J. Acoust. Soc. Am.* **57** 1341–1351 (1975).

Problems

6.1. A piezoelectric ceramic composite vibrator is designed to radiate sound from one end as part of a large array. The operating frequency is 2 kHz. Electroacoustic efficiency is 60 percent. Electrical power input is 500 watts. For purposes of simplicity, assume that the masses of the head and tail are identical point masses. The radiating face, area $A_R = 0.02$ m^2, is loaded acoustically with the radiation resistance of a plane propagating wave in water, i.e., the specific impedance is $\rho_0 c_0$. The ceramic cross sectional area is one fourth that of A_R. The ceramic is a Navy type I and consists of eleven identical rings of length 2 cm, poled axially (so that 33 coupling is used). These are connected electrically in parallel. The length of the ceramic stack is very small compared to the acoustic wavelength.

(a)   What is the displacement amplitude of the radiating face?

(b)   What is the maximum strain and the maximum stress in the ceramic?

(c)   If the maximum allowable strain is 10^{-4}, does this cause a limitation at this power?

(d)   If the cavitation threshold is 1 watt/cm^2, will cavitation be a limiting factor?

(e)   If all power losses were dissipated in the ceramic without heat transfer, what would be the temperature rise for a pulse duration of one minute? (Specific heat of the ceramic is 420 joules/kg °C.)

(f)   Determine approximate values of C_0, C_M, Z_{in}, voltage, and current amplitudes.

6.2. Explain why piezoelectric ceramics are often used as sound sources in water but seldom in air and why transducers involving a moving coil in a magnetic field are often used for generating sound in air but seldom for sound in water.

CHAPTER 7

MAGNETOSTRICTIVE TRANSDUCERS

7.1 Background

The magnetostrictive effect in nickel, discovered by Villari and studied quantitatively by Joule in the 1840's (1), was not used in any significant way until the 1930's and 1940's when it became important in the construction of sonar projectors and hydrophones. A brief history of the use and design of magnetostrictive sonar transducers may be found in ref. (2). Nickel and its alloys continued to be important in sonar transducers into the 1950's. Magnetostrictive materials have been largely supplanted by the ferroelectric ceramics in sonar projectors. However, there are still specialized applications where magnetostrictive materials are useful. For example, nickel may be useful in some appplictions where the transducer is lightly loaded or where mechanical toughness and low sensitivity to hydrostatic pressure are desired. Recently, new magnetostrictive alloys have been developed that have large electromechanical coupling coefficients and extremely large magnetostrictive strains. They appear to have the potential of becoming very effective in certain applications and their use in sonar projectors is currently being explored. For these reasons and because of the historical importance of this effect in sonar transducers, the student should be familiar with magnetostriction.

7.2 The Magnetostrictive Effect and Piezomagnetic Phenomena

Magnetostriction is a second order effect observed in almost all materials and is analogous to electrostriction, a second order effect found in almost all dielectric materials. Applying a magnetic field to the material causes a strain that is a nonlinear function of the applied field. Magnetostriction is exhibited to a significant extent only in ferromagnetic and ferrimagnetic materials. Some of the more useful have been the metals iron, cobalt, nickel, and their alloys and compounds. Magnetostriction occurs in the single crystal, in isotropic polycrystalline ceramics and metals, and in mechanically and magnetically oriented materials. Similarly, piezomagnetism is a linear magnetomechanical effect analogous to the linear electromechanical effect found in piezoelectric materials.

Unlike the piezoelectric ceramics which have a large remanent dielectric polarization, most acoustically useful magnetostrictive materials have a small remanent magnetic polarization. For this reason, the magnetic bias must be provided by external means, either by a steady current, which adds to the power loss, or by a permanent magnet, which often complicates the design. Since most magnetostrictive materials are reasonably good electrical conductors, eddy current losses may be large unless a laminated structure is used. Some ceramic materials, e.g., the ferrites, which are poor conductors, have been used in magnetostrictive transducers. The nonlinear behavior of the type observed in piezoelectric ceramics at large drive levels, described in Ch. 4, is also found in magnetostrictive materials.

It is believed that a naturally occurring piezomagnetic effect has never been observed (3,4). However, in magnetostrictive materials, magnetic polarization permits the achievement of a de facto piezomagnetic effect. The piezomagnetic effect does not depend upon domain wall motion but involves the reorientation of the magnetic dipole moment of the domains of the material. This is different from the effect in piezoelectric ceramics in which domain wall motion occurs. It enhances the strength of the piezoelectric effect although it is not necessary for the phenomenon.

In further analogy to the piezoelectric ceramics, the magnetically poled direction, either imposed or remanent, is chosen as the 3- or z-direction in the material. The material properties are independent of direction perpendicular to the z-axis but the axial symmetry is different from the piezoelectric ceramic materials. Due to the solenoidal character of the magnetic field, there is a plane of symmetry perpendicular to the z-axis that results in two additional coefficients, $d_{14} = -d_{25}$, which are zero in the piezoelectric ceramics (3). The nomenclature and symbology used here, which is very similar to the usage for piezoelectric ceramics, follows the recommendations in the *IEEE Standard on Magnetostrictive Materials* (5,6).

The matrix of elastic coefficients and the magnetic permittivity are similar to those of the piezoelectric ceramic. The matrix of piezomagnetic coefficients is:

$$\begin{bmatrix} 0 & 0 & 0 & d_{14} & d_{15} & 0 \\ 0 & 0 & 0 & d_{15} & -d_{14} & 0 \\ d_{31} & d_{31} & d_{33} & 0 & 0 & 0 \end{bmatrix}$$

The piezomagnetic relations, taken from Eqs. (3.43) and (3.45), are tabulated below for various combinations of dependent and independent variables. The correspondence to piezoelectric relations, Eqs.(3.55) through (3.59), is very close. The symbols c and s have their customary meanings as elastic stiffness and compliance coefficients. The arrays μ and ν, the inverse of μ, are the customary magnetic permeability and reluctivity constants, respectively. Superscripts indicate which variable is kept constant during the determination or specification of the coefficient, just as in piezoelectric materials. The piezomagnetic coefficients—d, e, g, and h—are analogues of the corresponding piezoelectric coefficients, where the analogies $H–E$ and $B–D$ are used. This leads to analogies between $\mu–\epsilon$ and between $\nu–\beta$. Thus, d and e may be called the piezomagnetic strain and stress constants, respectively.

The piezomagnetic relations for the cases where electric fields and temperatures are constant are tabulated below.

With T and H independent:

$$S_i = s_{ij}^H T_j + d_{mi} H_m \tag{7.1a}$$

$$B_m = d_{mj} T_j + \mu_{mn}^T H_n. \tag{7.1b}$$

With S and H independent:

$$T_i = c_{ij}^H S_j - e_{mi} H_m \tag{7.2a}$$

$$B_m = e_{mi} S_i + \mu_{mn}^S H_n. \tag{7.2b}$$

With T and B independent:

$$S_i = s_{ij}^B T_j + g_{mi} B_m \tag{7.3a}$$

$$H_m = -g_{mj} T_j + \nu_{mn}^T B_n. \tag{7.3b}$$

With S and B independent:

$$T_i = c_{ij}^B S_j - h_{mi} B_m \tag{7.4a}$$

$$H_m = -h_{mj} S_j + \nu_{mn}^S B_n. \tag{7.4b}$$

7.3 The Magnetomechanical Coupling Coefficient

Following the method used in the definition of the electromechanical coupling coefficient for piezoelectric materials, the magnetomechanical coupling coefficient may be defined as the ratio of the mutual energy density W_{Mut} to the geometric mean of the elastic energy density W_{Elas} and the magnetic field energy W_{Mag}:

$$k = \frac{W_{\text{Mut}}}{\sqrt{W_{\text{Elas}} W_{\text{Mag}}}}. \tag{7.5}$$

The total energy density is calculated (in matrix form) from:

$$U = \frac{ST}{2} + \frac{BH}{2}. \tag{7.6}$$

Using Eq. (7.4), in which S and B are the independent variables, the values for the components of the energy density are:

$$U = \frac{c_{ij}^B S_i S_j}{2} + h_{mi} B_m S_i + \frac{\nu_{mn}^S B_m B_n}{2}. \tag{7.7}$$

The energy density terms are easily recognized to be, in order: the elastic energy density, twice the mutual energy density, and the magnetic energy density. For the case where the magnetic fields and elastic fields have the same direction, namely the poled or 3-direction, the quasistatic magnetomechanical coupling coefficient is:

$$k_{33} = \frac{h_{33}}{\sqrt{c_{33}^B \nu_{33}^S}}. \tag{7.8}$$

7.4 Piezomagnetic Relations for a Bar

We now examine the case of a bar of magnetostrictive material polarized along its length in which the only elastic and magnetic variables of consequence lie along this direction, the 3-direction. Using Eq. (7.4) in which S and B are independent variables, the piezomagnetic equations reduce to a single pair:

$$T_3 = c_{33}^B S_3 - h_{33} B_3 \tag{7.9a}$$

$$H_3 = -h_{33} S_3 + \nu_{33}^S B_3. \tag{7.9b}$$

Several different elastic and magnetic boundary conditions are now considered. First, for a completely free bar, that is, T_3 is zero:

$$S_3 = \frac{h_{33} B_3}{c_{33}^B} \tag{7.10a}$$

and

$$B_3 = \frac{\mu_{33}^S H_3}{1 - \dfrac{h_{33}^2}{c_{33}^B \nu_{33}^S}} = \mu_{33}^T H_3. \tag{7.10b}$$

Eq. (7.10b) defines a magnetic permeability for the constant stress case that is larger than the permeability for the constant strain case. The difference involves the square of the magnetomechanical coupling coefficient defined in the preceding section:

$$\mu_{33}^T = \frac{\mu_{33}^S}{1 - k_{33}^2}. \tag{7.11}$$

If the bar is clamped so that the strain S_3 is zero, then Eq. (7.9a) gives:

$$T_3 = -h_{33} B_3 \tag{7.12}$$

and if the quantity H_3 is also zero, then Eqs. (7.9a) and (7.9b) together give:

$$T_3 = c_{33}^B \left(1 - \frac{h_{33}^2}{c_{33}^B \nu_{33}^S}\right) S_3 = c_{33}^H S_3 \tag{7.13}$$

which defines a stiffness modulus at constant H. This is smaller than the modulus at constant B:

$$c_{33}^{H} = (1 - k_{33}^{2}) \, c_{33}^{B}. \tag{7.14}$$

Thus, it is clear that the elastic properties of the material depend upon the magnetic conditions, just as the magnetic properties depend upon its elastic boundary conditions.

We see from Eq. (7.10b) that when a time varying field H_3 is applied, which would occur if an alternating current were made to flow in a conductor wrapped around the bar, there will be both a change in the magnetic flux density B_3 and a magnetically induced mechanical strain S_3. While the details of the interactions among B, T, and S will depend on the loads imposed on the bar by the external mechanical system, we see that this provides a mechanism for converting electrical energy into mechanical energy and that the bar may be a part of a sound source.

If the bar is subjected to a time varying external force, these equations give the resulting strains and the changes in the magnetic flux density. The time varying flux density would induce an emf in a conducting coil surrounding the bar. Thus the bar could be part of an acoustic sensor system in which mechanical energy is converted into electrical energy.

7.5 Properties of Magnetostrictive Materials

Nickel

This material has had a very wide use in sonar transducers but has been replaced by piezoelectric ceramics in almost all applications. Its advantages include mechanical toughness, chemical stability, and the independence of its properties from hydrostatic pressure. The major reason for the decline in its usefulness is its relatively low electromechanical coupling coefficient and the concomitant low operating bandwidth. The accompanying tables include data for nickel as a basis of comparison with other materials.

Metallic Glass Alloys

The metallic glasses are amorphous metallic alloys of a transition metal and a metalloid, produced by rapid quenching from the molten state. They are produced commercially (Allied Chemical Corporation) in very thin (15–50 micrometers) continuous–length ribbons in various widths. Those alloys containing iron, nickel, or cobalt are ferromagnetic and have been useful in transformer cores. When annealed with an applied transverse magnetic field, the alloys have optimum electromechanical coupling factors consistently larger than 0.7. Values of 0.96 have been reported by Modzelewski *et al.* (7). As in other magnetostrictive materials, linear piezomagnetic effects occur only when the material has been placed in a polarizing magnetic field. Meeks and

Hill (8) give values of d_{33} for the 2605 SC alloy that are the largest ever reported for any material.

The product of the piezoelectric constants d_h and g_h is often used as a figure of merit for a piezoelectric material in hydrophone applications. For this alloy, the product of the piezomagnetic constants g and d significantly exceeds the corresponding piezoelectric product for the very active piezoelectric ceramic, lead zirconate–titanate. For this reason, there is a significant potential for the use of these alloys in hydrophone design and there is currently development activity underway in several laboratories. A magnetic bias must be provided and because of the extreme thinness of the material the transducer must be built with a laminated structure. In some designs the metallic glass is laminated to an inactive material for support and the combination is operated in flexure. Additional data on the properties of these materials is given by Meeks and Hill (9). Some applications are described by Savage and Spano (10).

Rare Earth–Iron Compounds.

It was recognized in the early 1960's that the rare earths possessed unusual magnetic anisotropy properties. Measurements of the magnetostrictive properties of Tb and Dy at low temperatures by Levgold et al. (11) and Clark et al. (12) were the impetus for the search for materials with high magnetostrictive strains at room temperature. It has been found that the additions of elements such as Ni, Co, and Fe to the rare earths produces compounds which offer great potential for sonar transducer application. In some of these, the Curie point is above room temperature and the magnetostritive effects are large as well. A report on the development and properties of these compounds is given by Clark (13).

Properties of polycrystalline samples are sensitive to many variables. The elastic moduli are very sensitive to magnetic field intensity and orientation. Properties are also dependent on whether the grains are randomly oriented or have a dominant orientation. Properties of two rare earth iron compounds, $Tb_{0.7}Dy_{0.3}Fe_2$ and $Tb_{0.145}Ho_{0.855}Fe_2$, are given in Tab. 7.1.

The first of these is known as Terfernol D (14, 15). This compound has a large magnetostrictive strain; however, the relative permeability is fairly small and a large magnetic field intensity is required to obtain optimum magneto-strictive effects. Timme and Meeks (16, 17) concluded that the volume of copper required to provide the magnetic field at maximum power drive makes the effective energy density in this material less than it would be in a lead zirconate–titanate ceramic. The costs for these materials is also high. The data in Tab. 7.1 for the TbDyFe alloy must be considered as approximate since data for two compounds of slightly different composition are combined, one with the ratio of 0.3:0.7:2 and the other 0.27:0.73:2. There are some differences in the properties. In particular, the internal losses in alloys having the second mixture ratio are less. Butler and Ciosek (14) and Cohick and Butler (15) have described developmental transducers that utilize the Terfernol D compound. It appears that considerable development is needed before these new rare–

Table 7.1

Properties of Selected Piezomagnetic Materials[1]

Quantity	Units	Nickel[2]	Metglas[3] 2605 CO	Metglas[3] 2605 SC	TbDyFe[4]	TbHoFe[5]
k_{33} (opt)	—	0.15 to 0.31	0.76 to 0.79	0.84 to 0.90	0.53 to 0.60	0.34
d_{33} (opt)	10^{-9} Wb/N	~ -3.1	70 to 80	300 to 400	—	~ 2.6
μ_{33}^S/μ_0 (opt)	—	22	—	—	—	—
μ_{33}^T/μ_0 (opt)	—	—	700 to 1000	5000 to 7000	4.4	~ 9
g_{33} (opt)	10^{-5} m²/Wb	—	6.5 to 7.5	7 to 8	—	—
$g_{33}d_{33}$ (opt)	10^{-13} m²/N	—	45 to 60	200 to 300	—	—
s_{33}^B	10^{-12} m²/N	4.8	~ 8	~ 9	28	~ 10
s_{33}^H	10^{-12} m²/N	~ 5	~ 40	~ 30	—	—
ν^B	—	~ 0.3	—	—	—	—
s_{44}^B	10^{-12} m²/N	13	—	—	—	—
Q_M^H	—	50 to 250	—	—	~ 40	—
H (opt)	A/m	700 to 1000	~ 800	~ 60	$\sim 20{,}000$	$\sim 32{,}000$
B (opt)	Tesla	~ 0.4	—	—	—	—
B_{sat}	Tesla	~ 0.6	—	—	—	—
Saturation strain	10^{-6}	–33	50 to 55	50 to 55	1620	>250
Curie point	°C	358	—	—	—	—
Yield stress	Pa	$\sim 6 \times 10^7$	—	—	—	—
Critical dynamic stress	Pa	$\sim 3 \times 10^7$	—	—	—	—
Density	kg/m₃	8800	—	—	~ 8700	9270
Sound speeds						
c^B	m/s	5000	—	—	~ 2300	—
c^H	m/s	4850	—	—	—	—

[1] Properties often vary with heat treatment and magnetic field.

[2] Data from Berlincourt (3).

[3] Metglas is a registered trademark of Allied Chemical Corp. Data from Modzelewski et al. (7) and Meeks et al. (8).

[4] Tb₀.₃Dy₀.₇Fe₂ Data from Clark (13) and Timme and Meeks (17).

[5] Unannealed Tb₀.₁₄₅Ho₀.₈₅₅Fe₂ Data from Timme (16).

earth magnetostrictive compounds can replace the piezoelectric ceramics in sonar transducers. However, these new materials may be effective in applications in which a large displacement is important, e.g., low frequency projectors.

References

1. Frederick V. Hunt. *Electroacoustics.* Harvard University Press: Cambridge, MA (1954). Reprinted by the Acoustical Society of America (1982).
2. *The Design and Construction of Magnetostriction Transducers.* Summary Technical Report of Div. 6. Vol. 13. National Defense Research Committee: Washington, D.C. (1946).

3. Don A. Berlincourt, Daniel R. Curran, and Hans Jaffe. Piezoelectric and Piezo-magnetic Materials and Their Function in Transducers. Chapter 3 in *Physical Acoustics.* Vol. 1A. Warren P. Mason, Ed. Academic Press: New York (1964).

4. Warren P. Mason. *Crystal Physics of Interaction Processes.* Academic Press: New York (1966).

5. IEEE Standard 319-1971. On Magnetostrictive Materials: Piezomagnetic Nomen-clature. *IEEE Trans. on Sonics and Ultrasonics.* **SU-20** 67-76 (1976).

6. A. Balato. Corrections to Piezomagnetic Nomenclature. *IEEE Trans. Sonics and Ultrasonics.* **SU-30** 114 (1983).

7. C. Modzelewski, H.T. Savage, L.T. Kabacoff, and A.E. CLark. Magnetomechani-cal Coupling and Permeability in Transversely Annealed Metglass 2605 Alloys. *IEEE Trans. on Magnetics.* **MAG-17** (11) 2837-2839 (1981).

8. Steven W. Meeks and J. Clifton Hill. Piezomagnetic and Elastic Properties of Metallic Glass Alloys $Fe_{67}CO_{18}B_{14}Si_1$ and $Fe_{81}B_{13.5}Si_{3.5}C_2$. *J. Appl. Phys.* **54** 6584-6593 (1983).

9. S.W. Meeks and J.C. Hill. Magnetic Boundary Conditions for Metallic-Glass Piezomagnetic Transducers. *J. Acoust. Soc. Am.* **74** (5) 1623-1626 (1983).

10. H.T. Savage and M.L. Spano. Theory and Application of Highly Magnetoelastic Metglas 2605SC (invited). *J. Appl. Phys.* **53** (11) (1982).

11. S. Levgold, J. Alstad, and J. Rhyne. *Phys. Rev. Lett.* **10** 509 (1963).

12. A.E. Clark, R. Bozorth, and B. DeSavage. *Phys. Rev. Lett.* **5** 100 (1963).

13. A.E. Clark. Magnetostrictive Rare Earth-Fe₂ Compounds. Chapter 7 in *Ferro-magnetic Materials.* Vol. 1. E.P. Wohlfarth, Ed. North Holland Pub. Co. (1980)

14. J.L. Butler and S.J. Ciosek. Rare Earth Iron Octagonal Transducer. *J. Acoust. Soc. Am.* **67** (5) 1809-1811 (1980).

15. S.M. Cohick and J.L. Butler. Rare-Earth Iron "Square Ring" Dipole Transducer. *J. Acoust. Soc. Am.* **72** (2) 313-315 (1982).

16. R.W. Timme. Magnetomechanical Characteristics of a Terbium-Holmium-Iron Alloy. *J. Acoust. Soc. Am.* **59** (2) 459-464 (1976).

17. R.W. Timme and S.W. Meeks. Magnetostrictive Underwater Sound Transducers. *Journ. de Phys.* Colloque C5, suppl to No 5 Tome 40. May 1979. pp C5-280-285.

Problems

7.1 A magnetostrictive transducer designed for underwater use has a blocked resist-ance R_E of 20 ohms. When the impedance is measured in air, the diameter of the motional impedance circle D_A is 25 ohms with an inclination angle of 30 degrees. The diameter of this circle when the transducer is loaded in water is D_W. The efficiency is given by:

$$\eta = \frac{D_W(D_A - D_W)}{R_I D_A}$$

where R_I is the real part of the input impedance when the transducer is acoustically loaded.

(a) Maximize the equation for efficiency with D_W as a variable.

(b) What value of D_W will yield a maximum efficiency?

(c) What is the maximum possible efficiency?

CHAPTER 8

HYDROPHONES

8.1 The Hydrophone Design Problem

The word *hydrophone* as customarily used denotes an electroacoustic transducer that senses sound waves in water. The most commonly used hydrophones generate an emf proportional to the acoustic pressure. However, there are cases where it may be more desirable to use a transducer that is sensitive to another acoustic variable, such as the particle displacement, particle velocity, or pressure gradient. For many years the most frequently used hydrophones have employed a piezoelectric transducing material, generally a piezoelectric ceramic. For this reason, the major portion of this chapter is devoted to pressure sensitive hydrophones that use piezoelectric material.

The number of hydrophones used is very large and there is probably a greater variety of hydrophone designs than projector transducer designs. As a result, hydrophone design has significant economic aspects as well as technological considerations and the subject is a very complex one, indeed. The considerations and material presented here apply primarily to transducers intended to receive acoustic signals and not to those transducers intended to be projectors that may also act as receivers, although some of the considerations apply equally well to both. This is because the factors that optimize a transducer for one function are different from those that optimize the device for the other. For example, a dominant design consideration for high power projectors is the efficiency of conversion from electrical to acoustic energy. In devices intended to be acoustic sensors, conversion efficiency is almost never a dominant concern. Since noise is generally the limiting factor in the detection of signals, in most hydrophone applications the ratio of signal energy to noise energy is of greatest importance and the hydrophone is often designed to optimize this ratio. In addition, factors that also influence the noise levels, such as the hydrophone cables and the first stage of electrical amplification, must be taken into account in the design. Other noise sources, such as vibration–induced noise and pressure or velocity fluctuations due to fluid flow, may be important to the hydrophone design, but are addressed here only in a qualitative manner.

As stated earlier, hydrophone design is a very complex problem. It is not possible to include in one chapter all that one needs to know about hydrophone design. The treatment here presents the physical basis for hydrophone functioning and discusses several of the more basic considerations important to the practical design and use of hydrophones, such as pressure sensitivity, signal–to–noise ratio, internal impedance, and noise matching. Some simple examples of their application and a qualitative discussion of some of the more complex problems are presented. Material on other transducing and sensor mechanisms is given in Ch. 10. References to other sources of information are provided. In particular, LeBlanc (1) provides more complete and detailed coverage of hydrophone technology than is possible in a textbook such as this.

In the process of choosing specifications when designing a hydrophone for a specific purpose, a large number of factors must be considered. Some of the questions pertinent to this matter are:

a. What aspect of the acoustic field is to be sensed? Although acoustic pressure is most often used, there may be situations in which the sensing of another parameter is more desirable, e.g., acoustic particle displacement, particle velocity, or the pressure gradient.
b. What is the frequency range of the signals that are to be received?
c. Is a uniform response needed?
d. Is a directional sensor needed?
e. What is the expected signal pressure level?
f. Is background noise expected to be a significant factor?
g. What sensitivity is needed? Is an absolute calibration needed?
h. Is stability in response an important factor?
i. Is the transducer expendable?
j. Is cost an important consideration?
k. Is reliability a factor? How long must it survive?
l. Is there a preference for the transducing mechanism to be employed?
m. What are the environmental, mechanical, and electrical constraints? These might include ambient temperatures and hydrostatic pressures, extraneous mechanical forces such as fluid turbulence or flow, mechanical vibration and shock, spatial separation between the sensor and the detecting device or system, weight and dimensional constraints, electrical environment, and the electrical load to be placed on the sensor.

8.2 Definition of Hydrophone Sensitivity

In many applications, the dimensions of the hydrophone are small compared to the acoustic wavelength at the frequencies of interest, so the acoustic pressure is essentially uniform over the active or pressure–sensitive parts of the element and the response is essentially independent of the hydrophone's orientation relative to the angle of incidence of the acoustic wave. In these cases the sensitivity can be defined very simply in terms of the output from the electrical terminals per unit free–field acoustic pressure. The free–field pressure is what would exist at the location of the hydrophone if the hydrophone were not in place. The electrical output most often used in specifying sensitivity of a hydrophone is the open–circuit emf, customarily designated by the symbol M_0. The short–circuit current sensitivity, designated by M_s, is sometimes useful.

If the hydrophone is directional, the sensitivity must be defined in terms of the free-field acoustic pressure in a plane, propagating wave, and the angle of incidence of the wave relative to some reference direction. This is normally the angle relative to the direction of maximum sensitivity.

8.3 Equivalent Circuits of Simple Hydrophone Designs

In many cases, it is desirable for a hydrophone to have a sensitivity that is essentially independent of frequency in the frequency range of interest and is also independent of orientation. This is achieved in the piezoelectric ceramic hydrophone by making its dimensions small compared to the acoustic wavelength in the fluid and by making the structure's frequency of mechanical resonance significantly higher than the frequencies at which measurements are to be made. Under these conditions assumptions can be made which greatly simplify the analysis of hydrophone performance. As examples, we will now consider several commonly used piezoelectric ceramic hydrophone configurations. Two approaches of analysis will be used. One is based on the analysis of an equivalent network for the hydrophone. The second involves an analysis using the basic piezoelectric relations and the elastic and electrical boundary conditions.

Piezoelectric Hydrophone Analysis Based on an Equivalent Network
  If the dimensions of the hydrophone are small compared to the acoustic wavelength at frequencies of interest, and the motion can be represented by a small number of degrees of freedom, then the canonical equations and equivalent circuits developed in Chs. 2, 3, and 5 may be used to provide a relatively simple equivalent network that serves as a basis for calculating its sensitivity, frequency response, and a figure of merit.

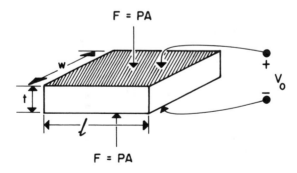

FIG. 8.1   A piezoelectric ceramic hydrophone constructed from a rectangular plate. Acoustic pressure acts on the electroded faces only. Sides are assumed to be shielded from acoustic pressure.

  Consider the case in which a rectangular plate of piezoelectric ceramic, as shown in Fig. 5.6a, is exposed to an acoustic pressure P on both of the electroded faces and the sides of the plate are shielded from the sound. The equivalent network of Fig. 5.6 is applicable if the applied forces are the product of the acoustic pressure and the area of the face. Redrawing Fig. 5.6a as Fig. 8.1, it is assumed that the voltage at the electrical terminals is the open–circuit value. We continue to neglect all damping effects. At frequencies that are small compared to the frequency of mechanical thickness resonance for the plate, the impedances Z_1 in the side arms of the T–network of Fig. 5.6b are small compared to Z_2 in the shunt arm. The consequences of this approximation were studied in Ch. 5 and the result for the open–circuit sensitivity of this device as a hydrophone was developed:

$$M_0 = \frac{Nw\ell C_m}{C_0} = \frac{w\ell C_M}{NC_0} \tag{8.1}$$

where C_m is the mechanical compliance of the plate for compression in the thickness direction and C_M is the corresponding element when it is transformed to the electrical side of the electromechanical transformer. If the mechanical elements are all transformed into electrical elements, the equivalent network is given by Fig. 8.2.

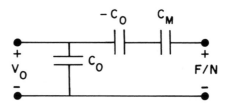

FIG. 8.2   Equivalent network for the piezoelectric ceramic disk hydrophone shown in Fig. 8.1. V_0 is the open–circuit output voltage.

A slightly different but similar result is found for the case of a longitudinal vibrator with transverse polarization used as a hydrophone, as illustrated in

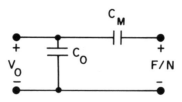

FIG. 8.3   Equivalent network for a piezoelectric ceramic long bar hydrophone with transverse field for stiffness-controlled conditions. V_0 is the open–circuit output voltage.

Fig. 5.4. In this case, the end faces are exposed to the acoustic pressure and the sides are shielded. The low frequency equivalent network is shown in Fig. 8.3 and its sensitivity as a hydrophone is given by:

$$M_0 = \frac{wt}{N} \frac{C_M}{C_0 + C_M}. \tag{8.2}$$

It is clear that the sensitivity of this type of hydrophone can be increased by using a thin diaphragm attached to one end of the bar, which will increase the effective area exposed to the acoustic field and thereby increase the force applied to the ceramic.

This form of equivalent network, consisting of a force generator associated with the acoustic pressure placed in series with a motional capacitance and a blocked capacitance, is typical of almost all piezoelectric hydrophones at low frequencies, i.e., at frequencies well below the frequency of mechanical resonance.

8.4 Hydrophone Analysis Using Piezoelectric Relations

Calculating the electroacoustic response of a piezoelectric ceramic hydrophone constructed from, say, a rectangular block, a cylindrical tube, or a hollow sphere can be somewhat simplified by making several assumptions. If the dimensions of the hydrophone are small compared to the acoustic wavelength in the fluid surrounding it, the acoustic pressure is essentially uniform over the dimensions of the cylinder. Because the frequency of operation is usually well below the frequency of mechanical resonance, wave propagation in the ceramic can be neglected and the dynamic elastic conditions are essentially the same as those for the static case. Because the voltages appearing at the electrical terminals are usually small, the elastic and piezoelectric calculations can be made independently without serious error.

In the following sections, a quasistatic analysis of piezoelectric ceramic hydrophones constructed in the configurations mentioned above is made using the piezoelectric and elastic relations.

Rectangular Ceramic Block Hydrophone

Consider a very simple piezoelectric ceramic hydrophone constructed using a rectangular block of dimensions w, ℓ, and t poled along the t-direction. The block is exposed to a homogeneous sound field so that all of its exterior surfaces experience the same acoustic pressure P, as indicated in Fig. 8.4. If the dimensions are small compared to the acoustic wavelength, then the acoustic pressure has the same amplitude and phase on all sides and the wave effects in the ceramic can be neglected. The stress components are:

$$T_1 = T_2 = T_3 = -P.$$

Using Eq. (3.58b):

$$E = -gT + \beta^T D \tag{3.58b}$$

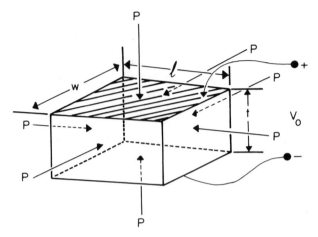

FIG. 8.4   A piezoelectric ceramic block exposed on all sides to the acoustic pressure P. V_0 is the open–circuit emf.

and neglecting the effect of the small surface charges induced by these stresses, the electric field in the poled direction is:

$$E_3 = (2g_{31} + g_{33})P. \tag{8.3}$$

The open–circuit potential difference between the electrodes is given by:

$$V_0 = E_3 t. \tag{8.4}$$

The sensitivity is thus:

$$M_0 = \frac{V_0}{P} = (2g_{31} + g_{33})t. \tag{8.5}$$

For a Navy type II ceramic, the values for the piezoelectric stress constants are approximately:

$$g_{31} = -11.4 \times 10^{-3} \qquad\qquad g_{33} = 24.1 \times 10^{-3} \quad \text{V/m/Pa}$$

so that the sensitivity will be about:

$$M_0 = 1.3 \times 10^{-3} \ \text{V/Pa} \tag{8.6}$$

where t is the thickness in meters. We see that a ceramic of this type is not a very sensitive hydrophone if the surfaces are all exposed to the acoustic pressure because the signs of the two constants are opposite and the value of $2g_{31}$ is not much different from g_{33}.

It is possible to define a volume coefficient of piezoelectricity for a piezoelectric material used in this configuration as:

$$g_h = 2g_{31} + g_{33} \tag{8.7}$$

where the subscript h stands for a hydrostatic stress constant. If the hydrophone material must be used in this mode, the hydrophone would be much more sensitive if materials such as lithium sulfate, lead metaniobate, porous ceramic, flexible ceramic, or piezoelectric plastic were used instead of the usual form of rather rigid ceramic. A comparison of relative sensitivities of several materials operating in this mode is shown in Tab. 8.1. It is shown in

Table 8.1

Comparisons of Low Frequency Pressure Sensitivity of Various Piezoelectric Materials Operating in the Hydrostatic Mode.[1] Compare with Table 4.10.

MATERIAL	$g_h d_h$ (10^{-15} m^2/N)	DENSITY (kg/m^3)	SENSITIVITY (–dB re 1 V/μP$_a$)	THICKNESS (cm)	RELATIVE PERMITTIVITY K_{33}^T
PZT–4	184	7,500	206	1.25	1,300
PbNb$_2$O$_4$	1,620	6,000	187	1.25	225
LI$_2$SO$_4$	1,990	2,060	187	0.64	10
SbSI (22 °C)	15,730	5,000	191	0.76	1,360
PZT Foam	13,600	3,200	180	1.25	190
PZT Epoxy	1,290	2,800	195	0.34	54
PZT/Rubber	17,300	2,800	—	—	170
Epoxy/PZT	16,500	5,400	—	—	410
PVDF (EMI)	1,260	1,800	203	0.06	14
PVDF/Nylon	973	1,800	210	0.03	11
PVDF (NBS)	250	1,800	209	0.06	11

[1] Data from Dr. R.Y. Ting, private communication.

Sec. 8.5 that the product of the piezoelectric constant $g_h d_h$ is a useful figure of merit on a unit volume basis for comparing materials used in a hydrostatic mode when hydrophone noise must be considered.

The Cylindrical Tube Hydrophone

A sketch of the ceramic cylinder is shown in Fig. 8.5, which also illustrates the coordinates used. We will want to examine the performance for several conditions of exposure of the cylinder surfaces to acoustic pressure and several conditions of poling and electroding of the ceramic. The procedure for determining the response of the piezoelectric ceramic hydrophone is to determine the components of stress caused by the applied acoustic pressure, and then to determine the emf generated at the electrodes by the stress induced electric fields in the piezoelectric ceramic. It should be expected that the result will depend upon the elastic boundary conditions and the details of the poling and electroding of the cylinder.

It is first necessary to determine the stress components in the ceramic for the

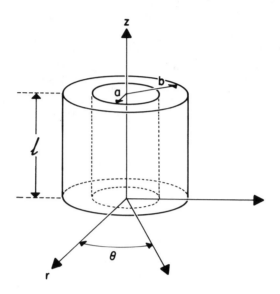

FIG. 8.5   Ceramic cylinder with coordinates.

various elastic boundary conditions. At low frequencies, the problem of finding the stresses in the hollow ceramic cylinder exposed to the acoustic pressure reduces to solving a boundary value problem in static elasticity. That is, one must solve the biharmonic equation:

$$\nabla^2 \nabla^2 \phi = 0 \tag{8.8}$$

where ϕ is the stress potential function, subject to the imposed stresses at the boundary. The Laplacian operator is the usual one in cylindrical coordinates:

$$\nabla^2 \phi = \left(\frac{\partial^2}{\partial r^2} + \frac{1}{r} \frac{\partial}{\partial r} + \frac{1}{r^2} \frac{\partial^2}{\partial \theta^2} + \frac{\partial^2}{\partial z^2} \right) \phi. \tag{8.9}$$

Cylindrical symmetry permits certain simplifications. The components of the tensile stresses are calculated (2) from the potential function by the operations:

$$T_r = \frac{\partial}{\partial z} \left(\nu \nabla^2 \phi - \frac{\partial^2 \phi}{\partial r^2} \right)$$

$$T_\theta = \frac{\partial}{\partial z} \left(\nu \nabla^2 \phi - \frac{1}{r} \frac{\partial \phi}{\partial r} \right) \tag{8.10}$$

$$T_z = \frac{\partial}{\partial z} \left((2 - \nu) \nabla^2 \phi - \frac{\partial^2 \phi}{\partial z^2} \right)$$

where ν is Poisson's ratio. It will be assumed that shear stresses are zero. A solution to Eq. (8.9), used by Langevin (3), is:

$$\phi = (A \ Ln \ (r) \ + \ Br^2 \ + \ C)z \ + \ Dz^3 \tag{8.11}$$

where the numerical constants A, B, C, and D must be determined from the boundary conditions. The stress components from Eq. (8.10) are given by:

$$T_r = \frac{A}{r^2} + (4\nu - 2)B + 6\nu D$$

$$T_\theta = -\frac{A}{r^2} + (4\nu - 2)B + 6\nu D \tag{8.12}$$

$$T_z = (8 - 4\nu)B + 6(1 - \nu)D.$$

Following the method used by Langevin (3), two additional constants are defined:

$$F = (4\nu - 2)B + 6\nu D$$

$$G = (8 - 4\nu)B + 6(1 - \nu)D \tag{8.13}$$

so that Eq. (8.12) now gives the stresses as

$$T_r = \frac{A}{r^2} + F$$

$$T_\theta = -\frac{A}{r^2} + F \tag{8.14}$$

$$T_z = G.$$

Langevin (3) calculated the results for the cylinder for three different boundary conditions: (a) acoustic pressure applied only to the exterior circumferential surface, (b) as in (a) but with the pressure also applied to the ends of the cylinder, and (c) as in (a), but with the pressure also acting on thin, rigid plates that cap both ends of the cylinder. Germano (4) used Langevin's results to make computations for PZT ceramic. Wilder (5) extended the work of Langevin by making calculations for additional cases, including one in which the interior surface of the cylinder is also exposed to acoustic pressure such as might occur in a free-flooding cylindrical hydrophone. In the following, Wilder's approach is used. The fractional part of the acoustic pressure acting on the inside, the outside, and the end surfaces is specified in terms of constants α, β, and γ, respectively. That is, if $\alpha = 1$, then the inner surface of the cylinder will be exposed to the entire acoustic pressure P or if $\alpha = 0$, the inner surface is shielded from the acoustic pressure. Intermediate values correspond to reduced pressure on the inside. For the case of capped ends a value of γ larger than unity may result.

It is assumed that a sinusoidally time varying acoustic pressure P exists in the fluid. In the following equations the time dependence is omitted. The boundary conditions are then:

At $r = a$, $T_r = -\alpha P$.

At $r = b$, $T_r = -\beta P$.

At $z = 0$, $T_z = -\gamma P$.   (8.15)

At $z = \ell$, $T_z = -\gamma P$.

Here, a, b, and ℓ are inner and outer radii and length of the cylinder, respectively.

Applying Eq. (8.15) to Eq. (8.14), gives, after some algebra:

$$T_r = -\frac{Pa^2b^2}{b^2 - a^2}\left(\frac{\alpha - \beta}{r^2} + \frac{b^2\beta - a^2\alpha}{a^2b^2}\right)$$

$$T_\theta = -\frac{Pa^2b^2}{b^2 - a^2}\left(\frac{\beta - \alpha}{r^2} + \frac{b^2\beta - a^2\alpha}{a^2b^2}\right) \qquad (8.16)$$

$$T_z = -\gamma P.$$

As an example, the result for shielded interior and ends, in which $\alpha = \gamma = 0$ and $\beta = 1$, is:

$$T_r = -\frac{Pa^2b^2}{a^2 - b^2}\left(\frac{1}{r^2} - \frac{1}{a^2}\right)$$

$$T_\theta = -\frac{Pa^2b^2}{b^2 - a^2}\left(\frac{1}{r^2} + \frac{1}{a^2}\right) \qquad (8.17)$$

$$T_z = 0.$$

It is a straightforward exercise to develop equations for the other cases.

Three different conditions of poling and electroding are practicable: radial polarization, with electrodes on the inner and outer circumferential surfaces; axial polarization, with electrodes at each end; and tangential polarization. For this last condition, it is assumed that there are an even number N of very thin electrodes lying in the radial–axial planes, equally disposed around the cylinder, as illustrated in Fig. 8.6, with alternate electrodes connected in parallel. In most designs, the ceramic cylinder is one continuous piece and the electrodes consist of thin conducting stripes applied along the axial direction on the outer and inner surfaces. With this method, some of the ceramic is not fully polarized and the resulting sensitivity is less than the values shown in

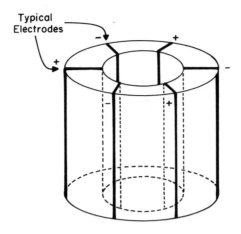

FIG. 8.6   Ceramic cylinder with electrodes for tangential polarization.

Fig. 8.7, a reduction estimated to be perhaps as large as fifteen percent (*1*).

In considering the piezoelectric equations, it is clear that the convention commonly used in piezoelectric ceramics of specifying the z-axis as the poled axis, convenient in rectangular coordinate geometry, leads to an awkward situation in the cylinder. Here, we will continue to specify the stress components in the radial, azimuthal, and axial directions by subscripts r, θ, and z,

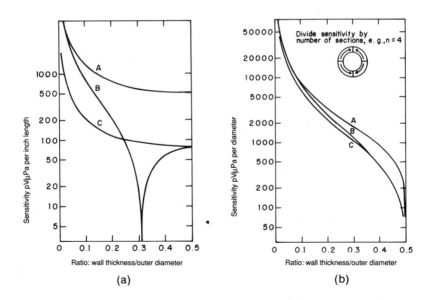

FIG. 8.7   Electroacoustic sensitivity of Navy type I ceramic cylinders with (a) longitudinal and (b) tangential poling for various elastic boundary conditions. A: Ends shielded. B: Ends exposed. C: Ends capped (After Germano (*4*)).

respectively. The directions of the electric field components and the piezoelectric stress constants will be designated by the subscripts 1 and 3, with the understanding that the 3–direction is the poled direction.

Consider first the case where the cylinder is radially polarized. We may use Eq. (3.58b):

$$E_3 = - g_{33}T_r - g_{31}T_\theta - g_{31}T_z. \tag{8.18}$$

The potential difference between the electrodes is given by:

$$V = \int_a^b E_3 dr.$$

Using Eqs. (8.16) and (8.18), this gives the result for the sensitivity of the radially polarized cylinder:

$$M_0 = b \left[g_{31} \left(\gamma(1 - \rho) + (\beta - \alpha\rho) \right) + g_{33} \left(\frac{1 - \rho}{1 + \rho} \beta + \alpha\rho \right) \right] \tag{8.19}$$

where $\rho = a/b$.

In the case with the interior and end surfaces shielded from the acoustic pressure, $\alpha = \gamma = 0$ and $\beta = 1$, the result is:

$$M_0 = b \left(g_{31} + g_{33} \frac{1 - \rho}{1 + \rho} \right). \tag{8.20}$$

We know that the two piezoelectric constants g_{33} and g_{31} have opposite signs and, therefore, the value of the sensitivity will depend significantly on the ratio a/b as well as the value of the piezoelectric constants. For a Navy type I ceramic, often used for hydrophones, $g_{33}/g_{31} = - 2.2$. For this value, the sensitivity will have a zero at a ratio of $a/b = 0.375$, which corresponds to a wall thickness–to–diameter ratio of about 1/3. It is clear that it would be well to avoid wall thickness/diameter ratios in this range.

In the case where the ceramic is polarized longitudinally or tangentially the stress varies along the direction transverse to the electrodes, so that Eq. (3.55b) must be used to calculate the electric displacement vector. This may be integrated over the electrode area to give a value for the charge q which will appear on the electrodes. The emf V can then be obtained from $q = CV$. In the case of longitudinal polarization:

$$D_3 = d_{31}T_r + d_{31}T_\theta + d_{33}T_z. \tag{8.21}$$

The surface charge on the electrodes is given by:

$$q = \int_a^b \int_0^\pi D_3 r \, dr \, d\theta \tag{8.22}$$

and, assuming there is no fringing, the capacitance is:

$$C_0 = \epsilon_{33}^T \pi \frac{b^2 - a^2}{\ell}. \tag{8.23}$$

Since the dielectric constant matrix for the ceramic is a diagonal matrix:

$$d_{33} = \epsilon_{33}^T g_{33} \qquad \text{and} \qquad d_{31} = \epsilon_{33}^T g_{31} \tag{8.24}$$

so that:

$$V = \frac{q}{C_0} = \frac{2\ell}{b^2 - a^2} \int_a^b [g_{31} (T_r + T_\theta) + g_{33}T_z] \, r \, dr \tag{8.25}$$

and the sensitivity of the longitudinally polarized cylinder is given by:

$$M_0 = \frac{V}{P} = \ell \left[2g_{31} \left(\frac{\beta^2 - \rho^2 \alpha}{1 - \rho^2} \right) + g_{33}\gamma \right]. \tag{8.26}$$

For the case where the interior and ends are shielded, the result is:

$$M_0 = \frac{2\ell g_{31}}{1 - \rho^2}. \tag{8.27}$$

For a cylinder poled in the tangential direction with N segments, Wilder (5) gives the sensitivity as:

$$M_0 = -\frac{2\pi b}{N \, \text{Ln} \, \rho} \left[g_{31} \left(\gamma(1 - \rho) + \frac{1 - \rho}{1 + \rho} (\beta + \alpha\rho) \right) + g_{33} (\beta - \alpha\rho) \right]. \tag{8.28}$$

Curves of the sensitivity for some of these cases and for a Navy type I ceramic are plotted in Figs. 8.7 and 8.8. It is clear from inspection of these curves that the sensitivity is considerably reduced for certain ranges of the wall thickness to diameter ratio. The reason for this is, of course, that the contributions from g_{33} and g_{31} oppose each other because of the difference in their signs. It is also clear that there is a considerable difference in sensitivity with different electrode and poling arrangements, since the tangentially polarized cylinder is more sensitive than either of the other cases. However, sensitivity alone is not a sufficient basis for choosing a hydrophone design. Other factors must also be considered in selecting a figure of merit for a hydrophone, as discussed later in this chapter.

At higher frequencies, the directionality must be taken into account. Trott (6) has computed the sensitivity for the capped or shielded end ceramic tube at frequencies for which the omnidirectional assumption is not valid.

The Spherical Ceramic Hydrophone

It is sometimes desirable to use a spherical shell of piezoelectric ceramic as a hydrophone. The primary advantage is that its response will remain

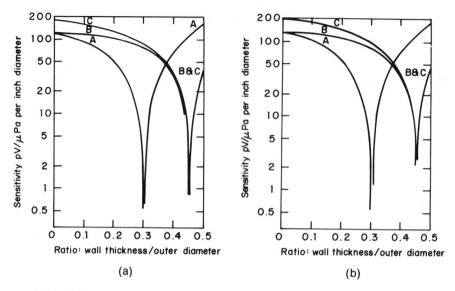

FIG. 8.8   Sensitivity of cylindrical tube ceramic hydrophones with radial polarization. (a) Navy type I. (b) Navy type II. A: Ends shielded. B: Ends exposed. C: Ends capped (After Germano (4)).

omnidirectional to a higher frequency than a cylindrical hydrophone of the same overall dimensions will. A secondary advantage is that, for a radially polarized sphere, the electrical shielding may be better than for the cylinder. Another may be, depending upon the application, that a radially polarized sphere has a higher blocked capacitance than does a radially polarized cylinder of the same volume (1).

Anan'eva (7) has worked out equations for the sensitivity of the spherical ceramic hydrophone using methods similar to those described in the previous section. A form of tangential polarization as well as radial polarization were considered. However, radial polarization is most often used. Some of the results of Anan'eva's analysis are now given.

The low frequency sensitivity for the spherical hydrophone is given by:

$$M_0 = \frac{b}{2(1 + \rho + \rho^2)} \left(g_{33}(\rho^2 + \rho - 2) - g_{31}(\rho^2 + \rho + 4) \right) \qquad (8.29)$$

where $\rho = a/b$ and a and b are the inner and outer radii, respectively.

Inspection of this equation leads one to expect that the sensitivity will be zero at a value of ρ which will depend upon the relative values of g_{33} and g_{31}, just as in the case of the cylindrical hydrophone. For $g_{33}/g_{31} = 2.4$, Anan'eva states that the sensitivity will be zero for the ratio of wall thickness to outside diameter ratio, $\chi = 0.402$, where:

$$\chi = \frac{b - a}{2b}. \qquad (8.30)$$

The zero value of sensitivity occurs at $\rho = 0.2$.

If $\rho = 1$, or $\chi = 0$, which corresponds to an infinitesimally thin shell, the sensitivity is:

$$M_0|_{\rho=1} = -bg_{31}. \tag{8.31}$$

If $\rho = 0$, or $\chi = 0.5$, which corresponds to a solid sphere, the sensitivity becomes:

$$M_0|_{\rho=0} = -b(2g_{31} + g_{33}). \tag{8.32}$$

In practice, the necessity of providing a hole for an electrical lead to an interior electrode should make the sensitivity smaller than that given by Eq. (8.29). Hydrophones have been constructed both in one piece and from two hemispheres cemented together (1, 7).

8.5 Hydrophone Noise

The ultimate useful sensitivity of a hydrophone system is limited by the noise at its output. This noise will normally have both acoustic and electrical origins. The level of the acoustic noise depends on the nature and distribution of the sources, which may include noises due to natural events, such as wind-induced wave splashing noise, biological noises, or man-made noises of many types. Other noises may originate in turbulent boundary layer pressure fluctuations or mechanical vibrations coupled to the sensor from its mounting platform. In addition to these sources, noise exists due to thermal motions of the medium and to processes internal to the transducer itself and in the electrical amplifier.

The hydrophone designer may have little or no control over the ambient acoustic noise perceived by the sensor. If the required operating frequency range permits it or if directionality of response may be employed, there is some potential for reducing the response to the ambient noise by limiting the hydrophone's frequency response or possibly using a directional sensor. Response to hydrodynamic fluctuations can be influenced by suitable fairings or proper location. For example, the "pseudo-sound" sensed by a hydrophone when a turbulent boundary layer flows past the sensor can be reduced by increasing the area over which the pressure is averaged. The analysis of the problem of controlling response to fluid flow fluctuations is a complex subject and is beyond the limits imposed on this book. For further details, the student is referred to Ross (8).

Response to mechanical acceleration due to the mounting platform can be affected by using vibration isolators or a vibration resistant design. A discussion of the effect of design on acceleration sensitivity is provided by Leblanc. The primary subject of this section is the noise inherent in the hydrophone and the requirements placed on the preamplifier to minimize its contribution.

Normally, a preamplifier is needed to match the electrical impedance of the hydrophone to the transmission cable and to raise the level of the signal to a value so high that noise in subsequent channels will not further degrade the signal–to–noise ratio. Thus, in cases where detection of signals near the acoustic noise threshold is important, care in the design of the preamplifier is often essential. It is seldom worthwhile to design the intrinsic internal hydrophone and preamplifier equivalent acoustic noise level to be very much smaller than the ambient acoustic noise in the environment in which the hydrophone is to be used.

The Ambient Noise Environment

Mellen (9) calculated the contribution due to thermal noise in the water. The mean squared spectral pressure is given by:

$$<p_i^2> = \frac{4\pi\rho f^2 K_B T}{c}$$
(8.33)

where K_B is Boltzmann's constant, $K_B = 1.38 \times 10^{-23}$ joules/degree, and T is the absolute temperature. For a temperature of 283°K, the thermal noise spectrum pressure level is:

$$L_N = -75 + 20 \log f \quad \text{dB ref } 1\mu\text{Pa}/\sqrt{\text{Hz}}$$

where the frequency is in hertz.

At frequencies below about 50 kHz, the ambient noise in the ocean is usually dominated by processes other than thermal noise in the water. Empirical data on the ambient noise in the ocean has been summarized by Wenz (10). Other convenient sources of ambient noise data are Urick (11), Kinsler and Frey (12), and Ross (8).

Noise in a Piezoelectric Hydrophone System

Transducer equivalent electrical circuits of the form seen in Ch. 5 can be used to analyze the electrical noise that appears at the output terminals of the hydrophone or the electrical preamplifier and the effects of electrical noise on signal–to–noise degradation. The circuit shown in Fig. 8.9, which includes a preamplifer, will be used as a basis for discussing receiver system noise. The form is inverted from the convention used earlier in order to emphasize that the source of energy in the hydrophone is in the mechanical part of the transducer, shown on the left, and the receiver is the electrical side, shown on the right. Although the magnetic field hydrophone has a different circuit from the one being considered here, the analysis of its noise behavior will be similar to the analysis for the piezoelectric hydrophone. The analysis of the piezoelectric hydrophone is simpler if the equivalent Thévenin circuit for a stiffness–controlled hydrophone, shown in Fig. 8.10, is used. The discussion here follows Young (13).

The radiation impedance elements are assumed to be a mechanical resistance

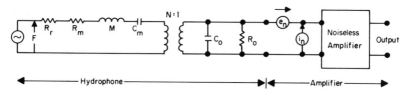

FIG. 8.9 Equivalent circuit model of hydrophone and preamplifier.

and inertance in series with the internal mechanical impedance of the mechanical elements of the hydrophone. The elements R_r, R_m, and R_0 contribute thermal noise. When the hydrophone is connected to a preamplifier, the noise contributions from the amplifier are assumed to be described by a pair of generators, a voltage generator and a current generator, coupled to a noiseless amplifier.

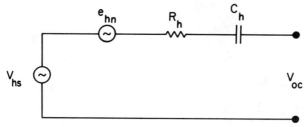

FIG. 8.10 Equivalent circuit for a stiffness–controlled hydrophone.

The hydrophone represented in Fig. 8.10 consists of two voltage sources, V_{hs} and e_{hn}, driving through the complex impedance of the series elements, a capacitor C_h, and a resistor R_h. The source e_{hn} arises from the thermal noise pressure associated with the acoustic medium. Its mean square value is:

$$<e_{hn}^2> = 4kTR_h$$

per unit bandwidth, where k is Boltzmann's constant and T is the absolute temperature. If M is the open circuit sensitivity, η is the hydrophone's transmitting efficiency, and D is its directivity factor:

$$<e_{hn}^2> = \frac{M^2<p_t^2>}{\eta D} \tag{8.34}$$

where $<p_t^2>$ is the mean squared thermal noise pressure in the medium (13).

The source V_{hs} represents the effect of acoustic signal pressure p_s and the nonthermal noise pressure p_n. In the case where the acoustic nonthermal noise is isotropic:

$$<V_{hn}^2> = M^2 \left(p_s^2 + \frac{<p_n^2>}{D} \right) \tag{8.35}$$

where p_s is assumed to be the amplitude of a plane acoustic wave incident from the direction of the major lobe of the directivity pattern of the hydrophone.

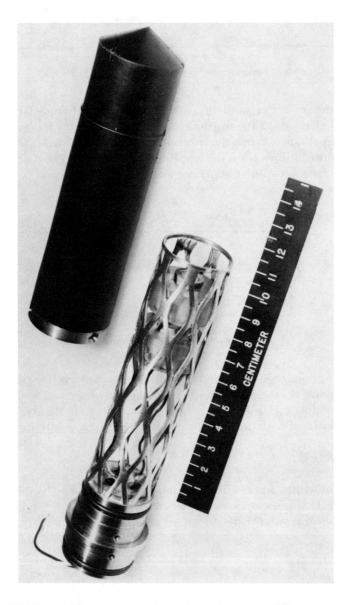

FIG. 8.11   USRD Type H–56 low–noise hydrophone before final assembly. The sensor element consists of a longitudinally polarized ceramic cylinder with capped ends that provides high sensitivity. The sensor output is connected to a low–noise preamplifier and gives excellent noise performance and good dynamic range. The vibration isolator, the metal supporting structure, and the rubber boot that provides protection for the sensor are shown. The interior is oil–filled at assembly. The photograph was provided through the courtesy of the U.S. Naval Research Laboratory, Underwater Sound Reference Division.

The correlation between the amplifier noise components, e_n and i_n, needs to be considered in an exact analysis. However, Woollett (14) has shown that their correlation has little effect on conditions of optimization and very little effect on noise level except near a resonance in the hydrophone. For uncorrelated noise, the mean squared output noise voltage from the amplifier is:

$$<V_{0n}^2> = A^2 \left(M^2 \frac{<p_n^2>}{D} + <e_h^2> + <e_n^2> + |Z_h|^2 <i_n^2>\right) \qquad (8.36)$$

where A is the amplification ratio.

The signal-to-noise ratio (S/N) at the output is then:

$$(S/N)_0 = \frac{<V_{0s}^2>}{<V_{0n}^2>} \qquad (8.37)$$

$$(S/N)_0 = <p_s^2> \left(\frac{<p_n^2>}{D} + \frac{<e_h^2>}{M^2} + \frac{1}{M^2}(<e_n^2> + |Z_h|^2 <i_n^2>)\right)^{-1}.$$

A factor F_D that represents the degradation of the S/N caused by the receiving system can be defined in terms of the S/N that can be achieved theoretically by a perfectly efficient hydrophone having the same directivity ratio and a noiseless preamplifier. Let:

$$(S/N)_a = \frac{<p_s^2>}{<p_a^2>D} \qquad (8.38)$$

where

$$<p_a^2> = <p_n^2> + <p_t^2> \qquad (8.39)$$

is the total ambient mean squared noise pressure. The degradation noise factor is defined:

$$F_D = \frac{(S/N)_a}{(S/N)_0} \qquad (8.40)$$

$$F_D = 1 - \frac{<p_t^2>}{<p_a^2>} + \frac{D}{M^2<p_a^2>} (<e_h^2> + <e_n^2> + |Z_h|^2 <i_n^2>).$$

Given the parameters in Eqs. (8.36), (8.38), and (8.39), a value for F_D can be calculated. The factor F_D is closely related to noise factors used in radio receivers.

The values of the noise sources e_n and i_n are often not available to the designer; more commonly, the preamplifier's noise factor F_A is given instead. This can be expressed in terms of the source resistance R and the noise sources by:

$$F_A = 1 + \frac{\dfrac{<e_n^2>}{R} + R<i_n^2>}{4kT_0}. \qquad (8.41)$$

It is easy to show by differentiation that F_A is minimized when the source resistance is matched to the so-called noise resistance of the preamplifier, i.e., when:

$$R = Z_N = \frac{<e_n>}{<i_n>}. \tag{8.42}$$

The minimum value of F_A is given by:

$$F_A|_{Min} = 1 + \frac{<e_n i_n>}{2kT_0}. \tag{8.43}$$

The degradation factor can then be written in terms of F_A. The explicit dependence of F_D on the noise sources can be removed by substituting Eqs. (8.33) and (8.42) into Eq. (8.40). By assuming that F_A behaves in the same way when driven by a source impedance Z_h as when the source impedance is R, the result for the degradation noise factor is:

$$F_D = 1 - \frac{<p_i^2>}{<p_a^2>} + \frac{4kT_0|Z_h|D}{M<p_a^2>} \left(\frac{R_h T}{|Z_h|T_0} + F_A - 1 \right) \tag{8.44}$$

where F_A is evaluated when driven by a source of impedance $|Z_h|$. Note that F_D is minimized when F_A is minimized, which occurs when the impedance of the hydrophone is matched to the noise impedance of the amplifier, $|Z_h| = Z_n$. In this case:

$$F_D|_{Min} = 1 - \frac{<p_i^2>}{<p_a^2>} + \frac{4kT_0|Z_h|D}{M^2<p_a^2>} \left(\frac{R_h T}{|Z_h|T_0} + F_A|_{Min} - 1 \right). \tag{8.45}$$

For frequencies considerably below 100 kHz and for nonresonant hydrophones, the ambient acoustic noise usually exceeds the acoustic thermal noise, i.e.:

$$<p_a^2> \gg <p_i^2>$$

and

$$|Z_h| \gg R_h.$$

Eq. (8.45) then simplifies to:

$$F_D|_{Min} \simeq 1 + \frac{4kT_0|Z_h|D}{M^2<p_a^2>} (F_A|_{Min} - 1). \tag{8.46}$$

Thus, the minimum noise degradation factor for the system is determined by the minimum noise factor for the preamplifier, the ambient noise level in the medium, and the characteristics of the hydrophone. Young (13) has chosen a quantity called the hydrophone spectral noise pressure as a noise figure of merit (FOM) for the hydrophone:

$$<p_h> = \left(\frac{4kT_0|Z_h|D}{M^2} \right)^{1/2}.$$ (8.47)

This quantity is an "inverse" FOM in that the lower its value, the better the system performance. Eq. (8.47) contains the factor M^2/Z_h which Woollett (15) uses as a measure of hydrophone noise performance. An advantage of using p_h as a FOM is that it has the units of rms spectral pressure and its value can be compared directly with the ambient acoustic noise spectral pressure. Using this definition, Eq. (8.46) becomes:

$$F_D|_{\text{Min}} \simeq 1 + \frac{<p_h^2>}{<p_a^2>} (F_A|_{\text{Min}} - 1).$$ (8.48)

For a small, stiffness-controlled omnidirectional hydrophone, the directivity ratio D is approximately unity and Z_h is dominated by the capacitance C_h resulting in:

$$<p_h> \simeq \left(\frac{4kT_0}{\omega C_h M^2} \right)^{1/2}.$$ (8.49)

For the very simple piezoelectric ceramic hydrophone of the type considered in Sec. 8.5 and sketched in Fig. 8.4, the sensitivity is given by:

$$M = g_h t.$$ (8.50)

The capacitance is:

$$C_h = \frac{\epsilon_{33}^T w\ell}{t}$$ (8.51)

so that:

$$C_h M^2 = \epsilon_{33}^T g_h^2 V_c$$ (8.52)

where V_c is the volume of the ceramic material. Also

$$<p_h> = \left(\frac{4kT_0}{\omega \epsilon_{33}^T g_h^2 V_c} \right)^{1/2}.$$ (8.53)

Two conclusions can be drawn from these results. First, the noise performance of the low frequency piezoelectric hydrophone can be improved by increasing the volume of the piezoelectrically active material. Second, the factor of desirability on a unit volume basis for the choice of a piezoelectric material is the product:

$$\epsilon_{33}^T g_h^2 = d_h g_h$$ (8.54)

where d_h and g_h are the piezoelectric coefficients for hydrostatic stress conditions.

References

1. C. LeBlanc. *Handbook of Hydrophone Element Design Technology.* NUSC Technical Document 5813, 11 Oct 1978. Naval Underwater Systems Center. New London, Connecticut.
2. S.P. Timoshenko and J.N. Goodier. *Theory of Elasticity.* 3rd Ed. McGraw–Hill: New York (1970), p. 381.
3. R.A. Langevin. The Electroacoustic Sensitivity of Cylindrical Ceramic Tubes. *J. Acoust. Soc. Am.* **26** 421–427 (1954).
4. C.P. Germano. Supplement to: The Electroacoustic Sensitivity of Cylindrical Ceramic Tubes, by R.A. Langevin. *J. Acoust. Soc. Am.* **34** 1139–1141 (1962).
5. William Doug Wilder. Electroacoustic Sensitivity of Ceramic Cylinders. *J. Acoust. Soc. Am.* **62** 769–771 (1977).
6. W. James Trott. Sensitivity of Piezoceramic Tubes with Capped or Shielded Ends Above the Omnidirectional Frequency Range. *J. Acoust. Soc. Am.* **62** 565–570 (1977).
7. Alevtina Aleksandrovna Anan'eva. *Ceramic Acoustic Detectors.* Translated from the Russian. Consultants Bureau: New York (1965).
8. Donald Ross. *Mechanics of Underwater Noise.* Pergamon Press: New York (1976)
9. R.H. Mellen. The Thermal–Noise Limit in the Detection of Underwater Acoustic Signals. *J. Acoust. Soc. Am.* **24** 478–480 (1952).
10. Gordon M. Wenz. Acoustic Ambient Noise in the Ocean: Spectra and Sources. *J. Acoust. Soc. Am.* **34** 1936–1950 (1962).
11. R.J. Urick. *Principles of Underwater Sound.* McGraw–Hill: New York (1975).
12. Lawrence E. Kinsler, Austin R. Frey, Alan B. Coppens, and James V. Sanders. *Fundamentals of Acoustics.* 3rd Ed. John Wiley & Sons: New York (1982).
13. J.W. Young. Optimization of Acoustic Receiver Noise Performance. *J. Acoust. Soc. Am.* **61** 1471–1476 (1977).
14. R.S. Woollett. Procedure for Comparing Hydrophone Noise with Minimum Water Noise. *J. Acoust. Soc. Am.* **54** 1376–1379 (1973).
15. R.S. Woollett. Hydrophone Design for a Receiving System in Which Amplifier Noise is Dominant. *J. Acoust. Soc. Am.* **34** 522–523 (1962).

Problems

8.1. A radially polarized piezoelectric ceramic cylinder, Navy type II, is to be used as a hydrophone. The ends are capped and the frequency of the sound for which it is to be used is much less than the frequency for mechanical resonance.
(a) If the outside diameter is 2.5 cm, the inside diameter is 2.0 cm, and the length is 4 cm, what is the open circuit sensitivity for pressure?
(b) What should be the nominal values of C_0 and C for the low frequency equivalent network?
(c) What would be the sensitivity if the inside diameter was 2.3 cm?
8.2. A radially polarized piezoelectric ceramic sphere of outside radius b and wall thickness t is to be used as a hydrophone. Assume that t is very small compared to b, that b is small compared to the acoustic wavelength, and that the inner surface of the sphere is free of stress.
(a) Using appropriate analysis and approximations, show that the low frequency

open circuit sensitivity is:

$$M_0 = bg_{31}.$$

(b)   What is the sensitivity if the material is Navy type II, b is 2.5 cm, and t is 0.32 cm?

CHAPTER 9

TRANSDUCER ARRAYS AND BEAM PATTERNS

9.1 Introduction

In many applications of sound in the ocean, it is desirable to use a transducer that has directional transmitting or receiving characteristics. For example, the use of a directional projector in an active sonar will permit the concentration of available acoustic power into a beam with a resulting increase in source level. A directional projector may also reduce undesired reflections from boundaries, e.g., shallow water propagation, and thereby reduce reverberation. The use of a directional receiver in both active and passive sonars may reduce the effects of interfering signals or noise from other directions and may permit more precise determination of the direction from which a sound arrives. There are occasions when a transducer because of its design structure or the manner in which it must be used acquires an undesired directionality. For these reasons, understanding the physical phenomena leading to directionality in transducers is important to the student.

In the design of a directional pattern for a transducer, the designer is concerned with specifying both the angular resolution of the principal beam and the relative level of secondary lobes and the necessary compromises between these two requirements. Thus, there is a need to understand the relationships between the physical parameters of the transducer and the characteristics of the beam pattern so that a desired pattern can be achieved in the design or a physically realistic pattern can be specified.

It is expected that the student is already somewhat familiar with at least the elementary theory of radiation patterns from distributed sound sources. However, the basic relationships will be reviewed here. The main concern is with the dependence of the sound pressure field on the geometrical distribution of the sources (or receivers) and with the effects on the pattern of varying the amplitude and the phase of different sources.

It will be assumed that the medium in which the radiation patterns exist is an ideal fluid and any reflecting objects are so distant that they may be ignored. It is also assumed that the amplitude of the simple harmonic waves is so small that nonlinear effects are negligible and linear superposition of sounds may be used. It will also be assumed that the distance at which the patterns are calculated is large compared to the dimensions of the array of sources. This allows considerable simplification in the analysis and is the usual practice. There are some important array problems in which these assumptions are not warranted, however.

Since the primary interest in this chapter is the relative amplitude of the pressure, it is convenient to disregard factors that depend on distance from the center of the sources and to normalize the amplitude pattern relative to unity in some direction, here chosen to be the direction of maximum amplitude. Thus, we define the pattern function or directivity pattern as the description of the angular functional dependence of the normalized sound pressure amplitude at a large fixed distance from the source.

In the following sections a discussion of the reciprocity theorem applied to arrays is presented. Next, the beam patterns for some simple linear point arrays are discussed in order to illustrate the effects of spacing, shading, phasing, and the number of elements on the beam patterns. Since it has not been feasible to include a complete discussion of the many kinds of acoustic arrays important to sonar systems, the remaining discussions of arrays are descriptive. The student is referred to other sources for analysis of arrays, e.g., Steinberg (1), Ziomek (2), and the other references given later in this chapter.

9.2 Acoustic Reciprocity Applied to Arrays

The reciprocity theorem is the basis for the fact that the directional pattern is identical whether a transducer is used as a projector or as a receiver. However, the term "directional pattern" must be understood in the proper sense. To illustrate this, the principle of reciprocity is stated somewhat differently than it was in Ch. 2. A very general form of the theorem is (3):

Consider an enclosed region that has bounding surfaces $S_1, S_2, \ldots$, and two distributions, generally different, of normal velocities v' and v'' over the bounding surfaces producing pressure fields p' and p'', respectively, in the enclosed region. Then:

$$\int_{S_1, S_2, \ldots} (p''v' - p'v'')dS = 0. \qquad (9.1)$$

The consequences of this theorem to the problem of interest here may be illustrated as follows. Let one of the bounding surfaces be the surface of a transducer used as a hydrophone, which may have a particular geometrical shape and associated reflectors and baffles, and the other the surface of a simple, spherically–symmetric source transducer of radius a, assumed to be small compared to the acoustic wavelength in the fluid filled space. Let the velocity v' be zero on all surfaces except the hydrophone and let v'' be zero on all surfaces except at the spherical source where it is the radial velocity of the surface. The strength of the spherical source is defined as the volume velocity of the source:

$$Q_s = 4\pi a^2 v''. \qquad (9.2)$$

Eq. (9.1) then becomes:

$$\int_H p''_H v' \, dS_H = Q_S p'_S \tag{9.3}$$

where p''_H is the pressure on the hydrophone when the simple source is a projector and p'_S is the pressure on the simple source when it is a receiver and the hydrophone is the projector. Eq. (9.3) leads to the conclusion that the pressure at any point S caused by a given velocity distribution on the hydrophone (when used as a projector) is the same as the total pressure on the hydrophone (when its surface is made rigid) caused by a source of unit strength at S, when the elements of area of the hydrophone are weighted in accordance with the original velocity distribution. Thus, since the location of the spherical source is arbitrary, we see that the directional characteristics of the sounds radiated from a transducer with a particular velocity distribution are the same as the receiving directional characteristics when the receiving sensitivity of each element in the transducer is in proportion to the original velocity distribution.

It is important to notice that this result depends on two assumptions: a) the receiving transducer has a rigid surface and b) the velocities at the projecting transducer are normal to its surface. That is, the theorem holds only for conjugate quantities. If the specific acoustic impedance of the transducer surface is not large compared to the specific acoustic impedance of the fluid, then the assumption that the surface is rigid during the reception of sound is not valid. There is no simple relationship between the motions of the surface during receiving or projection.

It is possible to extend the reciprocity principle to the complete electromechanical system. Ballantine (4) has developed a reciprocity theorem relating open–circuit voltage to short–circuit current as conjugate quantities that applies to any linear passive system, even when it includes damping forces—provided they are linear. If a voltage V' applied to the transducer produces an acoustic pressure p'_S at a point in the fluid and a source of strength Q''_S at the same point produces a current I'' when the transducer output is short–circuited, then the theorem gives the result:

$$\frac{p'_S}{V'} = \pm \frac{I''}{Q''_S}. \tag{9.4}$$

Correspondingly, if the terminating electrical impedance during reception is not zero, then the assumptions of the theorem are no longer valid. The voltages and currents in reception and in projection cannot be related without more detailed information about the terminating impedances of the circuits involved.

9.3 Beam Patterns of Point Source Arrays

This section is limited to the discussion of arrays of point sources of simple harmonic sound waves located in an infinite region of ideal fluid. It is assumed that there is no interaction between the sources, i.e., the source strength of any element is unaffected by the acoustic pressure at its location caused by any of the sources. The assumption of a point source insures that each source radiates uniformly in all directions.

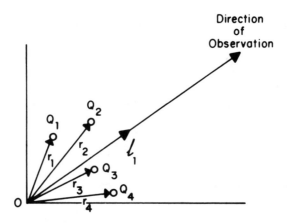

FIG. 9.1   The geometry of the array of point sources.

Consider an array of N such sources, located at positions given by the radius vectors $\mathbf{r_n}$, measured from an arbitrary origin, with source strengths Q_n and phase angles ψ_n, as indicated by the sketch in Fig. 9.1. Linear superposition of the sound from all the elements leads to the directivity pattern function:

$$P = P_0 \ \Sigma \ Q_n \ \exp \ [j(k(\boldsymbol{\ell}_1 \cdot \mathbf{r_n}) + \psi_n)] \tag{9.5}$$

where k is the propagation constant in the fluid, $\boldsymbol{\ell}_1$ is the unit vector in the direction of observation, and P_0 is the normalizing factor chosen to make P equal unity along the direction of the maximum sound pressure. Range dependence of the pressure and its simple harmonic time dependence have been suppressed. The suppression of range dependence caused by spherical spreading is inherent in the definition of the pattern function.

It is clear from Eq. (9.5) that the pattern function is determined by several independent parameters:

  a. The relative strengths of the sources, usually called shading.
  b. The geometric configuration of the array itself as determined by the number of elements and the relative spacing measured in terms of the acoustic wavelength.
  c. The relative phases of the sources.

The following paragraphs illustrate how each of these variables affects the pattern in a linear array. In the first example, we will consider a set of four point sources arranged symmetrically about the origin as shown in Fig. 9.2. The observation angle is measured from the perpendicular bisector of the

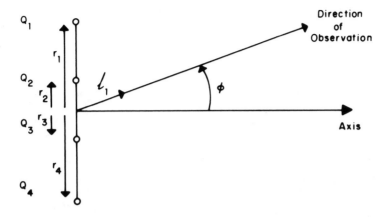

FIG. 9.2   The geometry of the four element point source linear array.

array line. In plotting the pattern function, only half of the pattern is plotted since there is an axis of symmetry through the line of the array. The pattern function plots are taken from ref. (3).

Effects of Shading

First consider a set of four sources arranged as shown in Fig. 9.2, but with equal separation a between adjacent elements, so that $r_1 = r_4$ and $r_2 = r_3$. All elements have the same phase, arbitrarily chosen to be zero. Now let $Q_1 = Q_4 = 1$ and $Q_2 = Q_3 = W$. That is, the strength of the inner pair of sources is W times the strength of the outer pair. Eq. (9.5) becomes:

$$P = P_0 \left(\exp j \frac{3ka \sin \phi}{2} + W \exp j \frac{ka \sin \phi}{2} \right.$$

$$\left. + W \exp -j \frac{ka \sin \phi}{2} + \exp -j \frac{3ka \sin \phi}{2} \right). \tag{9.6}$$

Combining terms and using standard trigonometric identities gives:

$$P = 2P_0 \left(W \cos \frac{ka \sin \phi}{2} + \cos \frac{3ka \sin \phi}{2} \right). \tag{9.7}$$

The maximum in the pattern, arbitrarily chosen to be unity, occurs along the line perpendicular to the line of the array. Thus, the normalizing factor is determined to be:

$$P_0 = \frac{1}{1 + W}$$

and the pattern function is:

$$P = \frac{1}{1 + W} \left(W \cos \frac{ka \sin \phi}{2} + \cos \frac{3ka \sin \phi}{2} \right). \tag{9.8}$$

By varying the parameter W, one can observe the effects of concentrating the source strength toward the center of the array (W greater than unity) or toward the ends of the array (W less than unity). The pattern functions for four values of W are shown in Fig. 9.3, where the value for a has been chosen to be one half

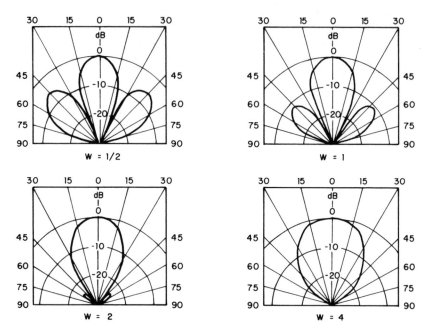

FIG. 9.3 Patterns of four point sources equally spaced one–half wavelength apart and having the same phase. W is the ratio of the strengths of the middle two sources to the two outer sources (After (3)).

of the acoustic wavelength, which gives the value of $ka = \pi$. The radius of the plot is proportioned to a logarithmic scale in decibels. Only half the pattern is sketched, since the pattern function for the line array has an axis of symmetry along the line of the array. As W is increased in value, more source strength is concentrated toward the array center, the minor lobes decrease in level, and the angular width of the central or major lobes increases.

The Effects of Relative Spacing

Next, suppose that each of the four sources has equal strength and phase but the distances between the elements is changed, keeping the overall length unchanged. Let the distances between elements 1 and 2 and between elements 3 and 4 be called a and the distance between elements 2 and 3 be called b. Eq. (9.5) now becomes:

$$P = \frac{1}{2} \left(\cos \frac{kb \sin \phi}{2} + \cos \frac{k(2a + b) \sin \phi}{2} \right). \tag{9.9}$$

The relative spacing between the inner pair of elements to the total length of the array is used as a parameter in the beam pattern plots:

$$W = \frac{b}{2a + b}.$$

Fig. 9.4 is a plot of Eq. (9.9) for four values of W when the overall length of the array, $2a + b$, is kept constant at one and one–half wavelengths. For $W = 1$, essentially we have a two element array with a spacing of $3\lambda/2$. As W decreases,

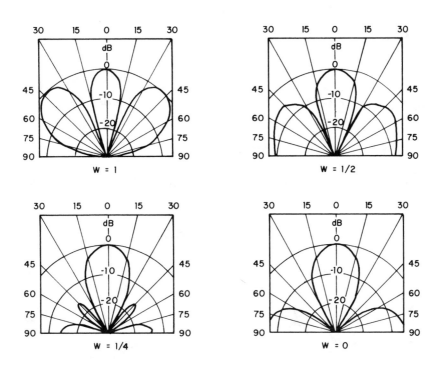

FIG. 9.4   Patterns of four point sources of equal strength and phase, symmetrically spaced on a line. W is the ratio of the distance between the inner point sources to the distance between the outer point sources, the latter being assumed fixed at one and one–half wavelength (After (3)).

more of the source strength is moved toward the array center and the central lobe increases in width and the levels of the secondary lobes decrease. At $W = 0$, we have essentially a three element array with the center element having twice the strength of the outer two and a spacing between elements of $3\lambda/4$.

Effects of Phasing

For this case, let the four elements have equal strengths and be placed uniformly at a separation a between adjacent elements. Let the phases of each source be different. Referring again to Fig. 9.1, it is clear that Eq. (9.5) becomes:

$$P = P_0 \left[\exp j \left(\frac{3ka \sin \phi}{2} - \psi_1 \right) + \exp j \left(\frac{ka \sin \phi}{2} - \psi_2 \right) \right.$$
$$\left. + \exp -j \left(\frac{ka \sin \phi}{2} - \psi_3 \right) + \exp -j \left(\frac{3ka \sin \phi}{2} - \psi_4 \right) \right].$$

$$(9.10)$$

Now consider the case where there is a progressive, equal phase shift from one end of the array to the other. That is, let:

$$\psi_1 = 3\psi \qquad \psi_2 = \psi$$

$$\psi_3 = -\psi \qquad \psi_4 = -3\psi.$$

Thus there is a progressive phase difference of 2ψ between adjacent elements. Eq. (9.10) now becomes:

$$P = 2P_0 \ \cos \left(\frac{3ka \sin \phi}{2} - 3\psi_1 \right) + \cos \left(\frac{ka \sin \phi}{2} - \psi \right) . \qquad (9.11)$$

In Fig. 9.5, where the spacing is set at one half of the acoustic wavelength, the pattern function is plotted for several different values of phase shift. Note that

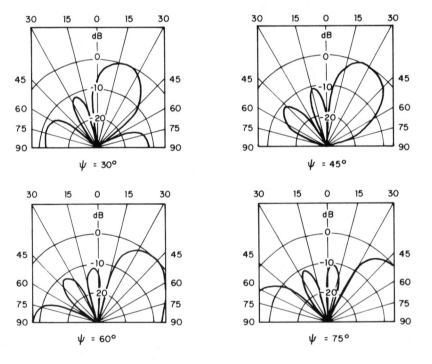

FIG. 9.5 Patterns of four point sources of equal strength equally spaced one–half wavelength apart and progressively phased by an amount 2ψ (After (3)).

as ψ increases, the central lobe is shifted toward one side by about 2/3 of ψ. At $\psi = 75$ degrees, one of the secondary lobes begins to get large.

Effects of Number of Elements and Length of the Array

If a linear array consists of N equally spaced, equally phased, equal strength elements, Eq. (9.9) becomes:

$$P = \frac{1}{N} \sum_{n=1}^{N} \exp jk \left(a_0 + (n - 1) a \sin \phi \right) \tag{9.12}$$

where a is the spacing and:

$$a_0 = -\frac{(N - 1)a}{2}. \tag{9.13}$$

This locates the reference point at the midpoint of the array. The sum in Eq. (9.12) reduces to:

$$P = \frac{\sin \left(\dfrac{Nka \sin \phi}{2} \right)}{N \sin \left(\dfrac{ka \sin \phi}{2} \right)}. \tag{9.14}$$

The effects on the beam pattern of changing the number N with the spacing set to one–half wavelength is illustrated in Fig. 9.6. Of course, the value of N

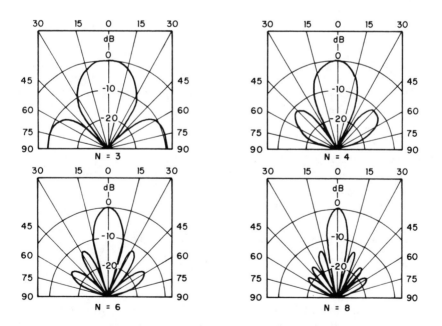

FIG. 9.6   Patterns of N point sources of equal strength and phase equally spaced one–half wavelength apart on a line (After (3)).

also controls the overall length of the array. As N increases, the central lobe of the pattern becomes narrower and the number of secondary lobes increases while their amplitude decreases relative to the central lobe.

9.4 Optimum Arrays

It should be clear from the discussion of linear point arrays in the previous sections that the directivity pattern has a major lobe and one or more minor or side lobes. Also, when amplitude shading is used so that there is a decrease in side lobe levels, there is a concomitant increase in the beamwidth of the major lobe. Conversely, when the shading results in a narrower major lobe, the amplitude of the side lobes usually increases. This is the basis for the notion of an "optimum" beam pattern, which is usually understood to mean that there is an optimum adjustment between major lobe beamwidth and minor lobe levels. Dolph (5) and Riblet (6) showed that for a given spacing and quantity of elements in a linear point array, a minimum beamwidth for the major lobe is achieved when shading is adjusted to make all minor lobes have the same amplitude as the largest minor lobe. Conversely, setting all minor lobes to the same specified level results in a minimum major lobe beamwidth for the specified level.

This approach has been developed further and applied by Pritchard (7) and Davids, Thurston, and Muesser (8). Dolph's method involves a design procedure that determines the amplitudes of the terms in the pattern function polynomial in terms of the Chebychev polynomial:

$$T_n(z) = \cos [n \cos^{-1}(z)] \tag{9.15}$$

where n is an integer and z may be complex. In this polynomial function, all extrema have the same amplitude. This type of array is often called a Chebychev array. Additional details on the properties of the Chebychev polynomials may be found in Abramowitz and Stegun (9) or other handbooks on mathematical functions. Design examples are presented in refs. (1) and (8). One disadvantage of this array is the necessity for precise control of the excitation functions for the elements.

9.5 Small Aperture Directional Arrays

The linear arrays discussed earlier in this chapter utilize a spatial distribution of sources or receivers in order to obtain a directional pattern. Generally, increased directivity is obtained only through increasing the number of elements and the overall dimensions of the array. Another important class of arrays utilize the difference in the patterns of colinear conventional arrays. Such arrays are often called super–directive or super–gain arrays. The patterns from them are often called difference patterns. The advantage of this form of array is that for a given number of elements and spacing the achievable directivity ratio is significantly larger than could be obtained with a conventional array.

Such an advantage is gained at the expense of a narrow operating frequency band and the requirement of precise control of the excitation amplitude and phase for each element. For a projector array, the radiation from some of the sources cancels that from others of the opposite phase, so that the source level is reduced. In a hydrophone array, the sensitivity is reduced, resulting in an increased demand on the intrinsic noise characteristics of the hydrophones and preamplifiers. The internally generated noises in the hydrophones are not coherent, so that subtracting the output of one hydrophone from another does not result in cancellation of internal noise. One example of a simple small aperture directional array is the dipole hydrophone which is used in the DIFAR sonobuoy system.

References

1. Bernard P. Steinberg. *Principles of Aperture and Array System Design*. Wiley: New York (1976).
2. L. Ziomek. *Underwater Acoustics, A Linear Systems Approach*. Academic Press, Inc. New York (1985).
3. *The Design and Construction of Magnetostrictive Transducers*. Summary Technical Reports of Div. 6. Vol. 13. National Defense Research Committee, Washington, D.C. (1946). Ch. 5.
4. Stuart Ballantine. Reciprocity in Electromagnetic, Mechanical, Acoustical, and Interconnected Systems. *Proc. I.R.E.* 17 (6) 929-951. June 1929.
5. C.L. Dolph. A Current Distribution of Broadside Arrays Which Optimizes the Relationship Between Beam Width and Side-Lobe Level. *Proc. Inst. Radio Engrs.* 34 335-348 (1946).
6. H.J. Riblet. *Proc. Inst. Radio Engrs.* 35 489-492 (1942).
7. R.L. Pritchard. Optimum Directivity Patterns for Linear Point Arrays. *J. Acoust. Soc. Am.* 25 (5) 870-801 (1953).
8. N. Davids, E.G. Thurston, and R.E. Muesser. The Design of Optimum Directional Acoustic Arrays. *J. Acoust. Soc. Amer.* 24 (1) 50-56 (1952).
9. Milton Abramowitz and Irene A. Stegun, Eds. *Handbook of Mathematical Functions with Formulas, Graphs, and Mathematical Tables*. Applied Mathematics Series, No. 55. National Bureau of Standards. U.S. Govt. Print Off., Washington, D.C. (1964).

CHAPTER 10

PROBLEMS OF TRANSDUCER DESIGN

10.1 Array Element Interaction

In Ch. 9, functions were developed that give the radiation pattern from a transducer array. It was seen that the pattern function is determined by the spatial distribution, the strength, and the relative phases of the sources. It was assumed that there was no interaction between the sources, i.e., the source strengths of the elements were unaffected by the acoustic pressure at each source. In Ch. 5, equivalent circuits were developed showing the relationships between the electrical impedance or admittance of the transducer and the acoustic radiation impedance presented to the transducer element. Thus, for a given applied drive voltage at the projector element input, the velocity achieved at the radiation face depends on the radiation impedance. The sensitivity to acoustic loading is enhanced by the use of materials that have a large electromechanical coupling factor.

The radiation impedance presented to each element of a projector array will be a function of the sound radiated by other elements in the array as well as the sound radiated by the element itself. The importance of this interaction can be appreciated in the case where the radiation resistance presented to a particular element becomes negative. In this case, the resultant acoustic pressure at the face of the element due to the sound radiated by all elements of the array is larger than and of opposite phase from the sound pressure that the element itself would radiate. If the velocity of the face is not zero, the element will then "receive" sound rather than "radiate" it. The acoustic intensity near the face of a large low frequency sonar projector is often very large so that the acoustic power delivered to the element in this manner can result in catastrophic failure in the transducer or its driver amplifier. At the least, the velocity of the element may be different in amplitude and phase from the design value, which may cause a degraded beam pattern and reduced power output. Similar difficulties have been experienced in the operation of high-powered loud speaker arrays.

The severity of this problem was recognized in the early 1960's when high-powered search sonars were being developed using the then newly available lead zirconate-titanate ceramics with good electromechanical coupling factors. It is not possible to discuss here the details of this problem. Prevention of destructive conditions or degraded performance requires the radiating element velocity to be controlled. Means for doing this have included the use of a tuning inductor with the transducers and feedback techniques employing a velocity sensor mounted on the radiating face. Much of the early work was done and reported by engineers at the Navy Electronics Laboratory; reports of this work were classified at that time and received limited distribution. Some of the basic theory of mutual radiation impedance is given by Pritchard (*1*) and Arase (*2*). Additional discussion of this problem is given by Greenspon and Sherman (*3*), Porter (*4*), Chan (*5*), and Stepanishen (*6*).

10.2 Comparison of Transducer Mechanisms

One means of comparing various mechanisms for converting electrical energy into acoustic energy is to tabulate the maximum stresses that can be obtained from each of them. Sherman (*7*) prepared a table of such values which are presented in Tab. 10.1. The maximum attainable stresses are a measure of a mechanism's suitability for use in sonar projector transducers. The electromechanical coupling factor is another perhaps more useful term for comparison. For hydrophone operation, the maximum obtainable force is not itself a useful criterion for comparison. However, for the reversible mechanisms, those capable of large forces when driven electrically are also capable of generating large electrical voltages when driven mechanically.

Table 10.1

Comparison of Transducer Mechanisms in Terms of Approximate Maximum Attainable Stress.[1]

MECHANISM	MAXIMUM STRESS Pa	CONDITIONS
Electrodynamic (moving coil)	8,000	2 A flowing in a 200 turn circular coil, 10 cm radius, in a field of 1 Wb m^2. Force applied to a piston of same radius.
Electrostatic	10	$E = 1500$ V cm, air dielectric
Variable reluctance	400,000	$B = 1$ Wb m^2 between the pole faces.
Magnetostrictive	1,000,000	Polarized nickel with $H = 1000$ A m.
Piezoelectric	8,000,000	Polarized lead zirconate–titanate with $E = 4000$ V cm.
Hydroacoustic	7,000,000	Hydraulic pressure variations of 1000 psi.

[1] Data from Sherman (*7*).

In some applications, especially at low frequencies, the requirement of a large volume velocity from a small transducer places more importance on the capability of a mechanism to provide a large displacement. An example is the frequent use of the moving coil transducer in low frequency projectors, especially when there is a need for a significant bandwidth at modest source levels. Other examples of low frequency projectors are described in Ch. 6.

10.3 Tuning for Transducer Matching

It should be clear at this point that the input electrical admittance or impedance of most projector transducers is a complex quantity, even in the neighborhood of mechanical resonance. The existence of a significant reactive component may give problems in matching an amplifier to the transducer, particularly at high drive levels where conversion efficiency is obviously very important and desirable. Optimum conversion efficiency occurs when the impedance of the load and the internal impedance of the driver are complex conjugates of each other. A transformer may be useful for matching the magnitude of the impedance, but the details depend upon the nature of the electrical generator.

For a piezoelectric projector, the electrical behavior in the neighborhood of mechanical resonance is approximated well by the equivalent circuit shown in Fig. 5.7b. Several methods for adjusting load impedance for the purpose of matching impedances between the driver amplifier and the transducer have been used. One method utilizes a transformer. Another is to tune out the reactance of the blocked capacitance C_0 by using an inductor either in series or in parallel with the transducer. Sometimes the need to obtain maximum power transfer regardless of efficiency requires that finely tuned matching be ignored. The subject of transducer impedance matching is discussed by Heuter and Bolt (8).

10.4 Laboratory Transducers

Transducers intended for use in conducting underwater measurements often operate under environmental conditions that are less severe than those for sonars in fleet operations. For example, the measurements may be made in fresh, relatively clean water in a laboratory environment. Or perhaps the measurements do not require submergence of the transducer for extremely long periods of time. In other ways, however, some of the requirements may be more restrictive than for a fleet sonar transducer. Very often, accuracy and long term stability of the calibration or other transducer performance parameters may be very important and tolerance for changes with time may be small. If submergence for extended periods is a requirement and reliability and stability are needed, then extreme measures to insure that water does not diffuse or leak into the transducer may be necessary. For example, a hydrophone intended for use in accurately measuring ship–radiated noise may be located on the sea floor at a considerable distance from shore. The cost of replacing such devices may be sufficient to warrant the expense of developing a very reliable transducer. For convenience in measuring, it is often very desirable for the response of the hydrophone or projector to be reasonably good and uniform over a wide frequency band. A large dynamic range is often needed. In some cases, a hydrophone with very low intrinsic self–noise may be essential. In order to achieve goals such as these, compromises in other parameters may be required.

An example of a transducer that was designed to provide operation over a

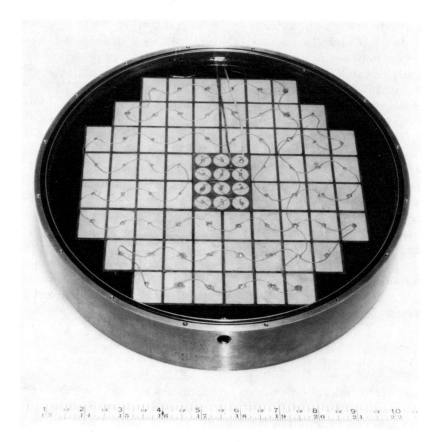

FIG. 10.1   USRD Type F-33 transducer, designed for broadband use in a laboratory environment. During final assembly, the active elements are covered with oil and a rubber boot. Photograph provided through the courtesy of the U.S. Naval Research Laboratory, Underwater Sound Reference Division.

wide band of frequencies for measurements in a laboratory environment is the USRD Type F–33 transducer, shown in Fig. 10.1. Two sets of piezoelectric ceramic disks, cemented to metal backing plates, are used. The outer section is designed to operate at lower frequencies and the inner section at higher frequencies. The useful frequency range is from 1 kHz to 150 kHz. The ceramic elements are potted in a clear polyurethane compound with pressure-release material around each piece. During final assembly, the elements are covered with oil as a coupling fluid and a rubber boot is attached as the outer covering. Another example of a specially designed measurement transducer is the USRD Type H–56 low–noise hydrophone described briefly in Ch. 8. The problems of designing hydrophones for deep submergence are discussed by Groves (9). Other transducers designed for measurement functions are described in the transducer catalog of the Naval Research Laboratory (10) and the catalogs of commercial transducer manufacturers.

FIG. 10.2   An array of piezoelectric cylinders designed to operate at the frequency of resonance of the cavity in each cylinder, which has led to its being called a "squirter" transducer. Applications are in high power, broadband operations where a toroidal beam pattern is desired. The photograph was provided through the courtesy of Channel Industries.

10.5 Other Transducer Mechanisms

There are other transducing mechanisms that are useful in sonar applications but do not meet the criteria of linearity, passivity, and reversability used to limit the discussions in this book. Space does not permit such discussion. However, the student may wish to become better acquainted with such transducers. Therefore, the following paragraphs describe the mechanisms very briefly and provide references to other literature that can be used for further study.

　　a. *Hydroacoustic Transducers.* There are a number of mechanisms that make it possible to control the conversion of kinetic energy or potential energy in a fluid into acoustic energy. One means that has been extensively studied and developed by Bouyoucos involves the modulation of the flow of hydraulic fluid acting on a piston. Called "hydroacoustic transducers" by the inventor, these transducers achieve control of the high pressure fluid flow by means of a shuttle valve positioned by a piezoelectric transducer. Alternating fluid flow results in an alternating change in pressure at the piston. The motion of the piston is coupled to a diaphragm that radiates sound into the water. These transducers are discussed by Bouyoucos (*11*).

　　b. *Parametric Arrays.* This mechanism converts sound energy at one frequency into sound at a different frequency. It depends on the fact that at large amplitudes, the medium transmitting the sound has nonlinear properties. For example, if sounds at different frequencies are generated in a piston projector at very high amplitude, the fluid near the projector behaves in a nonlinear manner so that intermodulation products of the various component sound waves are generated in the medium. Thus, sound at frequencies given by the differences and the sums of the primary sound frequencies is generated in the fluid in the column where the intensity is sufficiently large. The phasing of the newly generated sounds is such that the column of fluid acts as an end-fire acoustic array. Normally, the interest is in generating a narrow beam at a lower frequency, called the secondary frequency component.

The process is very inefficient. However, the directivity of the resulting secondary beam is very nearly the same as the primary beam and the temporal variations in pressure at the secondary component will follow rapid modulations of the primary frequency. This is achieved with a transducer having transverse dimensions that are much smaller than would be required to obtain the same directivity at the same frequency using a conventional array. The process can be used for a receiver as well as a projector. The use of this mechanism for a sonar system is described by Konrad (12).

c.   *Fiber-Optic Sensors.* Acoustic waves will affect the optical properties of thin transparent fibers. The use of these effects for acoustic sensing was first described by Cole and others in 1977 (13, 14). Since then, it has been extensively studied because of the fiber-optic sensor's important advantages. Compared to other transducer systems, it has very high sensitivity. There is also geometrical versatility in the possible shapes of the transducer, immunity to electromagnetic interference, and ruggedness. There are a number of configurations in which the effect of acoustic pressures on the properties of a thin fiber is sensed. In almost all of them, the sensing is accomplished in an optical detector that is sensitive to phase differences between light that has traveled some distance in a fiber exposed to the sound and light that has traveled approximately the same distance in a fiber that has been insulated from the sound. Because the optical interferometric method is so sensitive, the noise in the system caused by mechanical vibrations or temperature differences between the two optical paths is a troublesome factor. A survey of the process is given by Bucaro et al. (15). An application of the fiber-optic sensor as a pressure gradient hydrophone is described by Mills et al. (16). Sessler (17) gives a short summary of the status of fiber-optic sensors as well as other electro-acoustic transducers.

d.   *Chemical Acoustic Sensors.* The study of acoustical effects on chemical processes has been going on for many years. There appear to be several phenomena in electrolytes that permit sensing acoustic pressure by measuring electrochemical potential. For example, if an acoustic wave impinges on an electrode where gas is being liberated by electrolysis, an alternating component of the electrode potential is produced. In what appears to be a different phenomenon, if a layer of electrolyte-filled nonconducting fiber surrounds an electrode, there is also an electrokinetic effect in the fiber which changes the electrode potential relative to the surrounding electrolyte. These effects and some of their applications are discussed by Yeager *et al.* (*18*).

A microphone useful for measuring low frequency sounds in the atmosphere, called the solion infrasonic microphone, was developed by Collins *et al.* (*19*). This device depends on a chemical reaction which in turn depends on the flow of ions through an acoustic resistance placed in the electrolyte between the electrodes. The acoustic pressure acts on only one of a pair of diaphragms which changes the flow of electrolyte through the resistance. An alternating difference in the potentials between electrodes permits detection of the acoustic pressure.

10.6 Passive Materials in Sonar Transducers

This book has emphasized the electrically and magnetically active materials that provide the basic conversion medium between the electrical and mechanical parts of the electroacoustic transducer. However, electrically inactive materials—metals, elastomers, and fluids—are widely used in the construction of sonar systems. Metal parts are used as vibrating parts of the transducer and also serve as protective enclosures and mounting brackets. Applications of elastomers in transducers include transducer boots, encapsulating compounds, acoustic windows, spacers for vibration isolation, sound absorbers, and O-ring seals. Liquids of several types are used to fill some transducers in order to provide acoustic coupling. These materials must not only satisfy specific requirements in their mechanical and acoustic properties but they must function in a reliable manner. A collection of information on relevant properties of such materials has been made by Capps and Thompson (*20*).

Operational reliability of the sonar transducer is very important and, ideally, the operational lifetime between major servicing or overhauls should be long. In many cases, the extreme cost of obtaining access to an unreliable transducer in order to replace it, such as having to put a submarine or ship in dry-dock, puts even greater demands on transducer reliability. The sonar transducer often must operate in a harsh environment. It must operate in salt water over large ranges of temperature and pressure and survive exposure to many different organic and inorganic fluids. The materials may undergo many cycles of heating and pressurization. Some transducers may be deployed for long periods of time at a particular location. The passive materials may not only affect the survivability of the transducer but may also have a significant effect on the acoustic performance of the transducer.

The designer must choose materials that will satisfy the design specifications. However, he must rely on documentation of material properties that may not be complete. One problem is that the properties, especially of the elastomers, are a function of frequency, temperature, pressure, curing time and temperature, additives, compounding methods, and sample shape. Another problem is that the existing data are located in diverse publications or may not have been published.

Table 10.2

Typical Corrosion Rates and Pitting Characteristics of Various Metals and Alloys in Sea Water[1]

MATERIAL	CORROSION RATE (MEAN RANGE)	RESISTANCE TO PITTING	TYPICAL RATE OF PENETRATION IN PITS
70–30 Cu–Ni	0.2–3.8×10^{-2} mm/yr 0.1–1.5 mils/yr	Good	2.5–13×10^{-2} mm/yr 1–5 mils/yr
Copper	1.2–7.6×10^{-2} mm/yr 0.5–3.0 mils/yr	Good	15–30×10^{-2} mm/yr 6–12 mils/yr
Ni–Al Bronze	2.5–30×10^{-2} mm/yr 1.0–12 mils/yr	Good	5–33×10^{-2} mm/yr 2–9 mils/yr
Monel 400	[2]	Fair	13–38×10^{-2} mm/yr 5–15 mils/yr
316 Stainless	[2]	Fair	178×10^{-2} mm/yr 70 mils/yr
Armco 22–13–5 Stainless	Not available	Good	Unaffected after 9 mo in quiet sea water
Berylco 717C	Reported by manufacturer to have virtually the same corrosion characteristics as Std 70–30 Cu–Ni alloy		
7075–T6 Aluminum	[2]	Fair	28–51×10^{-2} mm/yr 11–20 mils/yr Always needs protection
6061–T6 Aluminum	[2]	Moderate	13–25×10^{-2} mm/yr 5–10 mils/yr May need protection
5086–H34 Aluminum	[2]	Excellent	$<2.5 \times 10^{-2}$ mm/yr <1 mil/yr Usually unprotected
5083–0 Aluminum	[2]		$<2.5 \times 10^{-2}$ mm/yr <1 mil/yr Usually unprotected

[1] Data from Groves (9).

[2] Characteristic form of corrosion makes overall weight loss data meaningless, since failure occurs by pitting.

It is beyond the scope of this book to provide all of the information in this area needed by a designer. Other sources, such as ref. (20), can help with that problem. The purpose here is to provide some insight into the problems of choosing such things as metals for the vibrating parts of transducers and housings, elastomers for supporting the vibrating elements or sealing the transducer from leakage of seawater, and fluids used to fill many transducers.

For elastomers, properties often of interest to the transducer designer include tensile strength, bonding capabilities, electrical resistivity, dielectric constant, thermal expansion coefficients, water permeability, density, hardness, chemical compatibility, bulk and shear moduli, and acoustic absorption coefficients or mechanical loss factors. For metals, properties of interest include the elastic moduli, density, mechanical loss factor, mechanical strength, and corrosion resistance under varying conditions. Fill liquids must meet acoustic property requirements as well as compatibility requirements for other materials in contact with the fluid and for the operations environment. For all, the factor of cost is an important one. Typical data on the acoustic or dynamic properties of these materials and some of the other mechanical and chemical properties which could serve as a basis for simple design exercises are also included in the accompanying Tabs. 10.2, 10.3, 10.4, and 10.5.

Table 10.3

Mechanical and Physical Properties of Various Alloys[1]

Alloy	Ultimate tensile strength MPa	0.2% yield MPa	Elonga- tion in 5 cm (%)	Modulus of elas- ticity 10^9 Pa	Density 10^3kg/m^3	Strength/wt (yield/dens) 10^2m
Berylco 717C (aged)	758.4	517.1	7	152	8.91	59.2
Std 70-30 Cu-Ni (MIL-C-20159-1	413.7	220.6	20	152	8.91	25.3
5% NiAl Bronze MIL-B-16033-1 (4) (heat treated)	758.4	413.7	5	131	7.72	54.7
316 Stainless MIL-S-18262-3	482.6	206.8	30	200	8.02	26.3
NiAl Bronze MIL-B-21230-1	586.1	241.3	15	131	7.53	32.7
MnNiAl Bronze MIL-B-21230-2	620.6	275.8	20	124	7.53	37.4
Armco 22-13-5 Stainless[2]	827.4	448.2	45	200	7.89	57.9
7075-T6 Aluminum	572.3	503.3	11	71.7	2.80	183.4
6061-T6 Aluminum	310.3	275.8	12	68.9	2.71	103.4
5086-H34 Aluminum	324.1	255.1	10	71.0	2.66	97.8
5083-O Aluminum	289.6	144.8	22	71.0	2.66	55.5

[1] Data from Groves (9).
[2] Annealed at 2050°F (1121°C) and water quenched.

Table 10.4

Properties of Rubber and Synthetic Compounds[1]

Property	Polyethylene		Neoprene	Butyl	Natural rubber	Nitrile rubber (NBR, Buna-N)[2]
	Low Density	High Density				
Physical						
Max operating temp	75°C	75°C	90°C	100°C	75°C	—
Elongation (%)	600	500	750	400	500	330
Tensile strength (MPa)	16.55	22.06	19.31	11.03	27.58	28.6
Low-temp flexibility (brittle temp)	–60°C	–60°C	–30°C	–55°C	–55°C	Poor
Abrasion resistance	Good	Excellent	Good	Fair	Fair	Excellent
Ozone resistance	Excellent	Excellent	Good	Very Good	Poor	Poor
Tear resistance	Very Good	Good	Fair	Fair	Fair	—
Flammability	Burns	Burns	Nonflam	Burns	Burns	—
Density ρ (g/cm^3)[3]	0.92	0.95	1.32	1.04	1.10	1.21
Sound speed c at 25°C (m/sec)	1950	2000	1525	1700	1525	—
Electrical						
D–C volume resistivity at 25°C (ohm–cm)[5]	10^{17}	10^{17}	8×10^{12}	1.5×10^{13}	1.9×10^{13}	10^{10}
Dielectric strength (volts/mil at 25°C)	1000	1000	4000	530	425	230
Power factor at 1 kHz	0.0002	0.0002	0.07	0.009	0.08	—
Dielectric constant at 1 kHz	2.34	2.26	6.7	3.1	5.4	—
Chemical Resistance						
Strong bases	Very good	Very good	Good	Good	Fair	—
Strong acids	Very good	Very good	Good	Very good	Fair	—
Oil and gasoline	Very good	Very good	Good	Fair	Fair	[6]
Castor oil	Very good	Very good	Very good	Very good	Very good	Excellent
Water permeability[4]	47×10^{-10}		379×10^{-10}	8×10^{-10}	413×10^{-10}	—

[1] Data from Groves (9).

[2] Data from Capps et al. (20)

[3] Density of sea water is 1.03 g/cm^3; sound speed is 1579 m/sec.

[4] Grams water/cm^2/cm/mm Hg water vapor pressure differential; 21-27°C. The water permeability of polyurethane (ether–based PR–1538) is 1000×10^{-10}.

[5] Volume resistivity will vary according to compound ingredients.

[6] Resistance to oil is good; resistance to aromatics poor.

Table 10.5

Fill Fluids for Sonar Transducers.[1]

	Castor Oil Baker DB Grade	Castor Oil Lubracin	Polyalkalene Glycol	Silicone D.C. 200.20
PHYSICAL PROPERTIES				
Volume Electrical				
Resistivity (Ohm-m)	6×10^{10}	5.2×10^{7}	7.8×10^{10} (dry)	—
Viscosity (25° C)	720 Centipoise	0.3 Stokes	3.6 Centipoise	19 Centipoise
Density (kg/m^3)(25° C)	966	—	973	949
Sound Speed (m/s)(25° C)	1490	1440	1395	992
Cavitation Level				
(dB/1 μPa)	233	—	—	—
Surface Tension (N/m)	0.06736	—	—	Low
Water Solubility Limit	1.4% at 25° C	—	—	—
COMPATIBILITY				
Neoprene W	Good	Poor	Fair	—
Neoprene 35003	Excellent	—	Poor	—
Butyl B252	Good	Good	Very Good	—
Chlorobutyl H862A	Excellent	Good	Very Good	—
Silicone	—	—	Very Good	—
Polyurethane	Good to Excellent	—	Poor	—
EPDM	—	—	Poor	—
Natural 35007	Excellent	Poor	Poor	—
Nitrile	—	—	Very Good	—
Viton	—	—	Good	—
Cork-Rubber Composites	Poor to Fair		Poor to Fair	—
Adhesives	EPON VI: Excellent	Vulcalock: Poor	—	—
Plastics				
Lexan Polycarbonate	Excellent	—	—	—
Syntactic Foam	Excellent	—	—	—
Vinyl Plastisol Dip	Poor	—	—	—
Toxicity	Very low	Low	Non Toxic	Non-toxic eye irritant
Ease of Cleanup	Moderately difficult	—	Readily removed	Difficult to remove
Cost	Low	Low	Low	Moderate
ADVANTAGES	Good compatibility, acoustic proper- ties	Low viscosity	Cheap, well defined, low thermal ex- pansion	Good compati- bility
DISADVANTAGES	High viscosity, esp. at low temp.	Incompatible with many transducer components	High water solu- bility, incom- patible with some elasto- mers	Low sound speed, troublesome handling prop- erties

[1]Data from Capps and Thompson (20).

References

1. R.L. Pritchard. Mutual Acoustic Impedance Between Radiators in an Infinite Rigid Plane. *J. Acoust. Soc. Am.* **32** 730–737 (1960).
2. E.M. Arase. Mutual Radiation Impedance of Square and Rectangular Pistons in a Rigid Baffle. *J. Acoust. Soc. Am.* **36** 1521–1525 (1964).
3. J.E. Greenspon and C.H. Sherman. Mutual-Radiation Impedance and Nearfield Pressure for Pistons on a Cylinder. *J. Acoust. Soc. Am.* **36** 149 (1964).
4. D.T. Porter. Self- and Mutual-Radiation Impedance and Beam Patterns for Flexural Disks in a Rigid Plane. *J. Acoust. Soc. Am.* **36** 1154 (1964).
5. K. Chan. Mutual Radiation Impedance Between Flexible Disks of Different Sizes in an Infinite Plane. *J. Acoust. Soc. Am.* **42** 1060 (1967).
6. P.R. Stepanishan. An Approach to Computing Time-dependent Interaction Forces and Mutual Radiation Impedance Between Pistons in a Rigid Planar Baffle. *J. Acoust. Soc. Am.* **49** 283 (1971).
7. C.H. Sherman. Underwater Sound—a Review I. Underwater Sound Transducers. *IEEE Trans. on Sonics and Ultrasonics.* **SU-22** 281–290 (1975).
8. Heuter and Bolt. *Sonics.* Wiley: New York (1955). pp 130–136.
9. Ivor D. Groves, Jr. *The Design of Deep-Submergence Hydrophones.* NRL Report 7339. Naval Research Laboratory, USRD, Orlando, FL. September 1971.
10. *Underwater Electroacoustic Standard Transducers.* USRD Transducer Catalog. Naval Research Laboratory, Underwater Sound Reference Division, Orlando, FL. 32856
11. J.V. Bouyoucos. Hydroacoustic Transduction. *J. Acoust. Soc. Am.* **57** 1341–1351 (1975).
12. W.L. Konrad. *Design and Performance of Parametric Sonar Systems.* NUSC Technical Report 5227. Naval Underwater Systems Center, New London, CT (1975).
13. J.H. Cole, R.L. Johnson, and P.G. Bhuta. Fiber-Optic Detection of Sound. *J. Acoust. Soc. Am.* **62** 1136–1138 (1977).
14. J.A. Bucaro, H.D. Dardy, and E.F. Carome. Fiber-Optic Hydrophone. *J. Acoust. Soc. Am.* **62** 1302 (1977).
15. J.A. Bucaro, N. Lagakos, J.H. Cole, and T.G. Giallorenzi. Fiber-Optic Transduction. Chapter 14 in *Physical Acoustics.* W.P. Mason and R.N. Thurston, Eds. Academic Press: New York (1982).
16. G.B. Mills, S.L. Garrett, and E.F. Carome. Fiber-Optic Gradient Hydrophone. *Proc. Soc. Photo-Optical Instr. Eng.* **478** 98 (May 1984).
17. G.M. Sessler. What's New in Electroacoustic Transducers. *IEEE ASSP Mag.* **1** 3–13 (1984).
18. E. Yeager *et al.* Ultrasonic Waves and Electrochemistry, I, II, III, IV. *J. Acoust. Soc. Am.* **25** 443–469 (1953).
19. J.L. Collins, W.C. Richie, and G.E. English. Solion Infrasonic Microphone. *J. Acoust. Soc. Am.* **36** 1283–1287 (1964).
20. R.N. Capps and C.M. Thompson. *Handbook of Sonar Transducer Passive Materials.* NRL Memorandum Report 4311, Naval Research Laboratory. Washington, D.C. (1981).

APPENDIX

Answers to Selected Problems

2.1 a. An equivalent circuit:

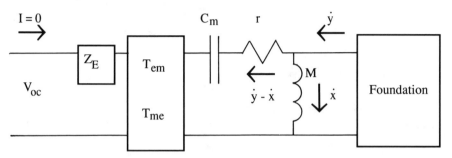

b.
$$M_V = \frac{BL\,(\omega/\omega_0)^2\,\cos\varphi}{\sqrt{[1-(\omega/\omega_0)^2]^2 + [2\zeta\omega/\omega_0]^2}}$$

where

$$\omega_0 = \frac{1}{MC_m}, \; \zeta = r/(2M\omega_0), \text{ and } \tan\phi = \frac{2\zeta\omega/\omega_0}{[1-(\omega/\omega_0)^2]}$$

c. For the mass-controlled case, $\omega \gg \omega_0$, $\phi \to 0$ and $M_V \approx BL$.

2.2 a. $f_s = 356$ Hz, $f_l = 227$ and $f_u = 560$ Hz.

c. $\eta = 0.55$ at resonance.

2.3 a. For maximum efficiency

$$D_W = -\frac{R_E}{\cos\Psi} \pm \sqrt{\frac{R_E^2}{\cos^2\Psi} + \frac{R_E D_A}{\cos\Psi}}$$

3.2 At low frequencies

$$\frac{V}{\dot{u}} = \frac{M}{N(1+C_0/C_M)} \quad \text{and} \quad \frac{V}{F_y} = j\omega\frac{V}{\dot{u}}$$

183

184

4.1 a. $V = s_{11}^E F / (d_{31} w)$

b. No, since $s_{11} \neq s_{12}$ and $d_{33} \neq d_{31}$

$$S_1 = \frac{(-s_{12}^E + s_{11}^E) F}{(w\, t)} \quad \text{and} \quad S_2 = \frac{(-s_{13}^E + \frac{d_{33}}{d_{31}} s_{11}^E) F}{(w\, t)}$$

4.2 a. Changes in length, mean diameter and wall thickness are in meters – 3.1 x 10⁻⁷, 1.2 x 10⁻⁷, and 2.9 x 10⁻⁸, respectively.

b. Tensile force, 176 N.

4.3 a. $T_1 = T_2 = T_3 = -P \quad T_4 = T_5 = T_6 = 0$

$$S_i = -s_{ij}^E T_j + d_{ni} E_n$$

$$m = d_{mj} T_j + \varepsilon_{mn}^T E_n$$

b. y-faces. See Table 4.5.

c. $V/P = 3.6$ mV/Pa. d. $V/P = 43$ μV/Pa. e. $V/P = 500$ μV/Pa.

4.4 a. $V/F_z = -\dfrac{d_{33} L_z}{\varepsilon_3^T L_x L_y}$

b. $V/F_y = -\dfrac{d_{15}}{\varepsilon_1^T L_x}$

5.2 $C_0 = 18$ μF, $k_{31}^2 = 0.044$, $f_r = 25.8$ kHz, $f_a = 26.3$ kHz, $N = 0.163$.

5.4 a.
$$\frac{V}{P} = \frac{N\,\omega\,C_0 \qquad \overline{-j\omega t}}{[\frac{Z_1}{N^2} + \frac{Z_2}{2N^2} - \frac{j}{\omega C_0}]}$$

b.
$$\frac{V}{P} = \frac{N\,\omega\,(C_0 + C_i) \qquad \overline{-j\omega t}}{[\frac{Z_1}{N^2} + \frac{Z_2}{2N^2} - \frac{j}{\omega(C_0 + C_i)}]}$$

5.5 a. 16.5 kHz b. About 31 kHz c. $N = 1.2$, $C_0 = 45$ nF, $R_r = 19,000$, $Z_0 = 14,000$, $v_b = 3,300$ m/s d. 3.

6.1 a. 11 μm b. 10^{-4}, 6.5×10^6 N/m^2 c. No d. Yes e. 3.4 C
f. $C_0 = 16$ nF, $C_M = 410$ μF, $Z_{in} = 1300 - j31$ ohms, $V \approx 800$ V rms, $I \approx 0.62$ A rms.

7.1 b. 10.2 c. 0.21.

8.1 a. $M_0 = 170$ pV/μPa b. $C_0 = 17$ nF, $C \approx 10$ nF (based on $k_p = 0.6$)
c. $M_0 = 0.02$ pV/μPa.

8.2 b. $M_0 = 290$ pV/μPa.

INDEX

Synopses of Reprint Classics
by Peninsula Publishing

Books can be ordered by mail or telephone.
See last page for instructions.

Acoustic Design — Michael Rettinger. Acoustic privacy and quiet living and working conditions essential to today's residential, industrial and business construction are highly dependent on effective isolation of undesirable airborne noise and vibrations. Acoustic Design, Volume I of a 2-book set, was revised and enlarged in 1977. It provides architects, builders, engineers community planners and environmentalists with understandable principles and practices for effective acoustic design of homes, buildings, rooms, industrial spaces, theaters and stages, grandstands, churches, hi-fi and music rooms.

Hardcover. 288 pages. Order Book No. P129. $41.95 USA, $43.95 Int'l.

Noise Control — Michael Rettinger. Companion to *Acoustic Design*. Contents cover the physics of sound, noise and noise reduction. Provides details of vibration control, absorptive treatment and barriers; noise effects and ratings; and basics of sound measurement. Easy-to-use formulas for estimation of noise from aircraft, helicopters, trains, cars, motorcycles, household appliances and for a wide variety of noise reduction techniques. *Noise Control* provides the means to predict potential noise problems and solve them before they become actual problems.

Hardcover. 400 pages. Order Book No. P128. $49.95 USA, $51.95 Int'l.

Ambient Noise in the Sea — Ambient noise, a subset of the ocean's total underwater noise, is defined as the residual, unwanted noise after all other noise sources have been identified. *Ambient Noise in the Sea* by Robert Urick encapsulates the body of knowledge on this subject. It discusses the sources of ambient noise, its variability, and its dependence on receiver depth, directionality and coherence. This book is a *must* for engineers in the field of active and passive sonars, underwater sensor and weapons systems, and underwater signal processing.

Hardcover. 205 pages. Order Book No. P114. $33.95 USA, $35.95 Int'l.

An Introduction to Statistical Communication Theory — Written by David Middleton, pioneer in statistical communication theory, this classic established a unified approach to the basic theory and applications of random signals in communication systems. The book provides a detailed account of systems and their elements as operations and changes on signal and noise ensembles; it addresses the adaptation of statistical *decision theory* to communication problems. The book emphasizes system optimization and evaluation of threshold detection and extraction, system design, comparison between theoretical optimum and actual suboptimum systems, and structure of optimum systems in terms of existing elements.

Hardcover. 1100 pages. Order Book No. P107. $63.95 USA, $65.95 Int'l.

Applied Acoustics — G. Porges. This book develops the basic theory of sound from first principles and applies the theory to obtain practical formulae for the transmission and absorption of sound, sound levels in enclosures and the radiation of sound from common noise sources. The behavior of sound waves in enclosures is explained, leading to practical formulae for predicting sound levels in closed spaces. The transmission of waves through solids is discussed to show how real-life problems of noise and vibration isolation can be tackled. The final chapters introduce the radiation of sound from solids into fluids and describe the major sources of unwanted noise experienced today. In keeping with the practical orientation of the book, the mathematics used is relatively elementary.

Hardcover. 190 pages. Order Book No. P115. $28.95 USA, $30.95 Int'l.

Digital Communications with Space Applications — This book defined an entire new technology for space communications. It was known, irreverently, as "The Bible" at the Jet Propulsion Laboratory.

Subjects addressed include: C³, data telemetry, tracking and ranging, coding, sequences and synchronization techniques. The authors, Solomon W. Golomb, Andrew J. Viterbi, Leonard Baumert, Mahlon Easterling and Jack Stiffer are among the foremost experts in the communications field.

Hardcover. 210 pages. Order Book No. P109. $21.95 USA, $23.95 Int'l.

ECM and ECCM Techniques for Digital Communication Systems — Ray H. Pettit. Presents an overview of contemporary concepts and techniques in the area of ECM and ECCM for digital communications. Focuses on applicable models and procedures, and gains and losses in systems performance.Graphic illustrations and practical examples.

Hardcover. 178 pages. Order Book No. P105 $25.95 USA, $27.95 Int'l.

Electronic Countermeasures — Originally published as a secret reference in the 1960s by the U.S. Army Signal Corps, the book is now declassified. Its 1100 pages cover signal intercept, jamming and deception fundamentals that are as valid today as when first written. Subjects include intercept probabilities, receiver parameters, detection and analysis, direction finding, jamming technique, IR and acoustic countermeasures. More than 600 references and a list of authors that reads like Who's Who in Electronic Warfare.

Hardcover. 1100 pages. Order Book No. P103. $48.00 USA, $50.00 Int'l.

Instruments of Darkness —The History of Electronic Warfare — Alfred Price. Regarded as the standard reference work on World War II radar battle. Enlarged and updated to include air actions over North Vietnam and the Middle East. Previous accounts of electronic warfare may have left the impression that the subject is completely shrouded in secrecy and too complex to be understood by the layman. These impressions are misleading. This book provides an excellent guide to electronic warfare from its beginnings until the present day.

Hardcover. 284 pages. Order Book No. P101. $25.95 USA, $27.95 Int'l.

Introduction to the Theory and Design of Sonar Transducers — Oscar Bryan Wilson. Written in 1985 as a text at the Naval Postgraduate School, this book provides a complete treatment of the fundamentals of transducer theory and design using equivalent circuit techniques. The book contains ten chapters, each ending with a list of literature references and a set of problems for the student. Subjects addressed include: introductory baseline and definitions, equivalent circuits, properties of materials: piezoelectric and magnetorestrictive, hydrophone design and transducer arrays. *Introduction to the Theory and Design of Sonar Transducers* will be useful not only to the sonar transducer designer but also to underwater acousticians and sonar system engineers who would like to gain appreciation of the problems of transducer design.

Hardcover. 202 pages. Order Book No. P122. $38.95 USA, $40.95 Int'l.

Machinery Noise and Diagnostics — Richard H. Lyon. Butterworth Publishers. Fundamentals of vibration, excitation, transmission and reception for designing quieter machinery and diagnostic systems which monitor operating conditions. Details signal processing techniques used to analyze vibration signatures. Addresses relationship of machinery noise and diagnostics, sources of vibration, structural response to excitation, vibration transmission in machine structures, and diagnostics using signal energy and signal phase.

Hardcover. 309 pages. Order Book No. P132. $54.95 USA, $56.95 Int'l.

Mechanics of Underwater Noise — Donald Ross. Originally published in 1976 this book continues to be the most authoritative work on the fundamentals of underwater noise radiated by ships, submarines and torpedoes. It features physical explanations of the basic mechanisms by which noise is generated, transmitted by structures and radiated into the sea. These complex phenomena are explained in a straightforward manner that concentrates on the dominant mechanisms.

Hardcover. 375 pages. Order Book No. P112. $51.95 USA, $53.95 Int'l.

Microwave Scanning Antennas — R. C. Hansen. Three-volumes bound into a single hardcover book. This classic reference covers all types of narrow beam antennas with emphasis on those that scan the beam. Comprehensively treats phased arrays and quasi-optical antennas. Includes multiple-beam arrays, time domain and synthetic apertures and adaptive antennas. Concentrates on narrow beam antennas, both mechanically steered and electronically scanned. Constraining equations and design tradeoffs along with practical examples. Volume I reviews on astronomy instruments and large radomes. Volumes II and III cover array theory, a variety of means for scanning such as phase shift, frequency and heterodyne, the systems technology of time domain and adaptive antenna systems.

Hardcover. 1200 pages. Order Book No. P110. $57.95 USA, $59.95 Int'l.

Noise Reduction — Edited by Leo L. Beranek. Classic book of fundamentals of noise control and noise reduction for the *general* engineer. Elementary beginnings leading to the advanced aspects of noise reduction for offices, residences, auditoriums and transportation vehicles. Case histories and abundant references.

Hardcover. 776 pages. Order Book No. P133. $63.95 USA, $65.95 Int'l.

Physics of Sound in the Sea — Classic work on underwater sound propagation resulting from the World War II program of studies organized by the National Defense Research Committee. Part I discusses the transmission loss of sound sent out from a projector. Part II deals with sound which has been scattered back. Part III deals with target strengths and echoes returned from submarines and surface ships. Part IV discusses the transmission of sound through wakes and echoes received from wakes.

Hardcover. 577 pages. Order Book No. P126. $50.95 USA, $52.95 Int'l.

Principles of Electronic Warfare — Robert J. Schlesinger. Provides an overview of EW technology and tactics in the space age. Written from an overall systems viewpoint, the book focuses on Electronic Warfare's contribution in the accomplishment of a military aircraft mission. Highlights radar countermeasure techniques, electronic intelligence (ELINT), elements of space environment, payload optimization between weapons and ECM, and air combat analysis.

Softcover. 213 pages. Order Book No. P104. $20.95 USA, $22.95 Int'l.

Principles of High-Resolution Radar — August Rihaczek. Step-by-step development of the theory of radar resolution beginning with basic measurements on single targets and proceeds through an analysis of the nature of the resolution problem. Capabilities and limits of radar and the details of waveform design. Synthetic aperture radar is used to illustrate the practical application of principles. Derivations are carefully spelled out and supported by extensive reasoning and interpretation. Conveys the theory of target resolution without resorting to advanced mathematics. Topics covered include: measurements, ambiguities, and pulse compression for single targets; target resolution and the limits on resolution performance; target detection in various forms of clutter and the relation to resolution; waveform design; higher order range derivatives, Doppler distortions, wideband signals, and general types of target motion.

Hardcover. 500 pages. Order Book No. P111. $45.95 USA, $47.95 Int'l.

Propagation of Short Radio Waves — Donald E. Kerr. Best known classic of the prestigious MIT Radiation Laboratory Series. Still today's most authoritative reference despite being written more than forty years ago, the book characterizes the phenomena of radio propagation of radar, communication and navigation systems in the frequency range of 100 MHz to 300 GHz. The first chapter introduces the reader to basic definitions and concepts. Ensuing chapters address: Theory of Propagation in a Horizontally Stratified Atmosphere; Refraction and Its Meteorological Characterization; Reflections from the Earth's Surface; Diffraction; Scattering; Atmospheric Attenuation; Radar Cross Section Theory and Measurements; Radar Targets and Meteorological Echoes; and Clutter. Technical information, data and formulas constitute a bedrock of theory and measurements.

Hardcover. 756 pages. Order Book No. P120. $49.95 USA, $51.95 Int'l.

Proposal Management Using the Modular Technique — The Modular Technique can help you achieve effective proposal results. It establishes a vehicle for the communication of complex ideas between manager and authors. It facilitates a large group of authors documenting ideas in a cohesive, easily-read proposal. The *Modular Technique*, based on storyboarding procedures as outlined in this book, provides the manager with the technique for planning the work, assigning design and writing tasks, implementing author-to-manager feedback and effecting document review in a timely manner.

Hardcover. 111 pages. Order Book No. P119. $23.95 USA, $25.95 Int'l.

Radar Signal Simulation — Richard L. Mitchell. Addresses modeling of radar signals including waveform modulation function, interaction of the scattering environment with the waveform and receiver processing. Presents radar environment model structures for simulation, mapping procedures, transformation techniques, sampled signals and generation techniques.

Hardcover. 200 pages. Order Book No. P116. $44.95 USA, $46.95 Int'l.

Side Scan Sonar Record Interpretation — Charles Mazel. Training manual produced by Klein Associates, Inc., manufacturer of side scan sonars. Applies to interpretation of all commercial side scan sonars. Covers basic interpretation. The 144 figures and photographs of actual sonar records depict mine and ship targets, shadows, clutter, noise, wakes and dolphins.

Softcover. 146 pages. Order Book No. P127. $44.95 USA, $46.95 Int'l.

Signal Detection and Recognition by Human Observers — Edited by John A. Swets in 1964, this book was the first to bring together into one volume a broad discussion coverage of modern signal detection theory applications to human performance, specifically in auditory and visual sensory tasks. Applications in the book address substantive problems in psychology including the integration of sensory information, signal uncertainty, auditory frequency analysis, speech communication, vigilance and recognition memory. *Signal Detection and Recognition* outlines how decision factors are centrally involved in even the simplest detection task and how sensory capacity can be assessed. The bibliography has been updated to 1988.

Hardcover. 734 pages. Order Book No. P124. $52.95 USA, $54.95 Int'l.

Signal Detection Theory and Psychophysics — David M. Green and John A. Swets. Summarizes the application of signal detection theory to the analysis and measurement of the human observer's sensory system. The theory provides a way to analyze the threshold or sensory limen, the basic unit of all discrimination studies, whether human or animal. The book outlines the theory of statistical decision making and its application to a variety of common psychophysical activities. It shows how signal detection theory can be used to separate sensory and decision aspects of discrimination responses. Signal detection theory is applied to a variety of other substantive problems in a sensory psychology. *Signal Detection Theory and Psychophysics* is an invaluable book for psychologists dealing with sensory perception, especially auditory, and for human factors engineers dealing with man/machine interfaces.

Hardcover. 521 pages. Order Book No. P125. $50.95 USA, $52.95 Int'l.

Sound Propagation in the Sea — Robert J. Urick. Subjects addressed: basic theory; speed of sound in the ocean; attenuation and absorption; surface ducts; the deep sound channel; caustics and convergence zones; computer models of sound propagation; shallow-water ducts; reflections and scattering by the sea surface; reflections and scattering by the sea bottom; temporal coherence; spatial coherence; and multipath in the sea.

Hardcover. 225 pages. Order Book No. P113. $34.95 USA, $36.95 Int'l.

Space-Time Information Processing — Charles Loda and A. Winder. Indispensable reference tool for audio signal processing and data analysis. Oriented to acoustics and sonar engineering. The book features Fourier transforms, statistical analyses, correlation and spectra. Especially valuable chapters address measurement of spatially and temporally-limited functions, optimal filtering procedures and interpretation of results.

Hardcover. 192 pages. Order Book No. P117. $29.95 USA, $31.95 Int'l.

Strategic Antisubmarine Warfare and Naval Strategy — Tom Stefanick. Lexington Books. Today's most comprehensive book on ASW strategy. Provides technical details of submarine detection available no where else in the unclassified literature. Summarizes fundamentals of acoustic and non-acoustic methods of submarine detection with assessments of effectiveness. Addresses submarine design, ASW forces of US and USSR, threats to SSBNs, sonars and sonar arrays, submarine acoustic signatures and their detection in noise, and submarine detection in the Arctic Ocean and Northern seas. Written in easy-to-read, understandable language for expert and layman.

Hardcover. 411 pages. Order Book No. P131. $54.95 USA, $56.95 Int'l.

The Strategy of Electromagnetic Conflict — Written by the Air Force Academy faculty. Contents include: electronic countermeasures and counter-countermeasures; electronic reconnaissance; tradeoffs in air defense; use of chaff for aircraft self-protection; communications intelligence, security and cryptoloty; vulnerability of space stations; countermeasures in the millimeter, IR, optical, laser and UV regions. Required reading for engineering and analysis personnel dealing with design and development of military electronic systems and the planning of air operations.

300 pages. Order Book No. P102. $27.95 USA, $29.95 Int'l.

Topics in Communication Theory — David Middleton. Provides a concise treatment of basic problems in statistical communication theory. Concepts are discussed and illustrated with simple but important examples. Chapter headings are: Communication from the Viewpoint of Decision Theory; The Detection of Signals in Noise; The Extraction of Signals from Noise; The Structure of Optimum Systems; and Critique, Extensions and Future Problems.

Hardcover. 125 pages. Order Book No. P108. $19.95 USA, $21.95 Int'l.

Traveling Wave Antennas — Carleton H. Walter. Useful in the design of "skin" antennas in high performance military aircraft. The book addresses traveling wave theory, analysis, synthesis, design and applications. Clearly written for designers and system engineers. References and problems at the end of each chapter. Generously illustrated with graphs and diagrammatic material.

Hardcover. 448 pages. Order Book No. P130. $44.95 USA, $46.95 Int'l.

Underwater Electroacoustic Measurements — Robert J. Bobber. Addresses the theory and practice of measuring electroacoustic parameters such as response, sensitivity, directivity, impedance, efficiency, linearity and noise limits of transducers used in sonars. Discussed in detail are wide band transducers used as measurement instruments, near field and far field methods, and measurements on auxiliary materials such as acoustic windows, reflectors, baffles and absorbers.

Hardcover. 341 pages. Order Book No. P123. $39.95 USA, $41.95 Int'l.

ORDERING INFORMATION

You can order by postcard, personal letter, telephone (415) 948-2511 or fax (415) 948-5004. For orders by letter, pay by check, VISA/MasterCard or money order. Book order numbers and prices for each book are listed in the synopses. Add $2.00 per copy for postage and handling. California residents add 7% sales tax. Make remittance payable to:

Peninsula Publishing, P.O. Box 867, Los Altos, CA 94023 USA

BUSINESS REPLY MAIL
FIRST CLASS MAIL   PERMIT NO. 722   LOS ALTOS, CA

POSTAGE WILL BE PAID BY ADDRESSEE

PENINSULA PUBLISHING
P.O. BOX 867
LOS ALTOS, CALIFORNIA 94023-9912

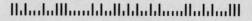

NO POSTAGE
NECESSARY
IF MAILED
IN THE
UNITED STATES

BUSINESS REPLY MAIL
FIRST CLASS MAIL   PERMIT NO. 722   LOS ALTOS, CA

POSTAGE WILL BE PAID BY ADDRESSEE

PENINSULA PUBLISHING
P.O. BOX 867
LOS ALTOS, CALIFORNIA 94023-9912

Enter my order as follows:

Book No.	Quanity	Unit Price	Total Cost
_____	_____	_____	_____
_____	_____	_____	_____
_____	_____	_____	_____
_____	_____	_____	_____
_____	_____	_____	_____
_____	_____	_____	_____

Total of Book Purchases _____

Calif. Residents add 7% SalesTax _____

Postage & Handling @ $2.00 Per Book _____

Surcharge for Air Mail _____

GRAND TOTAL OF ORDER US$ _____

Charge to: ☐ MasterCard ☐ VISA

Account Number: _____

Expiration Date: _____

_____
Signature as it appears on charge card

_____
Name (please print)

_____
Organization (if required for shipment)

_____
Address

_____
City   State   Zip

┌───┐
│ *Air Mail Service (surcharges per copy):* │
│ *US priority mail $3.00*   │
│ *Canada $5.00*   │
│ *Europe $15.00*   │
│ *Asia/Africa/Oceana $20.00*   │
│ *South and Central America $8.00*   │
└───┘

Peninsula Publishing • P.O. Box 867 • Los Altos, California 94023 USA

--✂-----

Enter my order as follows:

Book No.	Quanity	Unit Price	Total Cost
_____	_____	_____	_____
_____	_____	_____	_____
_____	_____	_____	_____
_____	_____	_____	_____
_____	_____	_____	_____
_____	_____	_____	_____

Total of Book Purchases _____

Calif. Residents add 7% SalesTax _____

Postage & Handling @ $2.00 Per Book _____

Surcharge for Air Mail _____

GRAND TOTAL OF ORDER US$ _____

Charge to: ☐ MasterCard ☐ VISA

Account Number: _____

Expiration Date: _____

_____
Signature as it appears on charge card

_____
Name (please print)

_____
Organization (if required for shipment)

_____
Address

_____
City   State   Zip

┌───┐
│ *Air Mail Service (surcharges per copy):* │
│ *US priority mail $3.00*   │
│ *Canada $5.00*   │
│ *Europe $15.00*   │
│ *Asia/Africa/Oceana $20.00*   │
│ *South and Central America $8.00*   │
└───┘

Peninsula Publishing • P.O. Box 867 • Los Altos, California 94023 USA

--✂-----